SIX SIGMA
SOFTWARE
DEVELOPMENT

Second Edition

Other Auerbach Publications in Software Development, Software Engineering, and Project Management

Accelerating Process Improvement Using Agile Techniques
Deb Jacobs
0-8493-3796-8

Antipatterns: Identification, Refactoring, and Management
Phillip A. Laplante and Colin J. Neill
0-8493-2994-9

Business Process Management Systems
James F. Chang
0-8493-2310-X

The Complete Project Management Office Handbook
Gerard M. Hill
0-8493-2173-5

Defining and Deploying Software Processes
F. Alan Goodman
0-8493-9845-2

Embedded Linux System Design and Development
P. Raghavan, Amol Lad, and Sriram Neelakandan
0-8493-4058-6

Global Software Development Handbook
Raghvinder Sangwan, Matthew Bass, Neel Mullick, Daniel J. Paulish, and Juergen Kazmeier
0-8493-9384-1

Implementing the IT Balanced Scorecard
Jessica Keyes
0-8493-2621-4

The Insider's Guide to Outsourcing Risks and Rewards
Johann Rost
0-8493-7017-5

Interpreting the CMMI®
Margaret Kulpa and Kent Johnson
0-8493-1654-5

Modeling Software with Finite State Machines
Ferdinand Wagner, Ruedi Schmuki, Thomas Wagner, and Peter Wolstenholme
0-8493-8086-3

Optimizing Human Capital with a Strategic Project Office
J. Kent Crawford and Jeannette Cabanis-Brewin
0-8493-5410-2

A Practical Guide to Information Systems Strategic Planning, Second Edition
Anita Cassidy
0-8493-5073-5

Process-Based Software Project Management
F. Alan Goodman
0-8493-7304-2

Project Management Maturity Model, Second Edition
J. Kent Crawford
0-8493-7945-8

Real Process Improvement Using the CMMI®
Michael West
0-8493-2109-3

Reducing Risk with Software Process Improvement
Louis Poulin
0-8493-3828-X

The ROI from Software Quality
Khaled El Emam
0-8493-3298-2

Software Engineering Quality Practices
Ronald Kirk Kandt
0-8493-4633-9

Software Sizing, Estimation, and Risk Management
Daniel D. Galorath and Michael W. Evans
0-8493-3593-0

Software Specification and Design: An Engineering Approach
John C. Munson
0-8493-1992-7

Software Testing and Continuous Quality Improvement, Second Edition
William E. Lewis
0-8493-2524-2

Strategic Software Engineering: An Interdisciplinary Approach
Fadi P. Deek, James A.M. McHugh, and Osama M. Eljabiri
0-8493-3939-1

Successful Packaged Software Implementation
Christine B. Tayntor
0-8493-3410-1

UML for Developing Knowledge Management Systems
Anthony J. Rhem
0-8493-2723-7

AUERBACH PUBLICATIONS
www.auerbach-publications.com
To Order Call: 1-800-272-7737 • Fax: 1-800-374-3401
E-mail: orders@crcpress.com

SIX SIGMA SOFTWARE DEVELOPMENT

Second Edition

CHRISTINE B. TAYNTOR

Auerbach Publications
Taylor & Francis Group
Boca Raton   New York

Auerbach Publications is an imprint of the
Taylor & Francis Group, an informa business

Auerbach Publications
Taylor & Francis Group
6000 Broken Sound Parkway NW, Suite 300
Boca Raton, FL 33487-2742

© 2007 by Taylor & Francis Group, LLC
Auerbach is an imprint of Taylor & Francis Group, an Informa business

No claim to original U.S. Government works
Printed in the United States of America on acid-free paper
10 9 8 7 6 5 4 3 2 1

International Standard Book Number-10: 1-4200-4426-5 (Softcover)
International Standard Book Number-13: 978-1-4200-4426-3 (Softcover)

Visit the Taylor & Francis Web site at
http://www.taylorandfrancis.com

and the Auerbach Web site at
http://www.auerbach-publications.com

Dedication

For Debra Racka, who has helped in so many ways. Thanks, Debbie. Here is another book for that special shelf.

About the Author

Christine B. Tayntor has been an IT manager and frequent contributor to technical publications for more than 30 years. She has worked in the insurance, banking, manufacturing, and consulting industries, most recently as director of Global IT Applications Sourcing for Honeywell International in Morristown, New Jersey, where she became a Six Sigma Black Belt and received her DFSS certification. She is currently a full-time writer and lecturer.

Acknowledgments

The second edition of this book would not have been possible had it not been for the following individuals.

- John Wyzalek, my editor. Thanks, John, for your support over the years and — most importantly — for suggesting that it was time for an update.
- Richard E. Biehl, of Data-Oriented Quality Solutions, who took time out of his busy consulting and teaching schedule to provide background materials. A special thanks, Rick, for demystifying the QFD.

Contents

List of Exhibits

Introduction

Fewer defects; faster, more reliable processes; increased customer satisfaction; greater profits. These are the reasons many companies initiate Six Sigma programs. Although they have the same goals, many information technology (IT) departments do not use Six Sigma techniques. Why not?

While many reasons can be cited, the most common fall into two categories:

1. *Skepticism.* This manifests itself in statements such as, "It will not work here," and has as its basis the beliefs that Six Sigma applies only to manufacturing or engineering processes and that it is impractical to implement Six Sigma in one department if the entire company has not committed itself to becoming a Six Sigma organization.
2. *Lack of awareness.* Although the business press has touted the successes of Six Sigma at companies such as Motorola and General Electric, many IT managers are unfamiliar with Six Sigma concepts and tools, and lack an understanding of how those tools can be used to improve the system development process.

This book has the following goals: removing the mystique surrounding Six Sigma and demonstrating how Six Sigma tools and concepts can be used to enhance the system development process. It provides:

- A clear explanation of Six Sigma concepts and their application, using a case study.
- A mapping of Six Sigma concepts and tools to all aspects of system development: traditional waterfall, rapid development, legacy systems support, packaged software implementation, and outsourcing.
- A proposal for the use of Six Sigma tools to evaluate and improve the overall performance of the IT department.

In addition to classic Six Sigma, this book introduces Design for Six Sigma (DFSS) and illustrates when and how DFSS tools and techniques can be used to increase the robustness and reliability of a new system.

Although "lean" techniques, which are designed to increase the speed of a process, are normally associated with manufacturing, this book shows how the judicious application of lean tools can reduce the complexity of IT processes, thereby shortening the time needed to translate customer requirements into completed systems and, not coincidentally, increasing customer satisfaction.

The book is divided into nine sections.

Section I provides an explanation of the basic concepts of Six Sigma, contrasts those to traditional Quality Assurance and the Software Engineering Institute's Capability Maturity Model, and — because change is an integral part of Six Sigma — it reviews the dynamics of change and the components of successful change. Section I also introduces DFSS, explaining the differences between it and classic Six Sigma.

Six Sigma is a process by which other processes are improved. Similar to most complex processes, it is divided into phases, creating what is referred to as the DMAIC model, where DMAIC is an acronym for the five phases: define, measure, analyze, improve, and control. Section II uses a case study of the fictitious Global Widget Company and its order entry process to illustrate the DMAIC model and the tools and techniques associated with each phase.

Many companies that have embraced Six Sigma have discovered that Six Sigma alone will not accomplish all of the quality goals they have set for themselves. DFSS is the answer to that dilemma. Utilizing another case study of the Global Widget Company, Section III presents the concepts, tools, and techniques associated with the five phases of DFSS.

Section IV outlines the traditional "waterfall" system development methodology or life cycle (SDLC), showing how Six Sigma tools can increase the probability of successful system development.

Although the traditional SDLC ends when the system is implemented, Section V describes the support of legacy systems, what is typically called maintenance, and introduces the concepts of steering committees and service level agreements as ways to increase customer focus and ensure fact-based decisions.

In response to the shortcomings of the traditional waterfall SDLC, the IT industry developed a number of different methods for developing systems, notably Rapid Application Development (RAD), prototyping, and spiral or iterative development. Section VI outlines these methods and the Six Sigma tools that enhance them, along with the technical challenges that accompany client/server and Web-based development projects and the measurement and analysis tools that can help identify and reduce the variation inherent in these technologies.

Another response to the lengthy delivery schedules of the traditional SDLC is the implementation of packaged software or, as it is sometimes called, a commercial off-the-shelf (COTS) solution. While there is no doubt that the correct COTS solution can help IT achieve the goal of "better, faster, and cheaper" system delivery, it is also undeniable that selection of the wrong package can be an expensive mistake. Section VII outlines the steps involved in package selection and implementation and shows how Six Sigma tools can assist in making a fact-based decision.

Outsourcing also holds out the promises of reduced costs and shortened delivery cycles; but like the acquisition of the wrong software, the selection of the wrong outsource supplier can have disastrous effects on both IT and its customers. Section VIII provides an introduction to outsourcing, explaining the differences between outsourcing and staff augmentation, and presents strategies for successful outsourcing, including the criteria to be used when deciding what to outsource as well as those to be used for the selection of the supplier.

While preceding sections have focused on using Six Sigma tools to improve specific functions within IT, Section IX proposes treating the entire IT function as a single process and applying Six Sigma tools and concepts to improve that process and create a nearly defect-free department that consistently satisfies its customers.

1

INTRODUCTION TO SIX SIGMA

Although at its most fundamental, Six Sigma is a measurement of quality, the term is now used to encompass concepts and tools, all of which are designed to help achieve the goal of nearly perfect processes. It has also become a management philosophy that includes in its credo the need for fact-based decisions, customer focus, and teamwork.

While some IT departments believe that Six Sigma can be applied only to manufacturing or engineering processes and that it has little or no relevance to the system development life cycle and the Information Technology (IT) department in general, Six Sigma has applicability to software engineering. The techniques for ensuring that customer requirements are understood, that the impact of proposed changes is measured and evaluated, and that the development process is made more reliable will benefit all IT departments.

Chapter 1 provides a general explanation of Six Sigma and debunks the myths surrounding its applicability to IT. The chapter also introduces Design for Six Sigma (DFSS) and explains why and when this extension to classic Six Sigma may be needed to reach desired quality levels.

Six Sigma is sometimes confused with Quality Assurance (QA) and the Software Engineering Institute's Capability Maturity Model (SEI CMM). As shown in Chapter 2, although there are common characteristics, the breadth of Six Sigma is greater than either QA or CMM.

Because Six Sigma by its very definition involves change, it is essential that anyone embarking on the Six Sigma journey understand the human effects of change, the roles people play in the process, and the attributes of successful transformations. Chapter 3 outlines those aspects of change and the effect that both formal and informal communications can have on promoting change.

Chapter 1

Six Sigma in Perspective

Although the term "Six Sigma" has become synonymous with highly efficient, customer-focused companies that have reduced costs while increasing customer satisfaction, at its most fundamental, Six Sigma is a measurement of quality. A process that operates at the six sigma level has so few defects that it is nearly perfect.

Defining Six Sigma

Six Sigma has its origins in statistics, and, in fact, the term is a statistical one. A statistician would explain that in addition to being the eighteenth letter of the Greek alphabet, sigma (σ) is the symbol for standard deviation. The same statistician would point out that a process that is at the Six Sigma level has six standard deviations between its process center and the upper and lower specification limits. In simpler terms, that process produces only 3.4 defects per million opportunities. If that sounds close to perfection, it is.

While there is no denying the statistical origin of Six Sigma or the fact that statistical analysis plays an important role in many companies' implementation of Six Sigma, it has become more than a simple measurement of defects. The term is now used to encompass concepts and tools, all of which are designed to help achieve the goal of nearly perfect processes, in many cases without relying on heavy-duty statistics.

More than Statistics

Six Sigma is more than statistics. While its objectives are to reduce variation and prevent defects, it has also become a management philosophy that includes in its credo the need for fact-based decisions, customer focus, and teamwork.

If this sounds like *déjà vu*, yet another productivity program *du jour* that will be supplanted next year, the results Six Sigma companies have achieved should dispel the skepticism. While some previous quality and productivity initiatives promised great benefits but frequently failed to deliver them, Six Sigma delivers. Streamlined processes and less rework result in lower costs. Add them to improved customer satisfaction, and the effect on the bottom line can only be positive. This is the power of Six Sigma.

How great can the improvement be? To put Six Sigma in perspective, most companies operate between three and four sigma. As shown in Exhibit 1.1, a four sigma process has greater than 99 percent accuracy. While that might appear acceptable, consider the third column in Exhibit 1.1. Four sigma processes have 6210 defects per million, compared to 3.4 for six sigma. If it took only one minute to correct each defect, a four sigma company would spend 103½ *hours* in error correction compared to less than 3½ *minutes*. Even at minimum wage, the difference is significant. Most defects, of course, require far more than a minute to correct.

More significantly, many are never corrected but instead are found by customers. While not all customers will return a defective product and demand a replacement, it is a rare one that will ignore poor quality. For the company that permitted defective products to ship, the result may be thousands of dollars of lost future sales.

Not Just Products

Although Six Sigma had its origin in manufacturing, it also applies to service industries. A defect is a defect. Whether a customer receives the

Exhibit 1.1   Comparison of Sigma Levels Three through Six

Sigma Level	Percent Correct	Number of Defects per Million Opportunities	Lost Time per Century
3	93.3193	66,807	3½ months
4	99.3790	6,210	2½ days
5	99.9767	233	30 minutes
6	99.99966	3.4	6 seconds

wrong sized widget or an incorrect answer to an inquiry, the result is the same: dissatisfaction, increased costs to correct the error, and potential lost sales.

Six Sigma companies focus on far more than the measurement and elimination of defects. For them, Six Sigma is the way they do business. It permeates their corporate culture and becomes one of the things that defines them and differentiates them from their competition.

Six Sigma is built on a foundation that includes the following tenets:

- Prevent defects
- Reduce variation
- Focus on the customer
- Make decisions based on facts
- Encourage teamwork

Defect Prevention

One way in which Six Sigma differs from previous quality initiatives is in its insistence that the way to eliminate defects is through prevention rather than correction. This is an important distinction. While it may seem that the results — zero defect products — appear the same to the customer, there is a fundamental difference between the philosophies of correction and prevention, just as there is a fundamental difference between fire fighting and fire prevention. Classic quality control inspected *products* to find the defects, then corrected them. Six Sigma analyzes the *process* to determine what causes the defects, then changes the process to prevent them. As shown in Exhibit 1.2, the effect of prevention is widespread and permanent.

Although the difference may not be immediately apparent to the customer, prevention of defects has a positive effect on the company's bottom line. That is because the cost of poor quality (COPQ) has been eliminated. Although some companies equate COPQ with warranty work

Exhibit 1.2 Comparison of Six Sigma and Quality Control

	Action Taken	Action is On	Effect Is	Effect is On	Need to Repeat
Quality Control	Inspect	Product	Correction of error	1 product	Constantly
Six Sigma	Analyze	Process	Prevention of defect	All products	None

and the cost of returned products, both of those are the result of customer-detected defects. Because the objective is to identify defects before they leave the factory, the COPQ should also include the following elements related to internal detection:

- *Scrap or waste:* the product or material that cannot be used or sold.
- *Rework:* the effort required to correct an error.
- *Inspection:* the cost of performing quality control.
- *Reporting:* the effort involved in developing and reviewing reports.

While many companies focus on the first two components, the cost of inspection and reporting can exceed scrap and rework, particularly in service processes. Sometimes whole organizations spring into existence to monitor quality. In other cases, employees develop informal methods of detecting and correcting defects before they reach Quality Control and can be reported. These processes are often referred to as "a hidden factory."

The COPQ can be significant. The need to reduce it was, in fact, the impetus for Motorola's initiating a Six Sigma program in 1979. For a four sigma company, the COPQ is estimated to be between 15 and 25 percent of sales; whereas for a six sigma company, it is less than 1 percent of sales. Reducing the COPQ can have a measurable effect on the bottom line. This is the reason Six Sigma companies place such a high emphasis on preventing rather than correcting defects. By "mistake-proofing" a process, defects are eliminated, and the COPQ is greatly reduced.

Reduced Variation

The second Six Sigma tenet is to reduce variation, or — to explain it in another way — to increase consistency. This is one way to prevent defects. Consistency is important because it is predictable. And what is predictable can be perfected. As shown on Exhibit 1.3, although it might appear that the dart player on the left is the better one, because she hit the bull's eye once, a Six Sigma company would prefer the consistency of the player on the right. Although he has never hit the bull's eye, and in fact has never even come close, this player's aim is consistent. Whatever he is doing wrong that keeps him from hitting the bull's eye is unvarying. As such, it can be corrected.

As detailed in Section II, for a Six Sigma company, the next steps would be to examine the process (i.e., throwing darts) to determine what has caused the defect (i.e., not hitting the bull's eye) and then change the process to eliminate the defect. Perhaps the player is holding the dart too high. Perhaps he has not considered the effect of the wind. Perhaps

Exhibit 1.3   Which Player is Better? A Pictorial Representation of Variation

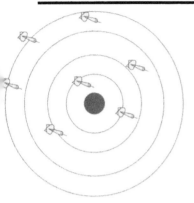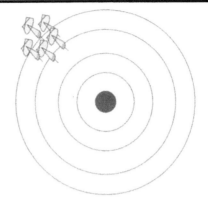
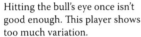

Hitting the bull's eye once isn't
good enough. This player shows
too much variation.

Although this player never hit the
bull's eye, the consistency of dart
placement means that a "process
shift" could result in consistent
bull's eyes.

his eyesight is not perfect. In any case, with training or improved tools (glasses), he should be able to hit the bull's eye consistently.

Consistent, on-target results are the goal of every company. Six Sigma helps them get there.

Customer Focus

Six Sigma companies spend a lot of time talking about — and to — customers. Whether they are external customers, the ones who buy the products or services the company sells, or internal ones, such as a department that uses a service another department provides, customers are the focal point of all activities. This is in direct contrast to many companies' focus on the bottom line. Six Sigma companies know that satisfying customers and increasing profits are not mutually exclusive but, rather, that increased profits are a direct result of having a strong customer focus. That is one of the reasons why eliminating defects is so important. Customers want — and deserve — perfect products and services.

Six Sigma projects begin by listening to the "voice of the customer." That means learning what customers need and which of those requirements are most important to them. But concern for the customer does not end when requirements are identified and the project is initiated. The entire project life cycle is characterized by constant communication, and it is much more than delivering periodic status reports. This is genuine two-way communication, ensuring that customers are a part of the process and that the results will satisfy their requirements.

The reason for such a high level of customer focus is simple: without the customer, there is no need for the company itself to exist.

Fact-Based Decisions

One of the hallmarks of a Six Sigma company is its insistence that decisions are based on facts. Although a project may be initiated because someone says, "*I think* we could improve our process by doing...," no action would be taken until the project team can state, "*We know* that our process will be improved if we...." Intuition and "gut feel" are second to incontrovertible facts. As detailed in Section II, getting from "I think" to "we know" requires an analysis of both the current process and the reason why the change is necessary or desirable. Although these analyses can be performed concurrently, neither can be neglected.

It is important to understand exactly how a process is operating before making any changes. That may sound basic, and it is, but all too often in the rush to show progress in solving a problem, companies fail to understand exactly what it is that they are changing before they begin to implement the modification. The result of this failure can be unexpected side effects or, in Six Sigma terms, defects.

Consider the Monster Cracker Manufacturer. When its best-selling crackers emerged from the oven apparently undercooked, the intuitive response would have been to raise the temperature of the oven. Instead, the company analyzed the entire cracker-making process and discovered that the problem was caused by excess humidity in the mixing room. Had the oven been adjusted rather than reducing the amount of liquid in the batter, the result would have been crackers that still did not meet the company's — or the customer's — standards.

Similarly, it is important to ensure that the change being made is the right one. This is a corollary to focusing on the customer. Before beginning any process changes, a Six Sigma company knows that it is essential to understand what the customer *really* wants, not simply the project team's perception of the customer's needs. A defect-free product is of no value if it is not one the customer will buy.

Like customer focus, the reason for insisting on fact-based decisions is simple. By having all the facts before making any change, a Six Sigma company eliminates the rework and waste caused by solving the wrong problem.

Teamwork

It is not insignificant that the previous paragraphs described the process of moving from "I think" to "we know," because teamwork is one of the characteristics of Six Sigma companies. Just as they recognize the importance of working on the right projects, these companies realize that the ability to understand what is currently happening, to determine what is causing the variation, and to develop methods of preventing defects requires having the right people working together to solve the problem. Individual heroics are much less important than the work that is accomplished by having the right group of people working together, sharing knowledge and expertise.

Although the corporate hierarchy does not disappear in a Six Sigma company, it is of little importance when a team is formed. This is why many meetings begin with the admonition to "check titles at the door." Team members are selected and valued because of their knowledge and expertise, not their position on an org chart.

Similarly, departmental rivalries and functional silos that discourage sharing of information have no place in a Six Sigma company. Because most processes span departmental boundaries, with one department providing input to a process and another using the output, teams are almost always cross-functional. The objective is to assemble the right group of people so that decisions are indeed fact based rather than being dependent on incomplete knowledge or assumptions.

Teams are, quite simply, the mechanism Six Sigma companies use to eliminate defects.

Tools and Training

Because one of their primary goals is to reduce variation, it is logical that Six Sigma projects would use a standard process and set of tools, rather than relying on each team to develop its own problem-solving techniques. Not only does this increase consistency, but it also reduces the time — and cost — of teams' reinventing processes.

Six Sigma projects are divided into five phases, with recommended tools for each phase. Section II describes the phases, tools, and overall process in detail.

Because Six Sigma companies recognize that training is a necessity rather than a luxury if their employees are to understand both the philosophy of Six Sigma and the best ways to implement that philosophy, there are three levels of formal training programs: (1) Green Belt, (2) Black Belt, and (3) Master Black Belt. Green Belt courses, which consist of up to two weeks of training, provide basic knowledge of the concepts and tools. Black Belts are given in-depth training, normally an additional four weeks, with more emphasis on the statistical analysis tools, while Master Black Belts receive specialized training in the statistical tools, enabling them to guide and mentor Black Belts on their projects.

Unlike many corporate training programs, these culminate in employee certification. Typically, participants may not attend training unless they are part of a team with an approved project. The reason for this stipulation is the understanding that learning is more effective when it includes applying concepts to "real-world" problems rather than simply using classroom examples. Having a project turns theory into practice. This approach has the added benefit of getting projects completed, because certification occurs only after the project is finished and the students can demonstrate both knowledge of the Six Sigma problem-solving process and that they used the tools in their project.

A Strategy, Not an Initiative

Six Sigma is often described as a strategy rather than an initiative. Although that may seem like semantics, it is not. Webster defines an initiative as an "introductory step," while a strategy is a "careful plan or method." The distinction is an important one. Six Sigma is more than a beginning or a first step. With its emphasis on analysis and fact-based decisions, it provides a method for improving a company.

To do that, three things must be right: the right *people* must be working on the right *problem* in the right *way*.

DFSS: The Logical Extension to Six Sigma

Six Sigma is a strategy and a highly effective one. It does, however, have limitations. Even when applied rigorously, companies have discovered that they are not reaching their goal of having six sigma processes, but in fact rarely exceed a sigma level of 4.5. This represents 1350 defects per million opportunities, a number that is still too high for most companies. The reason for this shortfall is that traditional Six Sigma focuses on improving existing processes. While there is no denying the benefit to be derived from reducing variation and eliminating defects in existing processes, this may not be enough.

Exhibit 1.4   Comparison of Six Sigma and DFSS

	Action Taken	Timing of Action	Action is On	Effects Are	Effect is On	Need to Repeat
Six Sigma	Analyze	At any point in the lifecycle of the process/ product	Any Portion of Existing Process	Prevention of Defects	All products	None
DFSS	Design	Before the process/ product is initially developed	Entirety of new process	Prevention of defects, increased quality, increased customer sat	All products	None

Classic Six Sigma assumes that the fundamental design of the process being optimized is a good one. It may not be. As Chowdhury states, "80 percent of quality problems are unwittingly designed into the product."[1] In that case, because the Six Sigma process begins after design is complete, it may be impossible to correct all of the problems and achieve the company's goal of near-perfection.

DFSS (Design For Six Sigma) tackles this problem by starting earlier in the process. As its name implies, it focuses on the *design* of the product or service. Using statistical methodologies and tools, DFSS has as its goal ensuring that the design fully meets the customers' requirements and results in a product that can be manufactured at the six sigma level.

IT professionals are familiar with the Five Ps (prior planning prevents poor performance). DFSS is the ultimate embodiment of those Five Ps. Exhibit 1.4 illustrates the difference between classic Six Sigma and DFSS.

Although DFSS is a powerful methodology, it should be noted that it is not applicable to all situations. As discussed throughout the remainder of this book, there are many projects that are better suited to classic Six Sigma. The strengths of DFSS are best applied to the development of new products or major reengineering of existing ones. Classic Six Sigma and DFSS are complementary strategies. A successful company will employ both.

Applying Six Sigma to System Development

Although it is doubtful that any IT manager would deny the importance of reducing defects, increasing customer satisfaction, and operating more efficiently, many IT departments have not adopted Six Sigma. While there are a number of reasons, some of which are discussed in Chapter 2, there are also two misconceptions that are frequently associated with Six Sigma and system development. The first is that, because Six Sigma has its basis in statistical analysis, it can be applied only to manufacturing or engineering processes and that it has little or no relevance to the system development life cycle and the IT department in general. The second is that IT cannot use Six Sigma techniques unless the entire company has adopted the Six Sigma philosophy. Both ideas should be debunked.

No Relevance to IT

There is some irony to the belief that Six Sigma applies to engineering processes but not to IT, because system development is sometimes referred to as software engineering. The truth is that the use of Six Sigma's disciplined approach and tools benefits service organizations as well as manufacturing processes. Both the tools and the techniques can increase the probability of successful system development by ensuring that the "three rights" are in place.

1. *The right people are involved.* Too often, projects fail either because all stakeholders are not represented or because they join the team too late to participate in the definition of requirements. With its emphasis on teamwork and the clear identification of customers, Six Sigma mitigates this problem. As explained in Section II, the definition of "customer" is broad and can include everyone who touches a product or process. Having these groups as active participants means that the right people are involved and helps to ensure the next "right."

2. *The right problem is solved.* Although meant as a joke, there is some truth to the classic cartoon that shows an IT manager speaking to his staff. "You start coding," he says. "I'll find out what they want." Six Sigma tools provide a clear way to identify not just the customer's requirements, but also the impact that a proposed solution will have on those requirements. Stringent use of the tools will help the team focus on the system components with the greatest value and will assist in separating nice-to-have features from those that are essential. In manufacturing terms, IT will produce the right product.

3. *The right method is employed.* Just as they can for a process on the manufacturing shop floor, Six Sigma tools can be used to assist the IT department in evaluating its processes and procedures to

determine where there is variation, why defects occur, and how to prevent them. If, for example, projects are consistently over budget, the use of Six Sigma techniques will help IT uncover the root cause and correct it. Following Six Sigma principles will ensure that decisions are fact based and risks such as modifying the wrong part of the process are avoided.

All or Nothing

The second misconception is that IT cannot benefit unless the entire company has adopted Six Sigma. While there is no denying that it is easier for IT to implement Six Sigma processes if the remainder of the company has embraced the philosophy, there are benefits to be derived from employing the tools and incorporating the process into system development, even if the corporation as a whole is not a Six Sigma company. Sections III through VIII describe ways in which Six Sigma tools can improve various aspects of system development. These tools are designed to be used in any IT department.

Six Sigma has applicability in software engineering. The techniques for ensuring that customer requirements are understood, that the impact of proposed changes is measured and evaluated, and that the development process is made more reliable will benefit all IT departments. The reasons for adopting these techniques are clear. Fewer defects, faster delivery, and increased customer satisfaction will result in a more effective IT department, one with enhanced value to the corporation.

Reference

1. Chowdhury, Subir, *Design for Six Sigma*. Chicago: Dearborn Trade, 2005, p. 9.

Chapter 2

The Six Sigma Difference

"We don't need Six Sigma. We already have a QA program."

"We don't need Six Sigma. We're making good progress moving up SEI's CMM."

The Six Sigma Difference

When asked why they have not implemented Six Sigma, some IT managers respond that they have no need for it. These arguments are common when IT organizations believe that there is no difference — or, at least, no important difference — between Six Sigma and quality assurance (QA) or between Six Sigma and the Software Engineering Institute's Capability Maturity Model (SEI CMM). The fact is that both QA and CMM are important and can contribute to the overall success of the IT department. Neither, however, is synonymous with Six Sigma, nor is either a substitute for it. Despite arguments to the contrary, IT needs Six Sigma because it encompasses more than either QA or CMM. The remainder of this chapter explains the differences.

Six Sigma and Quality Assurance

The quality assurance movement, which had its origins in W. Edwards Deming's principles of quality, seeks to prevent rather than correct defects.

It has as one of its precepts that quality assurance should be an integral part of the entire process, not a step that is tacked on at the end. The rationale for this is simple: the earlier that a problem is found and corrected, the less costly that problem becomes.

If this sounds like Six Sigma, it is no coincidence. Six Sigma had its foundation in the quality movement. What gives Six Sigma greater value and utility to a corporation is that while it encompasses QA principles, it also goes beyond them. The differences include:

- *Greater focus on the customer.* Although one of the goals of quality assurance is customer satisfaction, Six Sigma recognizes that to satisfy customers, it is essential to understand them and to ensure that their requirements are central to every decision that is made. In a Six Sigma company, there is nothing more important than the customer. The logical extension of this philosophy is that customers may be part of process improvement teams. Even when they are not active participants, there is frequent communication with customers to ensure that their needs are being met. After all, defect-free products are of little value if they do not meet the customer's requirements.

- *Focus on continuous improvement.* A Six Sigma company embraces change as a way of life. While quality assurance seeks to prevent defects in existing processes, a Six Sigma company encourages its employees to challenge the process, even if it is working well, and to find ways to make it better. As one slogan states, "Don't let being the best keep you from getting better."

- *Analysis and confirmation of facts before making decisions.* The fact-based decision making that is so integral to Six Sigma is not an explicit part of a QA program. Although QA is indeed based on facts, the procedures for analyzing processes and ensuring that the implications of making a change are fully understood before it is implemented are not incorporated into QA. Six Sigma, as noted before, is more than a concept. It includes the tools and procedures that can be used to convert ideas into reality.

- *Emphasis on teamwork.* Quality assurance can be performed by a single department or even by one individual, whereas Six Sigma projects normally cross departmental and functional boundaries. Because its scope is more limited, QA places no importance on the need to break down barriers between departments and functions, and it has no formal process for establishing and chartering teams.

- *Breadth and depth of program.* While QA tends to be more narrowly focused, Six Sigma impacts everyone and every aspect of a company. That is why it is sometimes referred to as a revolution. QA seeks to guarantee a better product; Six Sigma's objective is a better company.

Six Sigma and CMM

Although it can be considered a quality program, CMM is a specialized one. It addresses one and only one aspect of a company's operations, namely, software development. In response to the cost and schedule overruns that frequently plague software development projects, the Software Engineering Institute (SEI) at Carnegie Mellon University created the Capability Maturity Model (CMM). CMM is a methodology to improve the development and delivery of software by making the entire process more predictable. The objectives are to prevent runaway projects and to enable an IT department to produce every system on time and on budget. If that sounds easy, it is not.

The transformation of an IT department's software development process from unpredictable to the ultimate goal of what the SEI calls "optimizing" is a lengthy one, typically measured in years. Recognizing both the magnitude of the undertaking and the fact that benefits are derived even if an organization never reaches the final stage, CMM is often returned to as a maturity path with five milestones along the way. These are referred to as *maturity levels.*

As shown on Exhibit 2.1, each level has a name and its characteristics are clearly defined. The division into levels allows organizations to chart their progress and to celebrate their improvements. Like a project plan with

Exhibit 2.1 SEI CMM Levels

Level	Description	Characteristics
1	Initial	Results are unpredictable, because they are dependent on individuals' skills and efforts.
2	Repeatable	Basic processes have been established on a project level, making it possible to replicate performance on similar projects.
3	Defined	Standard processes have been integrated across the IT organization and are used consistently on all projects.
4	Managed	Detailed measurements and quantitative controls make it possible to predict results.
5	Optimizing	The organization actively seeks to improve the process through innovation.

clearly defined milestones and deliverables, each maturity level is composed of key process areas (KPAs), with each KPA consisting of activities.

As would be expected of a quality program, CMM has a formal assessment process that enables an organization to determine where it is on the maturity path and what steps must be taken to reach the next level. Some companies train internal staff to serve as assessors. There are also outside organizations that specialize in CMM assessment. The advantage of outside assessments is that they may be more objective.

The overall goal of CMM is to move system development from an immature process, typically characterized as ad hoc, to a mature, disciplined one where procedures are documented and followed and where quality is measured by objective criteria. The further an IT department moves up the maturity path, the less its success depends on individual expertise. Instead, the institutionalization of good procedures helps ordinary people deliver extraordinary results consistently.

Similar to QA, the CMM has many similarities to Six Sigma, yet there are important differences. Like QA, CMM does not have Six Sigma's intense customer focus, it does not emphasize teamwork, and it does not stress fact-based decision making. In addition,

- *CMM applies only to the software process.* In some respects, CMM can be viewed as a subset of Six Sigma, because — like Six Sigma — it focuses on reducing variation, quantifying performance, and improving processes. However, whereas Six Sigma is normally implemented across a corporation and is designed to improve all processes, CMM is limited to IT's software process.
- *CMM does not ensure that the right problem is being addressed.* While it is effective in helping IT organizations ensure that they are using the right method to develop software, CMM does not have any provision for verifying that the software will solve the most critical problems. It is possible to deliver software on time and on budget and yet have dissatisfied customers, simply because the system does not meet their highest priorities.

CMM can be viewed as the tool that tells a department *how* to develop software, whereas Six Sigma shows them *what* to develop. CMM can also be viewed as an IT-specific infrastructure for Six Sigma because it provides QA and documentation systems that can be used in the deployment of six sigma system development.

Although they have limitations, there is no denying the value of both quality assurance and the capability maturity model. From an IT perspective, they can be considered building blocks of Six Sigma, pieces that, when combined with others, form a powerful whole.

Six Sigma and Lean

When Six Sigma was first introduced, it was sometimes viewed as being in competition with lean techniques. Now, just as the Total Quality movement was often expanded to address speed issues, many companies have incorporated lean fundamentals into their Six Sigma programs.

The primary focus of lean is increasing the speed of a process by reducing waste. Although the term "waste" is often considered synonymous with defective products, as will be discussed in greater detail in Chapter 6, waste has a number of components, only one of which is scrap.

As noted above, Six Sigma has as its fundamental goal the improvement of quality, while lean seeks to increase speed. Rather than being considered mutually exclusive, lean and Six Sigma should be recognized as complementary. Lean, when applied in a vacuum, may decrease cycle time but have no effect on quality. The customer may be delighted by the speed with which he receives the product, only to discover that he has gotten a defective one. Similarly, in its narrowest definition, Six Sigma may eliminate defects but not address cycle time. The customer may receive a perfect product too late.

Although these examples are extreme, it should be obvious that the combination of greater speed with increased quality will result in improved customer satisfaction. And that is — or should be — every company's goal.

Chapter 3

Managing Change

No book about Six Sigma would be complete without a chapter addressing change. That is because one of the principles of Six Sigma is that improvement is continuous, and improvement by definition means change. The changes that result from Six Sigma process improvements can be major ones such as reorganizations or layoffs. They can be as small as changing the location of the tool crib. But the one constant is change, and the change is constant.

Although it becomes a way of life, Six Sigma companies recognize that change is a process, not an event, and — like all other processes — it must be understood and managed.

The Human Effects of Change

Moving the tool crib is simple. While it may involve planning, it is a single event with a clearly defined beginning and end. However, the human reaction to the relocated tool crib may not be so simple. Habits of many years may have to be broken and new work patterns developed because tools are no longer in the same place. Initially, tasks may take longer to complete, and accidents may occur because of the change. In short, a seemingly minor change may have unexpected effects on the employees who are directly impacted by it.

Although it is processes that are changed by a company's efforts to reduce defects, it is people who feel the effects of those changes. They are the ones whose lives are being altered; they are also the ones who must make the change happen. Depending on their personalities and their past experiences, they may welcome change, while others may resist it. It is not always possible to predict a person's reaction. What is important is understanding the effect change may have.

One exercise that is sometimes used in change management classes is to give participants a piece of paper and a pencil and ask them to sign their names. Although this frequently elicits puzzled looks, it rarely creates a problem. When the facilitator tells the participants to move the pencil to their other hand and repeat the exercise, the reaction is different. Nervous laughter is sometimes heard.

The third step in the exercise is for the participants to discuss the difference between the two experiences. Common responses are:

- It took longer.
- I felt awkward.
- My second signature is illegible.
- Why would anyone do this?

The point of the exercise is to understand that change is difficult, that — without adequate training — quality may suffer and schedules may not be met. Furthermore, people may resist change because it takes them out of their comfort zone.

In addition to understanding that some people will resist change, as Johnson shows in his fable about the reaction of two mice to corporate change, *Who Moved My Cheese?*,[1] it is important to recognize the stages that people typically experience when coping with major change. The stages are sometimes referred to as the SARAH model:

- *Shock:* surprise is sometimes mingled with disbelief and denial.
- *Anger:* the anger may be directed at either individuals or the corporation as a whole.
- *Resistance:* in this stage, there is an active lack of cooperation.
- *Acceptance:* although productivity may not return to normal in this stage, employees begin to participate in the change process.
- *Hope:* at this point, employees are able to focus on the future.

While the stages are shown in sequence, some people appear to skip one or more stages, while others who appear to be progressing have relapses and move back to a previous one. It is also important to note that change affects not only the people most directly impacted, but also those around them. "Survivor guilt" can be an effect of a layoff or reorganization, with the people who remain experiencing many of the same symptoms as their former colleagues.

The Roles People Play

The previous paragraphs describe the way people might react to change. It is also important to understand the roles that they might play as part of the change process.

In *Managing at the Speed of Change,*[2] Conner divides people into four categories: (1) sponsors, (2) agents, (3) targets, and (4) advocates. Sponsors are the champions of change, the ones who instigate it. Agents are the activists who make change happen, while targets are those who are changed, and advocates support the change.

In a typical system development project, IT is an agent. Although not directly impacted by the change, IT will not be successful unless those who are directly affected — the targets — accept the new system and the changes that it brings. It is, therefore, important for IT to understand the dynamics of change, how it affects people, and how to help lessen the negative effects.

Components of Successful Change

Virtually every company can cite an example of a major change that failed, whether it was the introduction of a product such as New Coke or an attempt to implement a new version of a software product. For it to be successful, change must be characterized by three things: (1) direction, (2) commitment, and (3) sustainability. Without all three, while it may appear to succeed initially, it will not achieve the desired long-term goals.

Direction, although often equated with vision, has three underlying components, of which vision is only one:

1. *A vision.* The "end state" must be clearly communicated and understood throughout the organization. There should be no doubt about what the desired result of the change will be.
2. *A reason.* Similarly, everyone should know why the change is being made. Additionally, the problem or underlying need that precipitated the change must be compelling enough to overcome the natural resistance to change. Change for the sake of change is rarely successful.
3. *A champion.* Also called the sponsor, the champion is a person with enough credibility, clout, and charisma to initiate the change and marshal the resources needed to implement it. The champion is the one who should communicate both the vision and the reason.

Although it is desirable to have all three attributes of direction, successful change must have at least one of them.

Commitment stands alone. It has no subcomponents, and it is mandatory. If a change is to be successful, all stakeholders — and that includes agents as well as targets — must be fully committed to turning the vision into reality. Mere acceptance is not enough.

Sustainability includes the attributes that ensure change will be lasting. Like direction, sustainability has three subcomponents:

1. *Methods.* Having a vision and commitment will not make change happen, whereas effective procedures and tools will.
2. *Measurement.* Unless the results of change are monitored, backsliding and reversion to the old ways are possible. Measurement adds a needed incentive to sustain change. It also helps quantify and communicate the results of the change, underscoring the validity of the initial reason for the change.
3. *Control.* Even measurement is not sufficient to prevent backsliding. A plan to bring the process back on course if the measurements demonstrate that there is a problem is also needed.

As was true for direction, while all three attributes of sustainability are desirable, at least one must be present for the change to be successful.

Building Commitment

Of the three components of change, commitment is often the most difficult to attain because it may mean bringing together disparate groups of employees whose priorities differ from those of the project. Although there are several steps involved in building commitment, the key is constant, effective communication. The goals of this communication are to:

■ Create a shared vision in which everyone recognizes the benefits that will be derived from the change.
■ Build a coalition of all stakeholders so that the change can occur and will not be thwarted by resistance.
■ Reduce affected employees' sense of isolation, including them in the process.

There are two types of communication: (1) formal and (2) informal. While informal communications are normally verbal, formal communication can be written (memos, e-mails, updates to Web sites) or verbal (speeches, teleconferences, meetings). The primary distinction between the two classifications is that formal communications are planned, whereas informal ones are not planned. Both have their uses and advantages.

Formal Communication

In the case of a major change, particularly one that involves staff changes, it is frequently desirable to not only plan the communication, but also to develop a written communication plan. The purposes of a formal plan are to:

■ Ensure that the right people are involved.

■ Develop a common message.

■ Identify the correct timing for delivery of the message.

That is, a communication plan outlines what will be communicated, by whom, and when. If layoffs or other major personnel changes are anticipated, it is critical that they be announced at the right time, and that the legal and human resource departments be active participants in both developing and delivering the message.

The contents of a communication plan include the key messages, a schedule of events, and a list of frequently asked questions (FAQs) and answers. All of these are prepared in advance and reviewed with the key communicators prior to the kickoff of the project.

■ *Key messages.* Particularly when sweeping changes are planned, it is essential to ensure that everyone affected understands the major elements. In journalistic terms, these are referred to as the five Ws (who, what, where, when, and why). The message should focus on:

■ What changes are being planned?

■ Why is the change needed?

■ When will it happen?

■ Who will be impacted?

■ Where will it happen? In many cases, the "where" aspect is of less importance, although for large companies that are centralizing previously decentralized groups, it is a critical component of the message.

When developing the key messages, it is important to keep them simple. Details will be presented in subsequent communications, and different groups may receive different pieces of information. The key messages, however, should be communicated to everyone at the project's initiation and should be repeated regularly until they have become incorporated into a shared vision.

■ *Schedule.* It is also important to know who will communicate what, to whom, and when. Building commitment begins by getting buy-in from advocates and agents at an early stage. These groups may be included in "pre-announcement" meetings so that they are prepared for the reactions when the general announcement is made.

Exhibit 3.1 illustrates a sample communication plan schedule.

Exhibit 3.1 Communication Plan Schedule

Date	Audience	Medium	Key Messages	Accountability
11/1 – 2 p.m.	Department heads	• Meeting (travelers to dial-in)	• Overview of project • Impact on employees • Timing • Overview of communications process • Next steps: Schedule meetings with your HR reps to review process for selecting employees	Sharon sponsor

11/2 – 11/6	HR Reps	• Memo
		• Meeting with HR reps
		
		(Dept heads to use memo as basis for discussion with their HR reps)
			• Overview of project
			• Impact on employees
			  • Selection criteria
			  • Alternative assignments
			• Timing
			• Overview of communications plan
				Department heads

11/8	Affected departments(all employees)	• Meeting	• Overview of project
			• Stress vision and need
			• Impact on employees
			  • Some layoffs
			  • Enhanced severance
			  • Internal posting for other jobs
			• Communications plan
			  • Weekly updates of project status
			  • Send questions to central e-mail box
			  • Answers posted weekly
				Department heads

■ *FAQs.* Any announcement of change will elicit a number of questions. To ensure that messages are not "lost in the translation," it is helpful to have a brainstorming session to outline all possible questions that may be raised and to develop answers for them. Putting both the questions and the answers in writing helps to prepare whoever will actually deliver the message and helps ensure consistency. (In Six Sigma terms, it reduces variation.) Some companies prepare a frequently asked questions (FAQ) document and distribute it to the affected groups. Others simply give the document to those who will be delivering the messages.

Informal Communications

Informal communications are often nicknamed "water cooler" communications because they tend to be ad hoc. While those conversations are important to helping employees feel involved, a more effective informal communication mechanism is the rumor control session (RCS). During a period of major change, the sponsor, department manager, or other person in a leadership role schedules regular RCSs. (Typically, these are held weekly.) Attendance is optional, there are no planned messages to be delivered, and the leader makes no speeches. Instead, he or she may begin the session by asking, "What's the latest rumor?" and either confirming or denying it. The leader also responds to questions. An honest "I don't know" or "I can't tell you that yet" are valid answers; silence is not, because the objective of an RCS is to allay fears and give employees a chance to gripe.

When dealing with change, it is important to understand that resistance is often because the employee feels a loss of control. Whether or not it is real, the employee's perception is critical. IT as an agent of change may not be able to restore any real control, but it can — by keeping all affected people informed of progress and including them in decision-making meetings — help to mitigate the sense of loss.

Change and Six Sigma are inseparable. In *Who Moved My Cheese?*, Johnson presents what he calls "the handwriting on the wall." These are seven statements that include "change happens" and "enjoy change."[3] A Six Sigma company might add an eighth: "find the opportunity to change."

References

1. Johnson, Spencer, M.D., *Who Moved My Cheese?* New York: G. Putnam's Sons, 1998, p. 76.

2. Conner, Daryl R., *Managing at the Speed of Change.* New York: Villard, 1992, pp. 106–107.
3. Johnson, Spencer, M.D., *Who Moved My Cheese?* New York: G. Putnam's Sons, 1998, p. 76.

II

THE BASICS
OF SIX SIGMA

Most complex processes are divided into smaller components. Six Sigma is no exception. It is typically divided into five phases, creating what is referred to as the DMAIC model, where DMAIC is an acronym for the five phases: define, measure, analyze, improve, and control.

Using a case study of the fictitious Global Widget Company and its order entry process, Section II shows how a project team is formed and how team members use the DMAIC model and Six Sigma tools to improve the process.

Chapter 4 provides an introduction to DMAIC, explaining the objectives of each of the phases and describing the background of the project. Chapters 5 through 9 detail the steps that the project team followed in each of the phases. During Definition (Chapter 5), the team is chartered, customer requirements are identified, and the current process is documented. Measurement (Chapter 6) quantifies the problem and determines the process's current sigma level and capability. In Analysis (Chapter 7), the team explores the causes of variation and defects, proposes process improvements, and assesses the risks associated with each of their proposed changes. The changes are approved and implemented in Improvement (Chapter 8). With Six Sigma, the process does not end with implementation. Instead, there is a fifth phase, Control (Chapter 9), which ensures that the benefits are sustained.

Like Total Quality and other continuous improvement movements, DMAIC is an iterative process. This means that even when the final phase of a process improvement project is completed, the team is not content with the status quo but continues to seek further improvements, repeating the DMAIC process.

Chapter 4

Introduction to DMAIC

Six Sigma has been described as a measurement, a philosophy, and a set of tools and techniques. It can also be described as a *process*. Because Six Sigma places great emphasis on understanding and improving processes, before explaining how it can be used to improve the system development process, it is important to understand the Six Sigma process.

Most complex processes are divided into smaller components. Six Sigma is no exception. It is typically divided into five phases, creating what is referred to as the DMAIC model. DMAIC is an acronym for the five phases:

1. *Define* the problem and identify what is important.
2. *Measure* the current process.
3. *Analyze* what is wrong and identify potential solutions.
4. *Improve* the process by implementing solutions.
5. *Control* the improved process by ensuring that the changes are sustained.

Exhibit 4.1 provides more information about each of the phases' objectives.

Like Total Quality and other continuous improvement movements, DMAIC is an iterative process. This means that when a process improvement project is completed, the team is not content with the status quo but continues to seek further improvements, repeating the DMAIC process. Exhibit 4.2 is a pictorial representation of the iterative nature of Six Sigma and the quest for ever better processes.

Exhibit 4.1 The DMAIC Model

Phase	Objectives
Define	Identify the problem and the customers; define and prioritize the customers' requirements; define the current process.
Measure	Confirm and quantify the problem; measure the various steps in the current process; revise and/or clarify the problem statement, if necessary; define desired outcome.
Analyze	Determine the root cause of the problem; propose solutions.
Improve	Prioritize solutions; develop and implement highest benefit solutions.
Control	Measure the improvements; communicate and celebrate successes; ensure that process improvements are sustained.

Exhibit 4.2 Continuous Improvement with Six Sigma

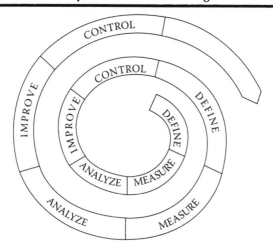

It must be noted, however, that the objective of a Six Sigma company is to continue to improve processes *only if the results are important to satisfying customer requirements*. The qualifying clause is italicized because the distinction is an important one. Six Sigma discourages tweaking or implementing improvements simply for the sake of changing the process. All decisions should be based on facts, with the benefits to the customers clearly defined.

The remainder of Section II uses a case study to illustrate the DMAIC process and the use of Six Sigma tools.

Background to the Case Study

The Global Widget Company (GWC) manufactures both large and small widgets for companies in a variety of industries. Customers range in size from multimillion dollar enterprises to small start-up companies, and — notwithstanding GWC's name — the majority of those customers are based in the continental United States. The company's sole manufacturing plant is located on the same campus as corporate headquarters, and — with the exception of the sales force — all employees are based in the same location.

Almost all order entry is done via telephone, using three shifts of operators, Monday through Friday. Although GWC's order entry process is still considered an industry benchmark, there are indications that problems may be developing. The CFO is concerned about rising costs, primarily salaries and benefits for the operators. Customers have complained about late deliveries and an increasing number of wrong items being shipped. The CEO worries about new competitors who are offering lower prices and 24/7 service to lure customers from GWC.

A year earlier, GWC made the decision to become a Six Sigma company. It hired outside consultants to train employees and guide the first process improvements. Currently, there are a number of certified Black Belts, and Green Belt training has been accelerated. It is GWC's objective to have all middle and upper managers certified as Green Belts before year-end. In the interim, there has been a major communication plan, designed to familiarize all employees with the Six Sigma vocabulary.

When concerns about the order entry (OE) process were raised at one of the Executive Committee meetings, the vice president of OE, Oscar Early, agreed that he would charter a project team to analyze the process and propose improvements. He further agreed that he would serve as the team's champion.

The Six Sigma improvement process had begun.

Chapter 5

The Definition Phase

The first phase in the DMAIC model is Definition. As might be expected of a philosophy that has as one of its tenets making fact-based decisions, the objective of this phase is to understand the problem to be solved and the process that will be changed as part of the problem resolution so that the correct decisions can be made.

The key steps within the Definition phase are:

1. Define the problem.
2. Form a team.
3. Establish a project charter.
4. Develop a project plan.
5. Identify the customers.
6. Identify key outputs.
7. Identify and prioritize customer requirements.
8. Document the current process.

The Project Champion

Before the project can begin, it is important to have a champion. Chapter 3 outlined the components of successful change and noted that having a champion is one of the three ways to obtain direction, with having a vision and a compelling reason for the change being the other two ways. Although pundits declare that change can be successful with only one of those three attributes, Six Sigma companies believe in maximizing their likelihood of success by insisting on all three, beginning with the champion.

Within GWC, Oscar Early had taken the first step in the DMAIC process when he agreed to serve as the project champion. Whether called a sponsor or a champion, this role is essential to the success of the project. The champion is the person who leads the change. He or she is the motivating force, the spokesperson, and the destroyer of roadblocks. Although the champion need not be involved in the day-to-day activities of the team, he or she must be accessible to the team.

An effective champion will:

- Believe in the value of the project
- Be fully committed to the project's success, including being willing to invest his or her own time to promote the project
- Have the authority to obtain funding and other resources
- Have enough political clout and persuasive skills to convince others of the project's value

Although it is not mandatory, it is helpful if the champion has a stake in the outcome, the proverbial "skin in the game." If the champion's budget or personal reputation is at risk, he or she will normally be a more effective advocate of change and will be viewed as having more credibility. It is, after all, easier to advocate change in another person's department than to be willing to implement it within one's own area of responsibility.

Step 1: Define the Problem

Before Oscar Early convened a team, he knew that he needed to develop a problem statement. He would then present this to the team as the reason it had been assembled. Oscar had learned in his Green Belt training that problem statements should be SMART. Like DMAIC, SMART is an acronym. This one defines the characteristics of a good problem statement and, later in the project, good requirements. SMART stands for:

- *Specific.* The problem must be quantified. Rather than attempting to cure world hunger, which in addition to being unlikely to be attainable, is a vague problem, the goal could be defined as "Increase the annual food supply in Country X by 50 percent for each person."
- *Measurable.* The results must be able to be measured. Using the previous example, unless the current per-capita food supply has been quantified, it is impossible to measure the increase.

- *Attainable.* The goal must be realistic. It may not be possible to increase the food supply by 50 percent, particularly not within a short timeframe.
- *Relevant.* The process improvement must satisfy an important customer requirement. In this example, the goal is relevant if the citizens of Country X suffer from malnutrition.
- *Timebound.* The expectation must be that the improvement will be achieved within a specified timeframe rather than being open-ended. In an ideal situation, the timeframe is measured in months rather than years. To make it timebound, the world hunger statement could be expanded to read, "Increase the annual food supply in Country X by 10 percent for each person by the end of the current calendar year and by 15 percent for each successive 12-month period."

Oscar Early's first problem statement was, "We need to improve customer satisfaction and reduce returned widgets without increasing costs of order entry." When he analyzed it, he realized it had met only one of the SMART characteristics. His problem was relevant to his operation. However, because the statement was phrased in general terms and no improvement levels or timeframes were specified, it was neither specific nor measurable nor timebound. This meant that Oscar had no way of determining whether it was attainable.

He revised his statement as follows: "Improve customer satisfaction by 10 percent and reduce returns by 20 percent by calendar year-end without increasing the costs of order entry." He believed he was now ready to establish the project team.

Step 2: Form a Team

Oscar knew that no matter how fervently he believed in the value of his project and no matter how much political clout he wielded, his project would be successful only if he assembled the correct team. He also knew that, although it might be easier to appoint only members of his department, because he could ensure that they had both the motivation and the time required to work on the project, he would have a higher probability of success if he involved all key stakeholders.

Because it was likely that the project would result in process changes, it was important to have buy-in from all affected groups. Although it is a basic tenet of Six Sigma, even before he attended Green Belt training, Oscar had learned from experience that if people were not involved at the early stages and did not believe that they were part of the change process, it was far more difficult to gain their acceptance later. Accordingly, when he began planning the team's composition, he included customer service representatives as well as members of the Information Technology (IT) department. The latter were included because Oscar believed that process changes might require modifications to the existing computer systems and wanted to ensure that IT was committed to the project. He also realized that the revised processes might involve changes in his department's responsibilities and asked Human Resources for an organizational design representative.

Oscar's creation of a cross-functional team was aligned with the Six Sigma concept of involving people who understand the current process so that decisions are made based on facts rather than intuition or guesses. Exhibit 5.1 provides a list of support departments that should be considered before finalizing the list of team members. It is important to note that while not all of these functions will be involved in every project, many will participate at some level. If they do not serve as active team members, they may be part of the improvement phase, working as individual contributors.

Exhibit 5.1 Support Functions to Consider for Team Membership

Function	*Reason for Including*
Communications	To assist with development of communication plan and package; this is particularly important when the change will impact customers and/or suppliers.
Customer Service	To provide a "voice of the customer"; this is especially helpful if actual customers cannot be involved.
Finance	To aid in developing benefit analyses
Human Resources	To provide assistance with change management, particularly when job functions will be eliminated or substantially altered.
Information Technology	To assist with identification of new technologies that may become part of the solution.
Internal Audit	To identify needed controls and ensure that company procedures are followed.
Legal	To identify any contractual issues that may result from proposed changes; if job functions will be eliminated or substantially altered, HR/Legal counsel should be obtained.
Procurement	To identify potential suppliers and the impact of proposed changes on existing suppliers.

Exhibit 5.2   Characteristics of Effective Team Members

- *Commitment.* The individual must believe in the project and be willing to do "whatever it takes" to make it successful.
- *Bias for Action.* The team member must have a sense of urgency and feel compelled to finish the project successfully.
- *Flexibility.* Since the team's charter is to recommend change, each team member must not only be able to adapt to change but must also embrace it.
- *Innovation.* Successful team members are able to not only embrace change but also to initiate it by finding new ways to accomplish the goal.
- *Personal Influence.* Since the team will become agents of change, it is highly desirable for all members to be well respected within their own communities. This is similar to the "personal clout" requirement for project champions.
- *Teamwork.* No matter how creative and committed individuals may be, unless they can work successfully as part of a team, they should not be part of the core team. Key "individual contributors" who lack cooperative and collaborative skills may be called on to provide expertise at various stages of the project.
- *Available Time.* Individuals who are close to burnout because of a too heavy workload should not be chosen for the team. Not only will they not be effective, but they may also create dissension within the team by missing meetings or failing to deliver on commitments.

In addition to ensuring that all key functions were involved, Oscar knew that it was important to invite the right individuals from each function. Not only did he want people with knowledge of their functional area, but he also wanted employees with a specific set of personal characteristics. Exhibit 5.2 lists the characteristics of effective team members.

Oscar was now ready to meet with Betty Blackbelt, a member of his department whom he planned to designate as the team leader. (Although it is not necessary to have a Black Belt as the leader, projects should have a Black Belt involved at least on an advisory basis.) Together, Oscar and Betty decided that the other team members should be:

- George Greenbelt, another member of the Order Entry department. George was about to take Green Belt training and needed an approved project. He was well regarded within the department and frequently advocated change.
- Irene Technowiz, a member of the IT department. As the IT staff member assigned to the Order Entry department, Irene was familiar with all the systems that the department used.
- Harold Resourceful, an organizational development specialist from the Human Resources department.

- Charlie Satiz, the member of the Customer Service department who had been responsible for developing the most recent customer satisfaction survey.

Although the group had never worked together as a team, they all met the personal characteristics that Oscar had identified as key success factors.

Oscar phoned each of the potential team members to invite them to join his team. Although Harold Resourceful mentioned that he was already a member of three other teams, he assured Oscar that he would have sufficient time to work on the Order Entry project. The other team members accepted the invitation with no reservations. Irene used this project as her impetus to register for Green Belt training.

The stage was set for the first team meeting. When Oscar convened the meeting, he opened with GRACE, the GWC meeting protocol. Although employees laughed because company lore claimed that GRACE was named in honor of the wife of GWC's founder, whose personal fortune paid for the manufacturing plant, no one disputed the value of the procedure.

GRACE was the company's acronym for the components it considered essential to set the tone for a meeting and to keep it focused:

- *Goal.* Without a clear objective, a meeting would founder. In this case, the purpose of the meeting was to kick off the Order Entry improvement project.
- *Roles.* Meetings within GWC had standard roles, some of which were not needed at all meetings. The team reviewed the list of roles shown in Exhibit 5.3 and decided to combine scribe and recorder. They also decided that the roles they chose would remain constant throughout the life of the project, although that was not mandated at GWC. Oscar had appointed Betty Blackbelt as the team leader. Irene Technowiz volunteered to become the time-keeper; Harold Resourceful agreed to be the conduct monitor, while Charlie Satiz accepted the role of scribe/recorder.
- *Agenda.* In accordance with GWC's company policy, 24 hours prior to the meeting, Oscar had e-mailed all attendees a copy of a tentative agenda. In this step, the group reviewed the agenda, adjusted timeframes as needed, and added a new item, a review of the project's constraints.
- *Code of conduct.* The Order Entry department had a standard code of conduct that was posted in all conference rooms. A sample code of conduct is shown in Exhibit 5.4. The attendees reviewed this and decided that no other items were required. They also stressed that it was important to check titles at the door, because the team

was composed of members at various levels within GWC. By "checking titles," everyone on the team had equal authority at the team meetings. The "no speeches" admonition limited participants to speaking for no more than 60 consecutive seconds, thus both avoiding some people's tendency to monopolize meetings and encouraging full participation.

■ *Expectations.* Each attendee expressed his expectations of the meeting. These were listed on flipcharts by Charlie and reviewed at the end of the meeting to determine whether they had been met. The most common expectations were to gain a better understanding of the project and to establish a basic project plan.

Exhibit 5.3   Sample Meeting Roles and Responsibilities

Role	*Responsibility*
Leader	Has overall responsibility for the success of the meeting; sets purpose and agenda
Timekeeper	Ensures that each agenda item starts and ends on time
Scribe	Is responsible for scribing ideas on flipcharts during the meeting
Recorder	Issues minutes of the meeting, including transcribing notes from flipcharts as appropriate
Conduct Monitor	Ensures that all attendees follow the code of conduct
Spokesperson	Serves as the official voice of the team

Exhibit 5.4   Sample Code of Conduct for Meeting

Start and end on time
Have an agenda and stick to it
Come prepared
No side conversations
Check titles at the door
Issue minutes within 48 hours
No speeches
No spectators; everyone participates
There are no bad questions or ideas
Attack ideas, not people
Have fun

The importance of checking titles at the door was evident when Oscar presented his problem statement to the team. Charlie Satiz, who had completed Green Belt training, pointed out that the statement outlined goals but was not a true problem statement. Even the problems that Oscar described were not specific enough to be included in a problem statement. In a truly hierarchical organization, Charlie might not have been comfortable making these assertions, but with titles "checked," he knew that Oscar would accept the criticism as constructive.

Charlie and the remainder of the team agreed that they did not have enough information to write a complete problem statement at this time, but that they were ready for the next step, which would help them prepare to finalize the problem statement.

Step 3: Establish a Project Charter

As its first major task, the team began to develop its project charter. The charter is one of the most important documents in a Six Sigma project because it serves as a summary of key information about the project. As would be expected of a strategy that has among its hallmarks an insistence on making decisions based on facts and the belief in teamwork, the charter is designed to help team members clearly understand why the team was formed, what it hopes to achieve, how long the project will take, and how much time the team members are expected to spend on it.

Documenting this information and ensuring that all participants and stakeholders receive copies may seem like common sense. The reality is that few companies — unless they have adopted Six Sigma — follow such a formal process. The benefits of a charter should be self-evident: fewer misunderstandings and greater focus. In short, less variation. Appendix A provides a sample charter with an explanation of what information is expected in each field.

The GWC OE team's initial project charter is shown in Exhibit 5.5. Many of the fields could not be completed during the first meeting. The team knew that this was normal, and that the charter would undergo several revisions before it was finished. Working with Oscar, the team agreed to a target project length of approximately six months. Although Irene Technowiz was concerned by the short timeframe, Betty Blackbelt reminded the team that its objective was not to resolve all of the problems in the order entry process. While the analysis might uncover a number of possible ways to improve customer satisfaction and reduce returns, the team would implement only the most important as part of this initial project.

Some companies refer to this as picking low-hanging fruit. George suggested that this would be only the first step in the continuous improvement

Exhibit 5.5 Initial Project Charter

Summary			
Process Impacted	Order Entry	Total Financial Impact	
Team Leader	Betty Blackbelt	Champion	Oscar Early
Start Date	June 1, 2001	Target Completion Date	December 15, 2001
Project Description	Improve customer satisfaction by 10% and reduce returns due to late shipments and wrong items by 20%.		

Benefits					
	Units	Current	Goal	Actual Achieved	Projected Date
Sigma Level					
COPQ					
Customer Sat					
Other Customer Benefits					

Team Membership				
Name	Role	Department	% Time	GB Trained?
Betty Blackbelt	Leader	Order Entry	50	Yes; BB
George Greenbelt	Team Member	Order Entry	30	No
Irene Technowiz	Team Member	Information Technology	20	No
Harold Resourceful	Team Member	Human Resources	20	No
Charlie Satiz	Team Member	Customer Service	20	Yes

Support Required	
Training Required	
Other Support Required	Team members will need access to the same shared network drive.

Schedule				
Milestone/ Deliverable	Target Date	Owner	Estimated Cost	Comments
Define	6/22/01			
Measure	7/20/01			
Analyze	8/24/01			
Improve	12/14/01			
Control	1/15/02			

Critical Success Factors and Risks	
Critical Success Factors	
Risks	

Approvals		
Role	Name	Date

Revision History		
Revision Number	Authors	Date
0	B. Blackbelt	6/1/01

process and that, once it was completed, the process would begin again as shown on Exhibit 4.2. In accordance with GWC company policy, the team's goal was to identify and achieve improvements quickly, normally selecting improvements that could be made within six months.

In addition to agreeing on a target completion date, one of the other important decisions the team made was to identify the amount of time each team member would devote to the project. Prior to the implementation of Six Sigma at GWC, project teams frequently failed because — although initial enthusiasm was high — team members' participation waned as the project progressed, leaving only a few individuals with the majority of the responsibility. The Six Sigma project charter served as a contract among team members, clearly delineating the amount of time each was expected to spend on the project. Although the amount of time might vary among team members, as was the case on the Order Entry project, each person understood his or her commitment and agreed to it.

Putting the time commitments in writing served several purposes. Not only did it assist the team in developing a realistic project schedule, but it also helped individual team members gain a commitment from their managers that they would be available to participate at the agreed-upon level. This written contract and the relatively short timeframe of projects at GWC increased the probability of success by ensuring that people would be available to participate when needed. It also helped foster the teamwork that is such an integral part of Six Sigma.

The Thought Process Map

At the same time it began to develop a project charter, the team started a thought process map (TMAP). The TMAP can be viewed as a repository of tribal knowledge about the project. Its purpose is to document the approach that the team used in problem solving so that other teams can understand why decisions were made. The TMAP lists questions that were posed, the answers to those questions, the methods that were used to determine the answers, and any Six Sigma tools that were employed in the development of the answers.

GWC has no standard form for a TMAP. Although some teams choose to use formal flowcharting techniques to document their TMAPs, the Order Entry team preferred a simple textual document as shown in Exhibit 5.6.

Refining the Project Scope

The first decision — and one of the most critical at this point in the project — is to establish a scope that can be accomplished within the desired

Exhibit 5.6   Initial Thought Process Map

ENTRY DATE: June 1, 2001

What facts do we know about the project?

- Customers have complained about late deliveries and an increasing number of wrong items being shipped.
- The CFO is concerned about the rising cost of order entry.
- The CEO believes new competitors with lower prices and 24/7 service will lure customers from GWC.

Questions:

What questions do we have at this point in the project?

1. What is the scope of our project?
2. How many deliveries have been late?
3. How does this compare to six months ago?
4. How many wrong items have been shipped?
5. What is the percentage of orders with wrong items?
6. How does this compare to six months ago?
7. What is the current level of customer satisfaction?
8. How does this compare to six months ago?
9. Do customers want 24/7 service?
10. What can we do to increase customer satisfaction?
11. Do we understand our current process?

What tools or methods will we apply to answer the questions? (Include action items, due dates and responsible person.)

1	Team meeting with champion.
2 – 3	Analysis of shipping records for past seven months. **Action:** HR to complete by 6/8.
4 – 6	Analysis of returns for past seven months. **Action:** IT to complete by 6/8.
7 – 8	Analysis of customer satisfaction for past seven months. **Action:** BB to complete by 6/8.
9 – 10	Customer focus group sessions. **Action:** CS to develop list of potential customers by 6/8.
11	Development of current process map. **Action:** GG to draft for 6/8 meeting.

Answers:

What were the answers to the questions? (Include reference to actual tools used.)

Question #	Date Answered	Answer	Tool Used
1	6/01/01	The project will focus on increasing customer satisfaction and reducing returns due to late shipments and erroneous items being shipped.	Brainstorming

timeframe. In most cases, this involves refining the problem statement to focus on one or two objectives. Teams typically have initial project scopes that are too broad. By narrowing the scope to a more manageable scale, the team has a greater likelihood of success.

As shown on the TMAP, the OE team listed three facts that were already known and which could be considered part of the scope. The team analyzed all three and determined that these were not different aspects of the same problem, but rather that there were three separate initiatives represented: (1) improve customer satisfaction by reducing late and erroneous shipments, (2) reduce or stabilize internal processing costs, and (3) determine whether pricing should be lowered.

Although all of these were valuable projects, the team determined that the reduction of late and erroneous shipments was the most critical problem and the one they should tackle first. A key reason that team members believed this was the most important problem was that it was the only one that had been raised by customers. While no one doubted the importance of the CFO and CEO, they all knew that their first priority must be to satisfy customers.

Furthermore, the team reasoned that if customers were dissatisfied with the service they were currently receiving, even lower pricing would not persuade them to continue buying widgets from GWC. Lower internal costs, while beneficial to the company, would have no direct, immediate effect on customers. The team agreed that reducing costs, which would ultimately translate into lower prices for customers, should be the goal of a different project.

Oscar Early concurred with the team's brainstorming session, and the revised problem statement became, "Improve customer satisfaction by 10 percent and reduce returns due to late shipments and wrong items by 20 percent." Although it was recognized that this was still a goal rather than a problem statement, team members agreed that until they could quantify the problem, this would remain the project description. They updated the project charter with this information.

The team then developed a list of questions that would help them quantify the problem and, as shown on the TMAP, determined how they would answer those questions. Because team members were committed to meeting their aggressive target completion date, they decided that they would meet for half a day each week. They also determined that to collaborate on documents and to have a single repository for the project's documentation, all team members would need access to the same shared network drive. Irene Technowiz volunteered to coordinate the network access. Because this would require service from IT, the team added it to the "Support Required" section of the project charter.

Step 4: Develop a Project Plan

The first step in planning the project was to establish a high-level schedule, showing when each of the DMAIC phases was expected to be completed. Although the team knew that each phase would consist of many smaller tasks, it decided to use these milestone dates as the summary schedule that it would show on the project charter. Their reasoning was that, although individual tasks might not be immediately comprehensible to people not on the project, anyone who would consult the charter would be familiar with the DMAIC phases and would quickly understand how the project was progressing.

Once that was complete, Betty Blackbelt reminded the team that, although the charter had a high-level schedule on it, it needed to develop a detailed project plan. Although it is possible to plan and track projects manually, GWC had adopted a PC-based project management package as part of its suite of office productivity tools and required all Green Belt candidates to use it. The company believed that having well-defined project plans and the ability to report progress against them added to the probability of a project's success.

George Greenbelt accepted responsibility for entering the team's schedule into the project management software. The team also adopted Harold Resourceful's suggestion that no task on the project plan last more than one week. Larger tasks would be broken into components of one week or less. Dividing the project into smaller deliverables and frequent milestones helps identify slippage before it becomes too difficult to correct.

Step 5: Identify the Customers

"We need to identify our customers," Betty Blackbelt told the team. Her statement met with laughter. "We know who they are," Charlie Satiz insisted. "Great Auto, Big Steel, Small Oil, . . ." He began to list the companies that bought GWC's widgets.

Betty shook her head, explaining that while those were external customers, they were not the only ones. She then led the team through an exercise to identify all of its customers, showing them that there were a number of different categories of customers:

- *External.* This group proved easiest for the team to identify, for these were the customers who placed orders, received widgets, and paid invoices. They were not, however, always the ultimate customers.
  - *Ultimate.* These external customers can also be classified as end users or consumers. If Great Auto incorporates GWC's widgets

on the cars it manufactures, the person who buys one of Great Auto's cars is GWC's ultimate customer.

■ *Internal.* Betty explained that other GWC employees would be classified as internal customers if they used the products or services that Order Entry generated. Although frequently overlooked by non-Six Sigma companies, internal customers are an important component in many processes. They come, Betty explained, in two varieties: immediate and intermediate.

- ■ *Immediate.* To help identify immediate internal customers, Betty asked the team to identify the product that the Order Entry department produced, then to determine who received that product. The product, the team agreed, was an order. Because the order was transmitted to the Packing department, Packing was an internal customer.

- ■ *Intermediate.* There was, however, another type of internal customer. George Greenbelt reminded the team that once Packing completed its work, widgets were sent to the Shipping department, where the orders were checked against the boxes of widgets. Was Shipping a customer of Order Entry because it used orders as part of its job? Betty explained that Shipping was indeed a customer and that it could be classified as an intermediate internal customer because it stood between Order Entry's first customer (Packing) and the external and ultimate customers.

As the team began to complete a chart (Exhibit 5.7), showing the customers they had identified and categorizing them, Irene Technowiz pointed out that some customers appeared to fit into more than one category. Big Steel, for example, was both an external and an ultimate customer. Betty agreed and explained that the primary reason for categorizing customers

Exhibit 5.7 Customers of the Order Entry Process

Internal		External	
Immediate	*Intermediate*	*External*	*Ultimate* (if different from External)
Packing department	Shipping department	Great Auto	Car buyer
Auditing department		Big Steel	
Customer service		Small Oil	
		Large Food	
		Little Telecom	Telephone buyer

was to help the team think beyond the traditional or external customer and consider everyone who used their products or services. Because one of the mantras of Six Sigma is to make decisions based on what will have the greatest positive effect on customers, it is vital to be able to identify all customers.

Once the team members identified customers by categories, they began to differentiate between customers within a category, creating a list of key customers. Some customers, they knew, were more important than others were, either because they purchased more widgets or because they used the product more often. Using that rationale, among internal customers, the Packing department was considered a key customer, while Auditing was not. The list of external customers was reduced until it included only the five largest customers. These companies accounted for 90 percent of GWC's sales.

The purpose of segmenting customers was to help determine who should be involved in focus groups and other "voice of the customer" activities that would be used to identify requirements and to aid in prioritizing those requirements. While small customers would not be excluded from either exercise, their requirements would bear less weight than those of major customers. The reason was simple. As a Six Sigma company, GWC wanted to make decisions based on facts. One incontrovertible fact was that increasing a major customer's satisfaction — and purchases — by 10 percent would have a greater effect than the same increase for a smaller customer.

Once team members had identified the customers of their process, they were ready to identify key outputs.

Step 6: Identify Key Outputs

Another round of laughter greeted Betty Blackbelt's declaration that the team's next task was to identify the outputs of the order entry process. "It's simple," Harold Resourceful said. "There is only one output: an order."

George Greenbelt was not so sure. While the order might be the most important output and the most tangible, he remembered Betty's saying that they needed to think about both products and services and consider everything that could be used to evaluate the Order Entry department's performance. Because orders were processed over the telephone, rather than having a separate Customer Service department to provide information about the types of widgets, the Order Entry clerks also served as sources of product information for customers.

"That is right," Charlie Satiz agreed. "You provide a customer service." The team expanded its list of outputs to include accurate information about GWC's products as well as courteous, prompt processing of orders. These were items that were routinely included on the customer satisfaction surveys that Charlie's department conducted and were one basis for evaluating the Order Entry department's performance.

As a Six Sigma company, GWC knew that outputs should include not just tangibles, such as the actual order, but intangibles such as speed of processing and accuracy of information.

Step 7: Identify and Prioritize Customer Requirements

The heart of Six Sigma is understanding and then delivering what customers need, what they expect, and what will transform them from simply being satisfied to being delighted. It is Customer Focus 101. That is why the team spent so much time identifying customers and why its next task was to determine customer requirements.

Clearly understanding requirements before making any process changes is not simply customer focus. It is also a key component of fact-based decision making. As discussed in Chapter 1, it is essential to understand why a change is needed and what impact it will have before making any modifications.

Customer requirements, or what is sometimes called "the voice of the customer," can be determined in a number of different ways. The most common techniques are shown on Exhibit 5.8, along with the advantages and disadvantages of each. Because team members already had access to customer satisfaction surveys and were going to gather information about returns and late shipments, they decided to conduct focus groups with representative customers as their primary method of identifying customer requirements.

In preparation for those focus groups, the team's final task during its initial meeting was to draft a customer requirements matrix. The purpose of this document was to identify what the team believed customers expected and what would delight them. This "straw man" document, which is shown in Exhibit 5.9, would be validated during the focus groups. Although it was possible to begin focus group sessions with a blank piece of paper and ask customers to list their requirements, the team believed that it would be helpful to have a starting place for the discussions.

Even if the requirements were inaccurate, this "priming the pump" would serve as both an ice breaker and the basis for establishing accurate requirements. The team would also be able to work with the customers to apply SMART criteria to the draft requirements, making them more specific.

Prior to conducting focus sessions or interviews, some teams complete the customer requirements matrix by entering their estimation of each

Exhibit 5.8 Tools for Determining Customer Requirements

Tool	Advantages	Disadvantages
Surveys	Relatively inexpensive to administer; require minimal effort from team	Unless carefully constructed, may not elicit important information
Focus Groups	Provide opportunity to digress from agenda and discover underlying problem; group setting may encourage participation and "building on" another's response	Require more time to conduct than surveys; group setting may intimidate some participants
Individual Interviews	Excellent way to discuss sensitive topics and to obtain specialized information that might be boring to others in a group setting; ideal for people who are uncomfortable in groups	Most time-intensive method
Site Visits	Excellent way to see the effect of problems and to meet customers who would otherwise be inaccessible	Can be expensive; customers may be unwilling to host site visits
Customer Complaints	Lowest cost	Provides only one perspective; does not address problems that other customers have not expressed; unbalanced, since it does not include positive comments
Returns	If reason for return is noted, clearly identifies problems	Too late to correct the problem

requirement's importance to the customer and the degree to which it is currently satisfied. The Order Entry team decided not to take this step, because it did not believe that it understood the customers' requirements and satisfaction level well enough to make meaningful estimates.

The team ended its first meeting by confirming the action items for the next meeting and documenting them on the TMAP.

Exhibit 5.9   Preliminary Customer Requirements Matrix

Customer: Great Auto

Requirement	Importance to Customer*	Current Satisfaction**
Order processed on time		
Order complete and accurate		
Information about products accurate		
Call answered promptly		

Customer: Packing

Requirement	Importance to Customer*	Current Satisfaction**
Order processed in time for shipping deadline		
All special requirements documented		

*Importance Ranking Scale:
1 = not very important
4 = moderately important
7 = very important
10 = extremely important
**Satisfaction Ranking Scale:
1 = not very satisfied
4 = moderately satisfied
7 = very satisfied
10 = completely satisfied

The Second Meeting

When the team met for its second meeting, the members reported the results of the action items that had been documented on the TMAP:

- *Questions 2 and 3.* Harold Resourceful indicated that out of 2570 shipments in the past six months, 310 (or 12 percent) were delivered later than the customer's specified date. This compared to an error rate of 5.5 percent seven months ago.
- *Questions 4 through 6.* Irene Technowiz reported that out of 185,005 widgets shipped over the past six months, 5521 (or approximately 3 percent) were returned with a return reason of "wrong

item." These items were part of 170 different shipments out of a possible 2570, or 6.6 percent. Another 175 widgets from five different shipments were returned with no reason indicated. Seven months ago, 28,316 widgets were shipped. "Wrong item" returns totaled 850, or approximately the same 3 percent. The returns came from 60 different shipments out of a possible 360, or 16.7 percent. There were no returns without a reason indicated during that month.

■ *Questions 7 and 8.* Betty Blackbelt told the team that her review of the customer satisfaction surveys showed that for the past six months, the average satisfaction was 3.7 on a scale of 1 to 5, with 5 being completely satisfied. Seven months ago, satisfaction was 4.2. Betty also noted that the trend was steadily downward over the past six months.

■ *Questions 9 and 10.* Charlie Satiz presented his list of potential customers for the focus groups. He suggested that large and small external customers be separated into two sessions and that there be another session for the Packing and Shipping departments. Because there would be costs associated with the focus group sessions, the team updated the project charter to include the costs of hosting focus group sessions as well as the other costs that it expected to incur during the next phases.

All of the team's findings were documented on the TMAP. In addition, the team added new questions. Exhibit 5.10 represents the status of the TMAP at the end of the second team meeting and shows the iterative nature of a TMAP.

Before reviewing the current process, the team decided to revise its project charter. Betty reminded the team that it had agreed to revise the problem statement once it had quantified the problem. The old problem statement, which was actually a goal, was: "Improve customer satisfaction by 10 percent and reduce returns due to late shipments and wrong items by 20 percent." The team revised this to: "Customer satisfaction has declined from 4.2 to 3.2 on a scale of 1 to 5 over the past seven months, while late shipments have increased from 5.5 percent to 12 percent over the same period, and returns due to wrong items remained constant at 3 percent of all widgets shipped. The project's goals are to:

■ Restore customer satisfaction to 4.2 within six months of the completion of the project (December 15, 2001) and increase it to 4.7 by the end of 24 months.

■ Reduce late shipments to 5 percent within three months of the completion of the project and reduce them an additional 1 percent during each of the next three six-month periods.

Exhibit 5.10   Thought Process Map After Second Meeting

ENTRY DATE: June1, 2001
What facts do we know about the project?
- Customers have complained about late deliveries and an increasing number of wrong items being shipped.
- The CFO is concerned about the rising cost of order entry.
- The CEO believes new competitors with lower prices and 24/7 service will lure customers from GWC.

Questions:
What questions do we have at this point in the project?
1. What is the scope of our project?
2. How many deliveries have been late?
3. How does this compare to six months ago?
4. How many wrong items have been shipped?
5. What is the percentage of orders with wrong items?
6. How does this compare to six months ago?
7. What is the current level of customer satisfaction?
8. How does this compare to six months ago?
9. Do customers want 24/7 service?
10. What can we do to increase customer satisfaction?
11. Do we understand our current process?

What tools or methods will we apply to answer the questions? (Include action items, due dates and responsible person.)
1   Team meeting with champion.
2–3   Analysis of shipping records for past seven months. **Action:** HR to complete by 6/8
4–6   Analysis of returns for past seven months. **Action:** IT to complete by 6/8
7–8   Analysis of customer satisfaction for past seven months. **Action:** BB to complete by 6/8
9–10 Customer focus group sessions. **Action:** CS to develop list of potential customers by 6/8
11   Development of current process map. **Action:** GG to draft for 6/8 meeting

Answers:
What were the answers to questions? (Include reference to actual tools used.)

Question #	Date Answered	Answer	Tool Used
1	6/01/01	The project will focus on increasing customer satisfaction and reducing returns due to late shipments and erroneous items being shipped.	Brainstorming

ENTRY DATE: June 8, 2001
Questions:
What questions do we have at this point in the project?
12. Why is the percentage of late shipments increasing?
13. Was the percentage of shipments with wrong items an anomaly seven months ago?
14. Why is customer satisfaction declining?

What tools or methods will we apply to answer the questions? (Include action items, due dates and responsible person.)
12   Will be determined during analysis phase.
14   Focus groups. **Action:** GG to schedule and lead groups by 6/15; all team members to participate.

Answers:
What were the answers to the questions? (Include reference to actual tools used.)

Exhibit 5.10   Thought Process Map After Second Meeting (continued)

Question #	Date Answered	Answer	Tool Used
2	6/8/01	12% (310 out of 2570 shipments) were late during the last six months.	
3	6/8/01	Seven months ago 5.5% shipments were late.	
4	6/8/01	3% (5,521 out of 185,005 widgets shipped) were returned as wrong items.	
5	6/8/01	6.6 % of the shipments contained wrong items.	
6	6/8/01	The percentage of items returned is constant at 3%; however, the percentage of shipments with wrong items has decreased from 16.7% seven months ago to 6.6% over the past six months.	
7	6/8/01	Current month customer satisfaction is 3.2. For the past six months, it averages 3.7.	
8	6/8/01	Seven months ago it was 4.2.	
11	6/8/01	We're making progress.	Top level, detailed and functional process maps.
13	6/8/01	We decided to focus on current shipments as part of the measurement phase.	

■ Reduce wrong item returns to 2 percent within four months of the completion of the project and reduce them an additional 1 percent during the next six-month period.

Team members reviewed these goals using the SMART criteria and believed that they met all five characteristics. They were now ready to review the current process.

Step 8: Document the Current Process

Although there are a variety of ways to document a process, most Six Sigma organizations use process maps rather than pure description. A process map provides a pictorial representation of the process being analyzed, showing the sequence of tasks along with key inputs and outputs. The purposes of a process map are to:

■ Make a complex process easier to understand by dividing it into smaller components (tasks).
■ Document the process flow, showing the sequence of tasks.
■ Understand the relationships between those tasks.
■ Provide facts with which to evaluate the process.

The development of process maps is typically an iterative process. The team will develop an initial map, which represents its understanding of how the process currently operates. As would be expected of a Six Sigma company that believes in including everyone who has knowledge of a process to ensure that the facts are known, the map is then reviewed by key people who understand the process and who are thus able to validate it. During this review process, it is not unusual to discover that steps — particularly rework loops — have been omitted.

Rework loops, as the name suggests, are breaks in the process where defects are identified and corrected, then reinserted into the process. In a rework loop, a widget with a rough edge might be taken from its shipping carton, returned to the polishing department to have the rough edge removed, and then placed back on the assembly line for shipping. Because one of the objectives of analyzing a process is to identify ways to prevent rather than correct defects, it is important to document all rework loops. They are normally among the first targets for improvement.

Types of Process Maps

The initial process map is frequently called an "as-is" map because it represents the process in its current state. Once the team has finished the Measure and Analyze phases of the DMAIC model, it will develop a "can-be" map, showing the proposed improvements. This is followed by the "to-be" map, which represents the agreed-upon end state. In many cases, "can be" and "to be" will be the same; however, when a number of improvements are recommended and phased implementation is required, there may be several interim steps before the final ("can be") state is achieved.

Top-Level Map

Similar to thought process maps, process maps can take several formats. Most teams begin the way George Greenbelt did, with a top-level map. As the name indicates, a top-level map attempts to reduce a process to major steps. It can be considered an outline of a process. Exhibit 5.11 shows the top-level map that George developed.

After reviewing the map, the team agreed that these were the basic tasks in the order entry process. While the top-level map provided a basic understanding of the process, if it were to recommend improvements, the team needed more detailed information. Under Betty's guidance, the team expanded the top-level map to show secondary or intermediate steps. The resulting process map is shown in Exhibit 5.12. While this is still a top-level map, the list of interim steps under each summary one provides additional information and documents decision points and rework loops.

In attempting to create the more detailed map, team members realized that they did not completely understand the packing and shipping processes. Recognizing what they did not know was a major benefit of creating the process map and was yet another step on the road to fact-based decisions. Team members agreed that they would add the intermediate steps once they had completed their interviews with the Packing and Shipping departments.

Exhibit 5.11   Top-Level Process Map

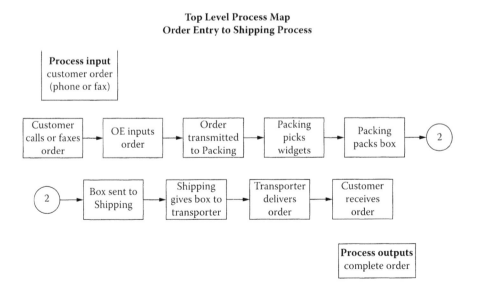

Exhibit 5.12   Top-Level Process Map with Intermediate Steps

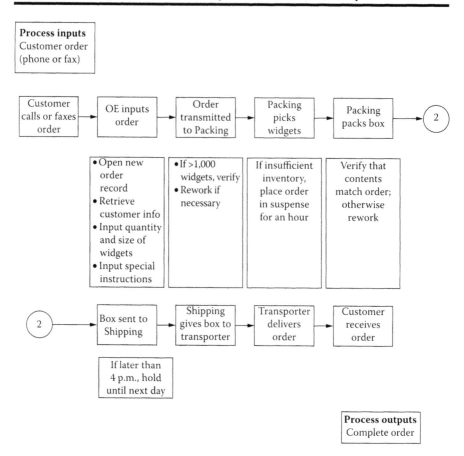

Detailed Process Map

The second format for process maps is the detailed process map. Unlike the top-level map, the detailed map displays each step, including intermediate ones, pictorially and includes decision blocks. If the top-level map is an outline, the detailed one is the text. It is particularly useful in later phases when a primary objective is to reduce non-value-added steps. Because each step is clearly shown, non-value-added steps can be color-coded for possible elimination. Identification and elimination of non-value-added steps are part of the application of lean techniques to Six Sigma.

Because the detailed map closely resembles the flowcharts that IT professionals use, Irene Technowiz volunteered to draw it. Exhibit 5.13 shows the detailed map equivalent of Exhibit 5.12.

Exhibit 5.13   Detailed Process Map

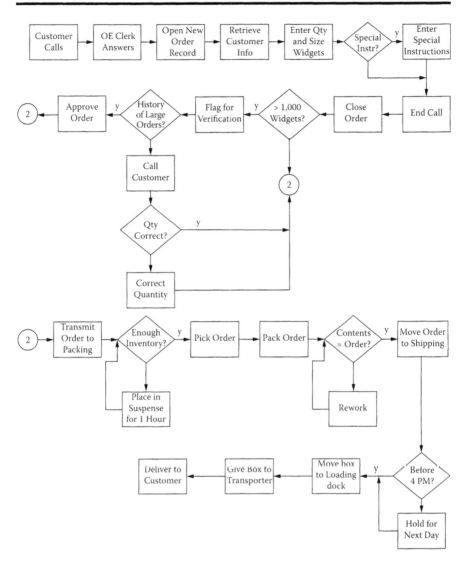

Functional Process Map

A third format for process maps is the functional map. This can be viewed as a hybrid version of a detailed map. The primary difference is that, while the detailed map showed steps in sequence with no regard for the department or function that performed them, the functional map clearly delineates responsibilities as well as the sequence of events. Functional maps are typically used for administrative processes, because one department rarely owns the entire process. They are also useful for building consensus among groups because they help identify boundaries and dependencies. Exhibit 5.14 provides a functional map of the order entry process. Appendix B details the creation of a functional map.

The process maps that were developed by the team during these initial meetings were preliminary maps and lacked some elements that would be needed for future phases. The team was, however, satisfied with them

Exhibit 5.14 Functional Process Map

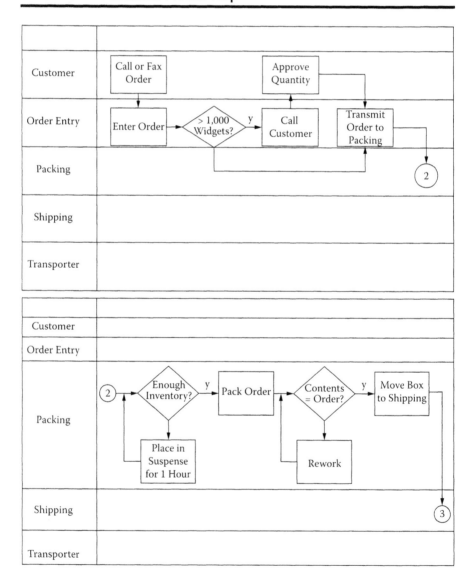

Exhibit 5.14 Functional Process Map (continued)

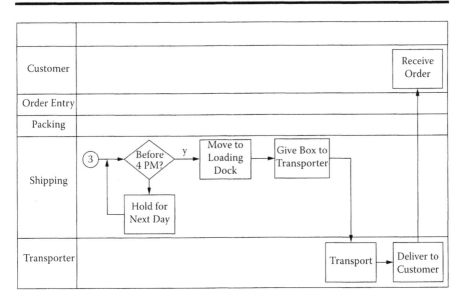

because members knew that meetings with customers and suppliers and the measurement phase would help them complete the maps by identifying key process input variables (KPIVs), key process output variables (KPOVs), and the minimum and maximum times required for each step.

The team was now ready to complete the definition phase by conducting focus group meetings with external customers and one-on-one interviews with key members of the Shipping and Packing departments. The objective was to complete the customer requirements matrix that it had begun the previous week.

Complete the Requirements Definition

The focus group meetings that the team held brought together representatives from each of the five major external customers. As they reviewed the preliminary customer requirements that the team had developed (see Exhibit 5.9), customers became animated. "No!" "Not quite . . ." "You forgot. . ." were frequent reactions. Customers clearly had concerns of which the team had been unaware. The team learned that "processed on time" was irrelevant to customers. What they wanted was delivery by the date they had specified. Customers wanted to be assured that they would receive their widgets in three or fewer working days from the date they placed the order without paying for expedited shipping.

Although the team had believed that "complete and accurate" were one requirement, customers explained that they were two separate requirements, with different importance ratings. It was more important to receive the correct number and size of widgets they had ordered than to have a complete order shipped the first time. Because it had been GWC's policy not to ship an incomplete order, believing that customers did not want partial shipments, this represented an "aha!" moment for the team. One of the ideas the team would explore in more detail would be changing the shipping policy — and process — to allow customers to get as many widgets as quickly as possible.

Similarly, customers' requirement that orders be shipped to the correct address pointed out a problem that the team had not known existed. It appeared that some orders were being shipped to the wrong division within a company. Rather than return the widgets, the division would forward the shipment to the correct address. This, however, resulted in delays, increased expenses to the customers, and decreased satisfaction. Had the team not held focus sessions and asked customers what GWC could do to improve services, it might not have known of the incorrect shipments. Charlie Satiz made a note to add a question about accurate delivery location to his department's survey form.

Customers also noted that calls were taking too long and added a requirement that they be completed within two minutes. The team realized that if it could reduce call length, not only would this improve customer satisfaction, but it would also delight the CFO because per-call costs would decrease.

Once customers had identified their additional requirements, the team worked with them to make them SMART. (As noted previously, SMART is an acronym for Specific, Measurable, Achievable, Relevant, and Time-bound.) There were few problems with the "measurable" and "relevant" characteristics, and specificity was relatively easy to define. The primary discussions revolved around whether or not a requirement was "achievable." Customers wanted guarantees that each requirement would be met 100 percent of the time, while the team insisted that not even Six Sigma processes operated at 100 percent reliability. The results of the discussion are shown on Exhibit 5.15.

Identifying requirements was only the first step in the focus group sessions. Once completed, the team asked customers to rank each according to its importance and then to measure the degree to which the process currently meets the requirement. The objective was to learn where changes could have the greatest effect on increasing customer satisfaction.

It should be noted that although the team uses a scale of 1 to 10, it asked customers to use only four values: 1, 4, 7, and 10. This simplified the ranking process and provided greater differentiation in the results.

Exhibit 5.15   Customer Requirements Matrix after Focus Group Meetings

Customer: Great Auto

Requirement	Importance to Customer*	Current Satisfaction**
Order delivered within 3 working days 95% of the time	10	4
Order delivered to correct address 95% of the time	7	4
Specified number and size of widgets delivered 99% of the time	10	7
Order complete on first shipment 95% of the time; remaining items delivered with in 7 days after first shipment 99% of the time	7	10
Information about products accurate 99% of the time	7	7
Call answered within three rings 99% of the time	4	7
Call completed within two minutes 98% of the time	4	1

Customer: Packing

Requirement	Importance to Customer*	Current Satisfaction**
Order received in time for shipping deadline (4 PM) 98% of the time	10	4
All special requirements documented 99% of the time	7	4

*Importance Ranking Scale:
1 = not very important
4 = moderately important
7 = very important
10 = extremely important

**Satisfaction Ranking Scale:
1 = not very satisfied
4 = moderately satisfied
7 = very satisfied
10 = completely satisfied

When the focus sessions were complete, team members reviewed the results to determine where they should place their emphasis. They knew that a requirement that is extremely important (10) and completely satisfied (10) has little or no room for improvement, whereas one with a very important score (7) that is not very satisfied (1) would warrant the team's attention.

Typically, teams ignore any requirements that receive satisfaction ratings of 10 and any that are assigned importance ratings of 1. Some teams create a priority ranking by multiplying the importance and satisfaction columns. The Order Entry team decided not to take that step because it believed that the results could be misleading. For example, both "order delivered to correct address" and "call answered within three rings" would have the same score (28), although customers clearly believed that the correct delivery was more important and more of a problem than the prompt answering of calls.

Reviewing the requirements matrix confirmed that late deliveries were the single largest problem but that the team should also resolve the problems of deliveries to incorrect addresses and shipment of wrong items.

In addition to reviewing the customer requirements matrix, the team asked the focus groups a number of open-ended questions, including, "What do you like best about ordering from GWC?" and "If we could change three things to make you more satisfied, what would those be?" The latter elicited comments such as, "Work on weekends," which confirmed the CEO's fear that 24/7 service was becoming a requirement.

As the team delved into that issue, one of the customers asked when GWC was going to join the 21st century and let its customers order online. "I used to call toll-free numbers to order clothes from JJ Carrot and Lake's Edge," the customer pointed out, "but now I can go to their Web site and order that way. It's easier." Another "aha!" moment had occurred as the team realized that one way to resolve some of the problems might be to replace telephone order entry with self-service online orders.

While team members might have reached this conclusion without the focus sessions, they would have been in the "we think" rather than the "we know" stage of problem resolution. By following the Six Sigma process, they knew what their customers wanted and were one step closer to making a fact-based decision.

The definition phase was complete. Although the team knew that it would update many of the documents that it had created during Definition, its members were now ready to proceed to the second DMAIC phase: measurement.

Chapter 6

The Measurement Phase

The second phase in the DMAIC model is measurement. Its objectives are to confirm and quantify the problem; to measure the steps in the current process; to revise and clarify the problem statement, if needed; and to define the desired outcome. Measurement is one more step along the road to making a fact-based decision.

When the team began this phase, Betty Blackbelt outlined the steps that the team would follow. The steps were:

1. Determine what to measure.
2. Conduct the measurements.
3. Calculate current sigma level.
4. Determine process capability.
5. Benchmark process leaders.

Although some companies include benchmarking within the analysis phase, GWC believed that it was part of measurement. The boundaries between the five phases — particularly among define, measure, and analyze — can appear fluid, in part because the process is not completely linear. It is not uncommon, for example, to do additional measurement during analysis. In reality, defining phase boundaries is of less importance than continuing on a well-defined path toward process improvement.

Step 1: Determine What to Measure

Because it has its foundation in statistical analysis, it is not surprising that Six Sigma would place a high level of emphasis on measurement. In fact, one of the tenets of Six Sigma is that measurement is a key to success. The team recognized the validity of this statement. It was, as Charlie Satiz pointed out, a corollary to the "if you do not know where you are going, any road will take you there" maxim. "If you do not know where you started," Charlie asked, "how will you know how far you have gone?" That was why the team wanted to understand not just what steps were involved in the order entry process, but also how long each step took, how many defects were created in each step, and where there were avoidable delays.

Betty reminded the team that its goal was to understand everything that affects the order entry process and then to eliminate defects. She had the team look at its top-level process map (Exhibit 5.11), which showed the major process steps as well as the input and output. She then wrote the following equation on the whiteboard:

$$y = f(x)$$

and said that was a mathematical explanation of the relationship between the inputs, outputs, and process. In the equation, y represents the ultimate output of the process, x is the input, and f is the process itself. That is, inputs are processed and turned into outputs or — in order entry terms — an order (input) is turned into a shipment of widgets (output).

"But," Irene said, "it is not that simple. There are several steps in the process." Betty agreed and said the equation should be:

$$y = f(x_1, x_2, x_3, \ldots)$$

where the multiple x values represent the various steps in the process. Delivering the correct number and size of widgets to the correct address happens only if each step in the process is defect-free.

Because opportunities for defects occur at each step, the goal is to eliminate them as early as possible in the process. To do that, it is necessary to understand what causes variation in each step. Typically, these are the inputs. To understand the causes of variation, it is necessary to measure the extent of that variation. However, the first step is to identify the inputs and decide which ones to measure.

Types of Variation

Although the team had identified the customer order as the primary input to the process, Betty asked the team to consider everything that had an impact on the process as a possible input or variable. When identifying variables, Betty suggested that the team use the "Six Ms" as a starting point. Exhibit 6.1 provides a definition of the "Six Ms": man, machine, material, methods, measurement, and Mother Nature. Like the exercise of identifying customers as internal, external, immediate, and intermediate, assigning inputs to a specific element was less important than simply identifying them. The "Six Ms" provided a framework for identifying variables. Exhibit 6.2 shows a portion of the team's work.

Exhibit 6.1   Elements of Variation: The Six Ms

Element	Explanation
Man	This is the human element, the differences that occur when more than one person operates a piece of equipment or performs a service.
Machine	Variances among different pieces of the same type of equipment are accounted for in this category.
Material	Raw materials or ingredients are included in this category.
Method	Standard operating procedures as well as the differences caused by having more than one way to perform a process affect variation.
Measurement	Some variances may not be true variances but may be the result of the measurement system. If measuring equipment is flawed or different observers record results differently, measurement may become an element of variability.
Mother Nature	Environmental factors, including temperature, humidity, and power availability are included in this category.

Exhibit 6.2   Order Entry Variables and the Six Ms

Six M Element	Order entry input variable
Man	Order entry clerks
Machine	System availability, telephone connection, fax quality
Material	Widget inventory
Method	
Measurement	
Mother Nature	Time of day

When the team had brainstormed input variables, Betty explained that in addition to assigning them to an element, those inputs could be classified as controllable and uncontrollable, and that controllable inputs could be subdivided into key (critical) and non-critical.

Controllable inputs are those that a person measuring the process can vary to determine their effect on the outputs. The team agreed that controllable inputs included the Order Entry clerks and the size of the widget inventory.

Uncontrollable inputs are those that affect the output variables but are difficult to control. Examples the team cited were system availability, poor telephone connections, poor quality of incoming faxes, and the time of day the order is received.

Critical variables, what some organizations call *key process input variables* (KPIVs), are those controllable inputs that have the greatest effect on the output variable. At this stage in the project, although team members had ideas of what the critical variables were, they made no assumptions because they knew that the measurement and analysis phases would enable them to clearly identify the KPIVs. Rather than make decisions based on opinions or intuition, the team would gather data and make informed, fact-based decisions.

The Lean Approach

While Six Sigma focuses on reducing variation, lean experts seek to eliminate waste. Waste, in this case, is defined as anything that consumes resources but generates no value. As might be expected, value is defined by the customer. In *Lean Six Sigma for Service,*[1] George defines seven types of waste. Exhibit 6.3 lists them and provides an example of each possible form of waste in GWC's environment.

The team reviewed the forms of waste as it had the Six Ms of Variation. Although it suspected that both inventory and overproduction might exist, neither was within the scope of the project. However, because it was GWC's goal to improve every process as much as possible, the team asked Oscar Early to propose a new project, focusing on inventory levels.

The team then began brainstorming what it would measure. Exhibit 6.4 shows the initial list of data elements the team proposed to collect. Although the team knew that not all of the fields would be critical to later analysis, it believed that the ones it had selected would enable the team to determine where delays occurred and where errors were being generated as well as to understand the current limits and capabilities of the process.

Exhibit 6.3   Seven Forms of Waste

Form	Description	GWC Example
Overprocessing	Doing more than is necessary to delight the customer	Removal of burrs on the inside of the widget. They create no problems but require an additional processing step to be removed.
Transportation	Unnecessary movement of materials or information	Moving orders packed after 4 PM to the "time out" corner of the warehouse, then back to the shipping lane the next morning.
Motion	Unnecessary movement of people	Packing clerk's moving order to and from the suspense file when there is insufficient inventory to fill it.
Inventory	Excessive work-in-progress	1,000 large widgets in the production line, when the current day's orders will not exceed 500.
Wait time	Delays in the process	Wait time caused by insufficient inventory being available for packing.
Defect	A product that does not meet the customer's specifications	Wrong size widget shipped to customer.
Overproduction	More finished product than needed for immediate use	500 large widgets completed at the end of the day but not needed for existing orders.

Measure What You Value

Another Six Sigma tenet is that it is important to measure what you value. George Greenbelt pointed out that, when describing their homes, most people mention either the number of rooms or the square footage, not the number of dust bunnies under a bed. The reason is simple: they value one and not the other.

Exhibit 6.4   Data Elements to Collect

Call Start Date
Call Start Time
Call End Date
Call End Time
*Length of Call
Number of Rings
Shift Code
Customer
Order Entry Clerk
Number of Small Widgets
Number of Large Widgets
*Total Widgets Ordered
Date Order Transmitted to Packing
Time Order Transmitted to Packing
*Minutes in Order Entry
Date Order Sent to Shipping
Time Order Sent to Shipping
*Minutes in Packing
Date Shipped
*Days in Shipping
Date Order Received by Customer
*Process Days (Call Start Date to Date Order Received)
*Number of Days Late (Process Days–2)
Number of Items Returned–Wrong Item
Number of Items Returned–Late Delivery
Number of Items Returned–No Reason
*Total Number of Items Returned
*Percent of Items Returned
*Number of Orders with Returns
Customer Satisfaction

* = Calculated field

Team members reviewed the proposed list of data elements to ensure that they were measuring what the customer valued. In comparing their initial list to the customer requirements matrix (see Exhibit 5.15), they discovered that, although the plan was to survey customers for their overall satisfaction, there was no method included to determine whether orders were delivered to the correct address. Although they believed that they would be able to determine whether the correct number and size of widgets were delivered by tracking "wrong item" returns, to ensure that they measured this accurately, they added another item to the customer satisfaction survey, asking whether the order had been complete and accurate.

Once they had determined that the data they proposed to collect had value to the customers, Betty asked the team members to use a different set of criteria to evaluate the measurements they planned to make. Just as requirements can be evaluated using the SMART system, Betty explained that an acronym can be used to describe characteristics of good measurements. Measurements should RAVE. That is, they should be:

- *Relevant.* For this project, there would be no relevance to measuring either the weight of packages that were shipped or the cost of raw materials. Neither has any bearing on customer satisfaction or on on-time delivery of widgets.
- *Adequate to detect process changes.* If length of call were measured in days rather than minutes, it would be impossible to determine whether the process had improved to the point of meeting the customers' requirement for calls to last no more than two minutes.
- *Valid and consistent from time to time.* When team members first proposed measuring process days, they envisioned a simple calculation: date order was received minus date order was placed. They soon realized that that was neither valid nor consistent, because it did not account for non-working days such as weekends or holidays.
- *Easy.* Although there might have been value in measuring time in seconds increments rather than minutes, the automated order entry system recorded only minutes. Using the existing system was easier than creating a new measurement technique, yet it still met the customers' requirements.

Accuracy of Measurements

Because measurements will be used to make decisions, a Six Sigma company places a high degree of emphasis on taking accurate measurements. The order entry team knew that there are risks associated with any measurement system. As shown on Exhibit 6.5, inaccurate measurements can result in good widgets being rejected or bad ones being passed through the system.

To help avoid these problems, the team knew that measurements should be repeatable and reproducible. If the same person measures the same item more than once and has the same results, the measurement is

Exhibit 6.5 Categories of Measurement Risk

	Alpha	Beta
Risk	Good items are rejected	Bad items are accepted
Group at Risk	Supplier	Customer
Effect on process	May be changed unnecessarily	Needed changes may not be identified
Other effects	Costs increase unnecessarily	Defects are created

repeatable. It is reproducible if a different person measures the same item and reports the same results as the first person.

Although the goal is to have all measurements be repeatable and reproducible, this goal is more difficult to achieve with subjective data, such as customer satisfaction or "pass/fail" evaluations that can vary depending on the rater or inspector. Objective data such as number of rings and length of call, neither of which requires any judgment, are more repeatable and reproducible.

To minimize the risks of subjective evaluations, the team knew it was important to define the measurement as clearly as possible. For example, if team members were measuring a "good" call, they could help ensure that the raters' scores were consistent if they defined "good" as:

- Call answered within two rings *and*
- Operator provided standard greeting ("GWC Order Entry department, Sandra speaking. How may I help you?") *and*
- Operator ended call by asking if there was anything else she could do to help the customer.

Without similar specifications, raters would have to rely on their own definitions of "good."

The team was now ready for the second step: actually measuring.

Step 2: Conduct the Measurement

Using the data element list it had developed (Exhibit 6.4), the team gathered data about orders for four days. Although more than 75 orders were processed during that period, because they were unable to obtain customer satisfaction ratings on all orders, it was decided to limit measurement to the 75 orders that had complete data, including customer feedback. When the collection step was complete, the team entered the data into a spreadsheet and performed some basic calculations to determine how closely

Exhibit 6.6   Comparison of Current Process with Customer Requirements

Requirement	Current Process	Importance to Customer
Order delivered within 3 working days of order date 95% of the time	26 orders (34.67 percent) were delivered within three days; average order processing time: 3.76 days	10
Order delivered to correct address 95% of the time	86.67% were delivered to correct address	7
Specified number and size of widgets delivered 99% of the time	Customers reported 49.33% of orders had problems; 29.33% of orders had "wrong item" returns	10
Order complete on first shipment 95% of the time; remaining items delivered within 7 days after first shipment 99% of the time	Not measured; only completed orders shipped under current process	7
Information about products accurate 99% of the time	Not measured	7
Call answered within three rings 99% of the time	Average number of rings: 3.08	4
Call completed within two minutes 98% of the time	Average call length: 3.33 minutes	4

the current process met the customer requirements that had been identified in the definition phase.

The team was appalled at the results. As shown in Exhibit 6.6, not one of the requirements was met. In addition, the team's calculations showed that 3.83 percent of all widgets were returned, an increase over the last period. Equally disturbing were the facts that 8 percent of all orders had items returned because of late delivery, and another 8 percent had returns with no reason specified. Although some orders had returns for multiple reasons, 42.67 percent of the orders had at least one widget returned. With return rates like those, the team was not surprised that customer satisfaction averaged 3.36 on a scale of 1 to 5.

Understanding Variation

The initial measurements confirmed that there was a problem and helped quantify its magnitude. Although in the past these measurements might have been enough to trigger a process improvement project, Betty cautioned the team against making decisions based solely on averages. She reminded team members that their goal was to eliminate defects, and any variation could be seen as a defect. To illustrate her point, she had the team load the data into a statistical software package and run some basic statistics on four of the fields that they had measured: (1) number of rings, (2) total call time, (3) work days in the process, and (4) customer satisfaction.

While it was clear from initial calculations that call time, process days, and customer satisfaction were problem areas, Harold Resourceful asked why they were continuing to measure the number of rings, because that had been close to the goal. The answer: variation. The object of Six Sigma is to reduce variation (in statistical terms, the standard deviation) so that the process is consistently close to its goal. Averages, as the team discovered, can mask a problem and should not be the only measurement used.

The goals and the averages achieved for each of these fields are shown on Exhibit 6.7. George Greenbelt reviewed the descriptive statistics that the software had generated (Exhibit 6.8) and asked the team to compare the range for rings and process days. For rings, although the mean (average) was 3.08, the range was from 1 to 6 (shown as minimum and maximum in the exhibit), and the standard deviation was 1.421. The variation was clearly too great.

Exhibit 6.7   Goals versus Average Actuals

Element	Goal	Actual
Number of rings	<3	3.08
Total call time (minutes)	2	3.33
Workdays in process	3	3.76
Customer satisfaction	4.2	3.36

Exhibit 6.8   Descriptive Statistics of Initial Measurements

Variable	N	Mean	Median	TrMean	StDev	SE Mean
Rings	75	3.080	3.000	3.030	1.421	0.164
Total Ca	75	3.333	2.000	2.851	3.147	0.363
Work Day	75	3.7600	4.0000	3.7313	0.6333	0.0731
Customer	75	3.3600	3.0000	3.3731	0.7822	0.0903

Variable	Minimum	Maximum	Q1	Q3
Rings	1.000	6.000	2.000	4.000
Total Ca	1.000	18.000	2.000	3.000
Work Day	3.0000	5.0000	3.0000	4.0000
Customer	1.0000	5.0000	3.0000	4.0000

Although the number of work days in the process was an obvious problem because only a third of the orders were delivered within the customer requirement of three days, the team was surprised to learn that the amount of variation for work days was less than call rings (a range of 3 to 5 with a standard deviation of 0.6333).

The situation was similar to the dart players shown on Exhibit 1.3 with its pictorial representation of the difference between consistency and variation. Because a key objective of any Six Sigma project is to eliminate variation, the team realized that, although the average appeared to be close to the goal, there was a problem with call rings. The team also knew that correcting the variation in call rings might present more of a challenge than reducing the number of process days. Because of this, the team decided that it needed more detailed measurement of call rings.

To begin to understand where the variation within call rings occurred, the team ran a number of reports from the statistical software. The first was a box plot (Exhibit 6.9) that showed the distribution of rings. The shaded area represents the 25th to 75th percentiles, with the vertical line showing the median. The horizontal lines that extend from the box show the full range of number of rings. From this chart, team members could see that the majority of calls were answered within two to four rings, but they had no idea how many calls were answered in each number of rings.

To obtain that information, they created a dot plot (Exhibit 6.10). Although they liked the simplicity with which it showed the distribution of rings and were encouraged by the fact that there appeared to be more calls being answered within one or two rings than at five or six rings, they did not like the fact that they could not tell how many rings fell into each category without counting dots. To solve that problem, they created a pie chart (Exhibit 6.11). This clearly showed counts and percentages for

Exhibit 6.9   Box Plot of Rings

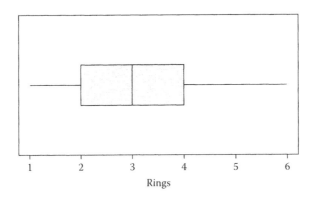

Exhibit 6.10 Dot Plot of Rings

Rings

Exhibit 6.11 Pie Chart of Rings

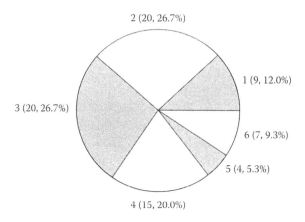

Exhibit 6.12 Histogram of Rings with Normal Curve

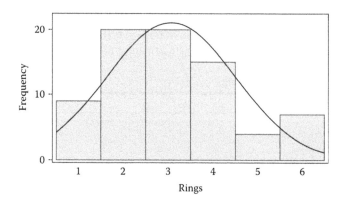

each number of rings. From this they could see that 49 calls (or 65.4 percent) were answered in three or fewer rings.

A histogram (Exhibit 6.12) added the normal curve. In a Six Sigma process, the normal curve is bell shaped and narrow. This one showed them that their distribution was close to bell shaped but too wide, meaning that there was too much variation. Although they already knew this from the standard deviation calculation, the chart provided a visual representation of the statistics.

While the team now knew how many calls were answered within each number of rings, it did not know when those calls had occurred. A time series plot (Exhibit 6.13) displayed this information. A run chart (Exhibit 6.14) showed the same spiked trends as the time series plot but added a line for the median and displayed basic statistics, including the fact that only 18 out of 75 calls were answered in three rings (number of runs about median on the chart). This further confirmed the fact that there was too much variation in answering phone calls.

In reviewing the time series plot and run chart, the team noted that the calls that took five or six rings to be answered were clustered together and wondered whether they occurred on a single shift. To obtain that information, they ran a scatterplot (Exhibit 6.15) to graph the relation between rings and shift. This showed that the high number of rings occurred on the third shift and that the first shift was the only one that answered calls in less than three rings.

A marginal plot (Exhibit 6.16) expanded the scatterplot by adding bar graphs in the margins to represent the number of calls for each dot. By reading the bars along the top of the graph, the team could see how many calls were answered in each number of rings. The bars on the right showed the count of calls by shift. This clearly pointed out that, although the third shift had the fewest number of calls, it also took the longest time to answer them.

Exhibit 6.13 Time Series Plot: Total Rings by Date Order Placed

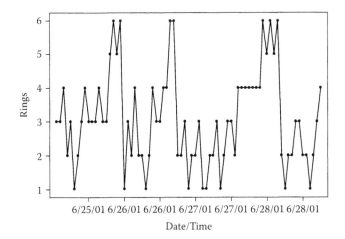

Exhibit 6.14   Run Chart for Rings

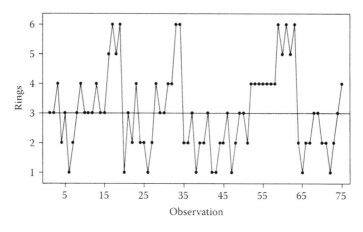

Number of runs about median:	18.0000	Number of runs up or down:	48.0000
Expected number of runs:	34.9733	Expected number of runs:	49.6667
Longest run about median:	17.0000	Longest run up or down:	6.0000
Approx P-Value for Clustering:	0.0000	Approx P-Value for Trends:	0.3220
Approx P-Value for Mixtures:	1.0000	Approx P-Value for Oscillation:	0.6780

Exhibit 6.15   Scatter Plot: Rings and Shift

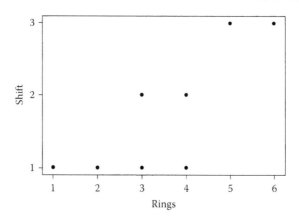

The fact that the first shift's performance was better than the others' was confirmed by another box plot (Exhibit 6.17). This showed that, although the first shift had the greatest variation in number of rings as measured by the length of the vertical line (from one to four), it also answered calls the fastest.

The team had completed its measurements. Although they had some theories about the causes of variation, they were not yet ready to analyze their findings. Instead, they prepared to calculate the sigma level of the current process.

Exhibit 6.16 Marginal Plot: Rings by Shift

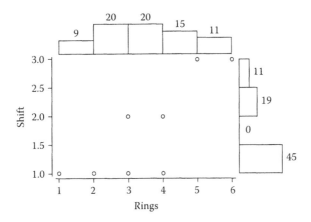

Exhibit 6.17 Box Plot: Rings by Shift

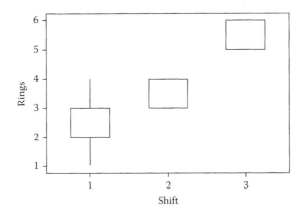

Step 3: Calculate Current Sigma Level

Because sigma level is a measurement of defects, the team knew that it was important to agree on the definitions of key terms before beginning the actual calculation. Those terms were defect, defective, unit, and opportunity.

■ *Defect:* a failure to meet the specification. For its project, the team identified the following as defects:
  1. A call that is answered in more than three rings
  2. A call that lasts more than two minutes
  3. An order that is delivered in more than three days

4. An order that is delivered to the wrong address
5. An order that is incomplete
6. An order that has the wrong number or size of widgets

The team counted 180 individual defects in the orders it had measured.

■ *Unit:* the smallest measurement of output. The team agreed that its basic unit would be the order, not a widget. For this project, 75 units were measured.

■ *Defects per unit (DPU):* the total number of defects in a sample divided by the total number of units in the sample. For this project, the DPU was 2.4 (180 defects divided by 75 units).

■ *Defective:* a unit with one or more defects. Unlike defects, which are measured at various points in the process, defectives are identified at the end of the process. Regardless of the number of defects found in a single unit, the measurement of defectives is binary: a unit is either defective or not. When the team reviewed the results of its initial data collection, they discovered that out of 75 orders (units), there were 40 defectives.

■ *Opportunity:* the chance to create a defect in a single unit. When the team brainstormed opportunities, it listed everything that had been identified as a possible defect and added the following:
1. Order remains in Order Entry more than ten minutes.
2. Order remains in Packing more than fifteen minutes.
3. Inventory is insufficient to fill order.
4. Order arrives in Shipping after 4 p.m.

The team added the six possible defects to these four opportunities to determine that there were ten opportunities for defects on each order.

■ *DPMO* (Defects per Million Opportunities): This metric, which is key to determining sigma level, is calculated as shown on the sigma calculation worksheet (Exhibit 6.18). Even without taking the next step, converting the results to a sigma level, the team knew that more than 53,000 DPMO was too high.

To calculate its process's sigma level, the team compared the DPMO that it had calculated using the sigma calculation worksheet against the sigma conversion table (Exhibit 6.19). The result, a sigma level of 3.1, confirmed what the team knew: that its process had much room for improvement. More importantly, it told the team exactly how much room for improvement it had.

Although the team calculated the sigma level for the process in its entirety, it is also possible and frequently desirable to perform the calculation for each step in the process. This helps determine which portions of the process have the greatest opportunity for improvement.

Exhibit 6.18 Sigma Calculation Worksheet

Step	Action	Result
1	Count the number of units processed	75
2	Count the number of units with defects	40
3	Compute the defect rate (Step 2/Step 1)	0.533
4	Count the opportunities for defects	10
5	Compute the defects per opportunity (Step 3/Step 4)	0.0533
6	Compute the defects per million opportunities (Step 5 × 1,000,000)	53,300
7	Convert DPMO into sigma value using table	3.10

Exhibit 6.19 DPMO to Sigma Conversion Table

DPMO	Sigma
933,193	0.00
926,471	0.05
919,243	0.10
911,492	0.15
903,199	0.20
894,350	0.25
884,930	0.30
874,928	0.35
864,334	0.40
853,141	0.45
841,345	0.50
828,944	0.55
815,940	0.60
802,338	0.65
778,145	0.70
773,372	0.75
758,036	0.80
742,154	0.85
725,747	0.90
708,840	0.95
691,462	1.00
673,645	1.05
655,422	1.10
636,831	1.15
617,911	1.20
598,706	1.25
579,260	1.30
559,618	1.35
539,828	1.40
519,939	1.45
500,000	1.50
480,061	1.55

Exhibit 6.19   DPMO to Sigma Conversion Table (continued)

DPMO	Sigma
460,172	1.60
440,382	1.65
420,740	1.70
401,294	1.75
382,088	1.80
363,169	1.85
344,578	1.90
326,355	1.95
308,537	2.00
291,160	2.05
274,253	2.10
257,846	2.15
241,964	2.20
226,627	2.25
211,856	2.30
197,663	2.35
184,060	2.40
171,056	2.45
158,655	2.50
146,859	2.55
135,666	2.60
125,072	2.65
115,070	2.70
105,650	2.75
96,800	2.80
88,508	2.85
80,757	2.90
73,529	2.95
66,807	3.00
60,571	3.05
54,799	3.10
49,471	3.15
44,565	3.20
40,059	3.25
35,930	3.30
32,157	3.35
28,717	3.40
25,588	3.45
22,750	3.50
20,182	3.55
17,865	3.60
15,778	3.65
13,904	3.70
12,225	3.75
10,724	3.80
9,387	3.85
8,198	3.90
7,143	3.95
6,210	4.00
5,386	4.05
4,661	4.10
4,024	4.15

Exhibit 6.19   DPMO to Sigma Conversion Table (continued)

DPMO	Sigma
3,467	4.20
2,980	4.25
2,555	4.30
2,186	4.35
1,866	4.40
1,589	4.45
1,350	4.50
1,144	4.55
968	4.60
816	4.65
687	4.70
577	4.75
483	4.80
404	4.85
337	4.90
280	4.95
233	5.00
193	5.05
159	5.10
131	5.15
108	5.20
89	5.25
72	5.30
59	5.35
48	5.40
39	5.45
32	5.50
26	5.55
21	5.60
17	5.65
13	5.70
11	5.75
9	5.80
7	5.85
5	5.90
4	5.95
3	6.00

Step 4: Determine Process Capability

What the team had measured to this point was the current performance of the process. The next step was to determine the process's capability. The reason for calculating process capability is to compare the process's normal variation against the customers' specification limits. This is sometimes referred to as a comparison of the "voice of the process" with the "voice of the customer."

The "voice of the process" tells how much variation occurs normally. The "voice of the customer" indicates how much variation customers will

Exhibit 6.20 "Within Spec" Process

Process Data

USL	10.0
Target	*
LSL	1.0
Mean	4.6
Sample N	75
StDev (Within)	0.787081
StDev (Overall)	0.857133

Potential (Within) Capability

Cp	1.91
CPU	2.29
CPL	1.52
Cpk	1.52
Cpm	*

Overall Capability		Exp. "Within" Performance		Exp. "Overall" Performance	
Pp	1.75	PPM < LSL	2.39	PPM < LSL	13.34
PPU	2.10	PPM > USL	0.00	PPM > USL	0.00
PPL	1.40	PPM total	2.39	PPM total	13.34
Ppk	1.40				

Observed Performance

PPM < LSL	0.00
PPM > USL	0.00
PPM total	0.00

tolerate. The ideal process is centered within the customers' specifications and has substantial range on either side of its normal variation.

Exhibit 6.20 is a graphical representation of a process that is within spec. The "voice of the customer" says that the order should spend between one and ten minutes in Order Entry; these are the lower and upper specification limits. The "voice of the process" says that the average time an order spends in Order Entry (the mean) is 4.6 minutes, and the range is between 2.5 and 8.5 minutes. As shown by the histogram and normal distribution curve, the process is well centered within the customers' specification limits (LSL and USL), and normal distribution is not close to either specification limit. The customer should be satisfied with this process.

Capability Indices

To further quantify process capability, Six Sigma organizations use two indices, C_p and C_{pk}. The formulas for each are:

$$C_p = (USL - LSL) / 6\sigma$$

$$C_{pk} = min [(USL - \mu/3), (\mu - LSL/3)]$$

where

 USL = upper specification limit
 LSL = lower specification limit
  σ = standard deviation
  μ = mean of the process

It should be noted that both indices are important; C_p reflects the ability to produce consistent results, while C_{pk} indicates whether or not those results meet the goal. The dart player on the right in Exhibit 1.3 has a high C_p because the results are consistent. C_{pk}, however, is low. No matter how consistent, these results do not meet the goal of hitting the bull's eye.

The process depicted in Exhibit 6.20 has a C_p of 1.91 and a C_{pk} of 1.52. Because a process is considered as being at the six sigma level if C_p is equal to or greater than 2.0 *and* C_{pk} is equal to or greater than 1.5, this process is close to six sigma. In layman's language, it has so little variation normally (C_p) and is so well centered within customer requirement levels (C_{pk}) that even if variability should increase, the process would still meet the customer's expectations.

Betty Blackbelt asked the team to consider the effect a specification shift might have on the same process. What would happen if, instead of agreeing that an order should spend between one and ten minutes in Order Entry, the "voice of the customer" required it to remain in Order Entry between three and thirteen minutes? Although the process itself did not change, the shift of LSL and USL in Exhibit 6.21 had a dramatic effect on the process capability. The histogram that represents the process has shifted to the left, and some orders are below the LSL. Because the process is no longer centered within customer requirements, a minor variation at the lower level causes it to be out of spec.

The capability indices reflect this shift from the center. C_p shifts from 1.91 to 2.12. Considered by itself, this would seem to be a six sigma process, because C_p is greater than 2.0. It is critical, however, to note that C_{pk} has shifted from 1.52 to 0.68, making it well below the 1.5 threshold for a six sigma process. The two capability indices measure different aspects of a process. That is the reason why organizations consider both of them when determining whether a process is truly at the six sigma level.

The team generated process capability charts for rings (Exhibit 6.22) and work days (Exhibit 6.23). While neither of those processes met customer specifications, the wider variation experienced for rings gener-

Exhibit 6.21 "Uncentered" Process

Process Data

USL	13.0
Target	*
LSL	3.0
Mean	4.6
Sample N	75
StDev (Within)	0.787081
StDev (Overall)	0.857133

Potential (Within) Capability

Cp	2.12
CPU	3.56
CPL	0.68
Cpk	0.68
Cpm	*

Overall Capability		Exp. "Within" Performance		Exp. "Overall" Performance	
Pp	1.94	PPM < LSL	21035.01	PPM < LSL	30972.57
PPU	3.27	PPM > USL	0.00	PPM > USL	0.00
PPL	0.62	PPM total	21.035.01	PPM total	30972.57
Ppk	0.62				

Observed Performance

PPM < LSL	0.00
PPM > USL	0.00
PPM total	0.00

ated a lower C_p than for work days. Rings had a higher C_{pk} than work days because that process was more centered than work days.

Cycle Time

Because one of the primary project objectives was to reduce late deliveries, the team wanted to determine where in the process delays were occurring. In addition to quantifying wait time, a form of waste, team members sought to identify variation as they had in their measurements of call rings. They already knew how long the entire order-to-delivery process took and had a preliminary idea of where delays occurred. The next task was to determine which process steps had the greatest variation.

Team members reviewed the data they had collected and discovered the major steps' minimum and maximum times. The results are shown in Exhibit 6.24.

Exhibit 6.22   Process Capability Analysis for Rings

Process Data	
USL	3.00
Target	*
LSL	1.00
Mean	3.08
Sample N	75
StDev (Within)	1.00501
StDev (Overall)	1.42627

Potential (Within) Capability	
Cp	0.33
CPU	−0.03
CPL	0.69
Cpk	−0.03
Cpm	*

Overall Capability		Exp. "Within" Performance		Exp. "Overall" Performance	
Pp	0.23	PPM < LSL	19243.66	PPM < LSL	72371.76
PPU	−0.02	PPM > USL	531722.71	PPM > USL	522365.13
PPL	0.49	PPM Total	550966.37	PPM Total	594736.89
Ppk	−0.02				

Observed Performance	
PPM < LSL	0.00
PPM > USL	346666.67
PPM Total	346666.67

They updated their process flowchart to show the minimum and maximum times for each step. By summing the minimum times for all steps, they were able to determine the shortest time in which the process could be completed. Summing the maximums showed how long the process could take under the worst circumstances. Although neither of these times necessarily corresponded to any of the actual elapsed times they had measured, they were useful in determining the best- and worst-case scenarios.

Like the calculation of sigma level for each process step, the individual step times were helpful in determining where delays were occurring and would be used in the analysis of possible process improvements.

Step 5: Benchmark Process Leaders

Once team members understood their process, they were ready to benchmark. The objectives of benchmarking are to:

Exhibit 6.23   Process Capability Analysis for Work Days in Process

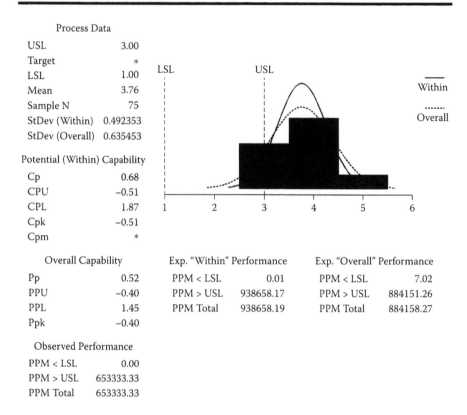

Process Data	
USL	3.00
Target	*
LSL	1.00
Mean	3.76
Sample N	75
StDev (Within)	0.492353
StDev (Overall)	0.635453

Potential (Within) Capability

Cp	0.68
CPU	−0.51
CPL	1.87
Cpk	−0.51
Cpm	*

Overall Capability		Exp. "Within" Performance		Exp. "Overall" Performance	
Pp	0.52	PPM < LSL	0.01	PPM < LSL	7.02
PPU	−0.40	PPM > USL	938658.17	PPM > USL	884151.26
PPL	1.45	PPM Total	938658.19	PPM Total	884158.27
Ppk	−0.40				

Observed Performance

PPM < LSL	0.00
PPM > USL	653333.33
PPM Total	653333.33

Exhibit 6.24   Major Steps' Minimum and Maximum Times

Step	Minimum	Maximum
Call received and completed	1 minute	18 minutes
Order processed by OE	2 minutes	9 hours, 36 minutes
Order picked and packed	5 minutes	11 hours, 5 minutes
Order processed by shipping	Same day	Next day
Order in transit	3 days	5 days

■ Identify those companies that perform the process best. It should be noted that for complex processes, a team might benchmark more than one company, because there may be different leaders for different portions of the process. The GWC Order Entry team planned to benchmark three different companies, one each for answering calls, packing product, and shipping.

■ Quantify the leaders' performance.

■ Learn what differentiates the leaders from their competition and from GWC. In the next phase (Analysis), the team knew it would review the results of the benchmarking and determine how to apply them to improving GWC's processes.

Although benchmarking is typically performed as a visit to the process leader's site, it is also possible to gather key information through telephone interviews. In either case, benchmarking's effectiveness is increased when the team compiles a list of questions in advance. These questions might include the volume of work processed, throughput, error rates, and quality measures, as well as a discussion of how improvements were achieved, how long the current procedures have been in place, and what the company's next objectives are for improving the process.

When team members completed their benchmarking, they had learned that:

■ Although two companies had implemented Web-based order entry, their telephone order volumes had decreased by only 15 percent.
■ Calls were answered in two or fewer rings.
■ Calls to place orders were completed within 90 seconds.
■ All orders were shipped the same day, even if they were partial shipments.
■ The shipping leader owned its own fleet of trucks.

At this point, the team members made no judgments. They recorded their findings on the TMAP and prepared for the next phase: analysis.

Reference

1. George, Michael, *Lean Six Sigma for Service*. New York: McGraw-Hill, 2003, pp. 259–262.

Chapter 7

The Analysis Phase

The third phase of the DMAIC model, analysis, has as its objective to analyze the data that was collected in the previous phase, determine the root cause of the problems, and propose solutions to them. As they entered the analysis phase, Betty reviewed the steps that the team would follow. They were:

1. Determine what caused the variation.
2. Brainstorm ideas for process improvements.
3. Determine which improvements would have the greatest impact on meeting customer requirements.
4. Develop a proposed process map.
5. Assess the risks associated with the revised process.

Step 1: Determine What Caused the Variation

Although it was clear from the measurements that they had taken that there was too much variation in the order entry process, team members had not yet determined the causes of that variation. Identifying the causes was the next step in gaining a thorough understanding of the current process and being able to design new processes based on clearly identified facts.

As she frequently did at the start of a phase, Betty provided the team with several definitions of terms. The first were common and special causes of variation. As shown on Exhibit 7.1, common causes are the ones the team would try to eliminate. Reacting to special causes and tweaking the

Exhibit 7.1   Common and Special Causes of Variation

Characteristic	Common	Special
Synonyms	Controlled Consistent	Uncontrolled Changing
Explanation	Normal, random variation	Severe, one-time deviation
Example	Quality of telephone line	Power outage
Mitigation	Improve process	Determine what was different

Exhibit 7.2   I (First Chart) and MR (Second Chart) Control Chart for Rings

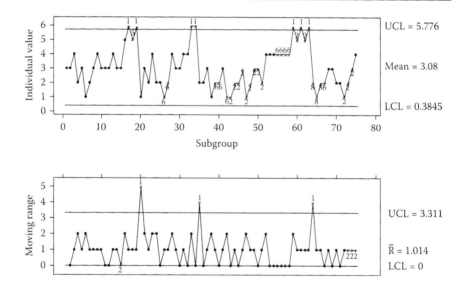

process to prevent them can in itself cause variation. As a result, it is important to distinguish between common and special causes, so that only common ones are addressed.

When team members asked how they could identify special causes, Betty explained that the statistical software they had used during the measurement phase could help them. Run charts such as the I & MR (individual and moving range values) one shown in Exhibit 7.2 help to distinguish between common and special causes of variation. Variation, of course, is represented by the spikes on the chart. From the chart it would appear that the points marked "1" might be the result of special causes. Using the same statistical software allowed the team to test for and identify

Exhibit 7.3   Special Cause Tests Applied to I and MR Control Chart

```
Test Results for I Chart
TEST 1.One point more than 3.00 sigmas from center line.
Test Failed at points: 17 19 33 34 59 61 63

TEST 2.9 points in a row on same side of center line.
Test Failed at points: 43 44 45 46 47 48 49 50 51 60 61 62 63 72 73 74

TEST 5.2 out of 3 points more than 2 sigmas from center line
        (on one side of CL).
Test Failed at points: 17 18 19 34 43 60 61 62 63

TEST 6.4 out of 5 points more than 1 sigma from center line
        (ononesideofCL).
Test Failed at points: 19 26 27 34 39 40 42 43 44 45 47 48 55 56 57 58
59 60 61 62 63 67 73

TEST 8.8 points in a row more than 1 sigma from center line
        (above and below CL).
Test Failed at points: 58 59 60 61 62 63 64 65 66 67

Test Results for MR Chart
TEST 1. One point more than 3.00 sigmas from center line.
Test Failed at points: 20 35 64

TEST 2.9 points in a row on same side of center line.
Test Failed at points: 15 73 74 75
```

special causes on the chart. The numbered points on the graph correspond to the description of special cause tests shown in Exhibit 7.3.

Noise Variables

Betty explained that some variables are characterized as noise; and although they result in variation within the process, they are treated like special causes. That is, as shown in Exhibit 7.1, the objective of mitigation is to determine what caused the variation but not to modify the process in response to it. Noise variables are typically divided into three groups:

1. *Positional:* variation from machine to machine or operator to operator. The team believed that some of the variation in the number of rings for answering the phone depended on the operator. To determine whether that was true, they ran a box plot, showing the number of rings by clerk. As shown in Exhibit 7.4, Ann and Eric had the highest number of rings. The variation between Ann and Eric's rings and the other clerks' confirmed the team's suppositions.

2. *Sequential:* variation from piece to piece or process step to process step. The time series plot the team had already run (see Exhibit 6.13) showed the variation from piece to piece. At this point, the team was not certain that the variation was caused by sequential noise.

3. *Temporal:* variation from hour to hour, shift to shift, day to day. Another box plot showing rings by call date (Exhibit 7.5) showed no marked differences among dates, other than on June 25. The team was able to identify the variation on June 25 as being caused by the absence of data from the third shift that day. The team had already run a box plot of rings by shift (see Exhibit 6.17) and had

Exhibit 7.4 Box Plot: Rings by Clerk

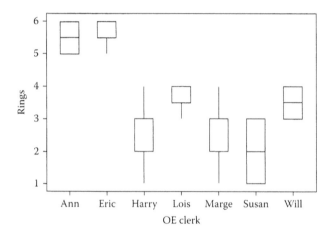

Exhibit 7.5 Box Plot: Rings by Call Date

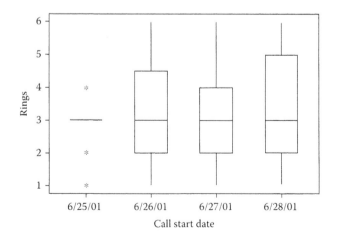

discovered that the number of rings was highest on the third shift. Because Ann and Eric were the third shift operators, this test confirmed that the process on the third shift should be investigated.

Team members were now ready to begin further investigation into the causes of variation. As they did, Betty reminded them that they needed to identify root causes. Root cause is determined by taking apparent causes and asking "why?" The process is repeated until no more causes can be found. The final cause identified is the root cause and the one that should be corrected.

When team members investigated the reasons why customers were given inaccurate product information, they learned that one order entry clerk had not received any training about large widgets. Instead of assuming that the cause of the problem was inadequate training, the team asked why the clerk had not been trained, as training was normally part of the new-hire process. They were told that classes for the last quarter had been cancelled. Again, the team asked why. This time they learned that the training budget had been cut to provide more money for a company picnic. Again, the team asked why, and learned that the manager had not realized the implications that reduced training would have on customer satisfaction. The root cause, the team determined, was the manager's ignorance of the importance of training. The solution was to educate the department manager about the importance of training so that the programs would be reinstated.

The team returned to its analysis of call rings. Because they had determined that the greatest variation in rings occurred on the third shift, Charlie Satiz volunteered to observe the process on that shift to see if the cause was obvious. It was. Because call volume was lower during the night, the third shift was responsible for entering faxed orders into the computer system. Operators would leave their workstations regularly to check the fax machine for incoming faxes. It was during these times that the phone would ring five or six times before it was answered. The team identified this as a form of waste, specifically motion, and realized that eliminating this waste would help improve the process. They made a note of the problem and also updated their process maps to show the retrieval and entry of faxed orders, two steps that had not been included on the original maps.

The causes of late deliveries were less obvious. When the team members were unable to find any one cause for the delays, Irene Technowiz suggested that they analyze the process map they had developed to determine which steps were not value-added. Those might be the reasons for the delays.

Steps are considered to be value-added if:

- The customer recognizes the value.
- They change the product.
- They are done correctly the first time.

Typical non-value-added tasks include waiting, inspecting, approving, correcting, and moving data or product between departments. The team recognized that the transportation, motion, and wait time forms of waste were, by definition, non-value-added.

Using these criteria, the team determined that the following steps were non-value-added:

- Verifying large orders
- Reworking large orders, if they were found to be erroneous
- Placing orders with insufficient inventory into suspense
- Verifying contents of packed boxes
- Reworking packing, if errors were found
- Holding shipments until the next day

After observing the process and reviewing the results of their measurements, team members held a brainstorming session to identify potential causes. As was normal for their brainstorming sessions, each team member was given a pad of adhesive notes and, working as individuals, was asked to write one cause per sheet. When they had exhausted their ideas, they pasted them onto a flipchart in pre-established logical groupings. When all team members had placed their ideas on the chart, they reassembled as a team and began to review each idea. Duplicates were eliminated and, when needed, groupings were changed.

Although the team began by classifying causes using the Six Ms (see Exhibit 6.1), when they found that the majority of the delays were caused by methods, they decided to group causes for delays by function or department. In each case, when they agreed that the cause was a valid one, they would ask "why?" until they were satisfied that they had discovered the root cause. These causes and their relationships were documented as shown in Exhibit 7.6.

Because they knew that it was important to work on the right problem, team members analyzed their data to determine which causes were the most significant. To do that, they counted the frequency with which each cause of delays had occurred in their sample data. The frequency was also documented in Exhibit 7.6. Frequency, the team knew, was similar to the importance ranking customers gave their requirements: it served as a guide to the relative importance of an item. The team used the frequency data to create a Pareto chart (Exhibit 7.7).

Exhibit 7.6 Root Cause Analysis

Function	Delay	Causes	Secondary Cause	Frequency
Order Entry	Verification of orders > 1,000 widgets	Policy	Desire to reduce returns	6
	Verifications processed only twice a day	Conflicting priorities		4
Packing	Insufficient inventory	"Complete shipment" policy	System cannot handle partial shipments	33
Shipping Department	Verification of contents	Policy	Desire to reduce returns	2
	Package received later than 4 PM	Shipper picks up at 4 PM		5
Shipper (External Supplier)	Delivery by truck	Need to minimize costs		15

Exhibit 7.7 Pareto: Causes of Delays

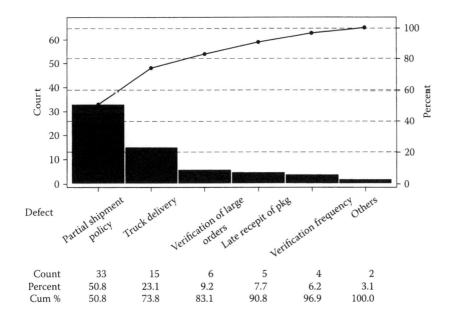

Count	33	15	6	5	4	2
Percent	50.8	23.1	9.2	7.7	6.2	3.1
Cum %	50.8	73.8	83.1	90.8	96.9	100.0

By ranking causes by frequency and providing a graphical representation, the Pareto clearly showed where the team should place its emphasis. Based on this analysis, they knew that the insufficient inventory/partial shipment problem was the first one they should tackle, followed by the shippers' delays.

The team repeated these analysis steps to determine the causes of overly long calls, incorrect items being shipped, and deliveries being made to the wrong address. They were then ready for the next step.

Step 2: Brainstorm Ideas for Process Improvements

Once team members had what they believed to be a comprehensive list of the causes of variation in their process, they began to consider ways to eliminate that variation. Again, they used brainstorming to introduce ideas.

When they had completed the process, they had the following suggestions:

- Move the fax machine next to order entry workstations to eliminate delays in answering the phone, which they had characterized as motion waste.
- Replace telephone entry with a self-service, Web-based system to provide seven-day order entry and eliminate call delays.
- Link the existing order entry system to inventory records so that customers can pre-authorize partial shipments.
- Eliminate verification of large orders, because verification causes delays in the process and is not value-added. The team considered that this might be a form of overproduction waste.
- Develop a system to track partial shipments.
- Separate multi-sized widget orders into separate orders for each size to reduce the need for partial shipments.
- Ship by air instead of truck to ensure that all deliveries are made in three or fewer days.

Although team members knew that some of these recommendations would be costly and would require more time to complete than others, they did not discard any of them at this point. They did, however, create a simple ranking (high/medium/low) of the cost and time needed to implement each change, the result of which is shown as Exhibit 7.8. Then they proceeded to the next step.

Exhibit 7.8   Cost and Time Ranking of Proposed Process Improvements

Improvement	Cost	Time
Move fax machine	Low	Low
Develop self-service web-based system	High	High
Link existing system to inventory records	Medium	Medium
Eliminate verification of large orders	Low	Low
Develop system to track partial shipments	Medium	High
Separate multi-sized widget orders into two orders	Low	Low
Ship by air instead of truck	Unknown	Medium

Step 3: Determine Which Improvements Have the Greatest Impact on Customer Requirements

If GWC were not a Six Sigma company, the team's recommendations would be simple. They would implement the three improvements that involved both low cost and minimal time to develop (moving the fax machine, eliminating verification of large orders, and separating orders by widget size). However, those changes might not satisfy their customers' requirements.

The team members knew better. They knew that satisfying customers was of paramount importance, and so they sought to determine which improvements would benefit customers the most. In accordance with the precept that decisions should be based on facts, team members evaluated each of their proposed process improvements against the customer requirements that had been established in Exhibit 5.15 and created a Process Improvement Ranking spreadsheet (Exhibit 7.9). (Appendix C provides detailed instructions for the use of a Process Improvement Ranking spreadsheet.)

It is significant to note that the team deliberately removed the customers' importance ranking and current level of satisfaction when they first created their ranking. This was to add objectivity to their ranking of the process improvements.

The team's initial step was to list the customer requirements and the proposed improvements, then rank each improvement according to the degree to which it would satisfy each requirement. As done in the past, the team used a 1-4-7-10 scale and recorded its rankings in the "effect" columns. Once all effects had been rated, the team added the customers'

Exhibit 7.9   Process Improvement Ranking

| Customer Requirement | Importance Ranking | Improvement Steps and Effects | | | | | | | | | | | | | Total Impact |
| | | Move Fax Machine | | Develop Self-Service System | | Link Existing System to Inventory Records | | Eliminate Large Order Verification | | Develop Partial Shipment Tracking | | Separate Orders by Widget Size | | Ship by Air | | |
		Effect	Impact on Cust	Effect	Impact on Cust	Effect	Impact on Cust	Effect	Impact on Cust	Effect	Impact on Cust	Effect	Impact on Cust	Effect	Impact on Cust	
Order delivered within 3 working days	10	1	10	4	40	1	10	7	70	7	70	7	70	10	100	370
Order delivered to correct address	7	1	7	10	70	1	7	1	7	1	7	1	7	4	28	133
Specified number and size of widgets delivered	10	1	10	4	40	7	70	1	10	1	10	1	10	1	10	160
Order complete on first shipment 95% of time	7	1	7	4	28	10	70	1	7	7	49	7	49	1	7	217
Information about products accurate	7	1	7	10	70	1	7	1	7	1	7	1	7	1	7	112
Call answered within three rings	4	10	40	10	40	1	4	1	4	1	4	1	4	1	4	100
Call completed within two minutes	4	7	28	10	40	1	4	1	4	1	4	1	4	1	4	88
Degree of Satisfaction from Implementing Improvement			109		328		172		109		151		151		160	

importance rankings. The spreadsheet did some basic calculations, multiplying importance by effect to determine the impact on the customer, and totaling columns and rows.

By comparing the values in the "Total Impact" column, team members could see the relative effects that their proposed changes would have on the customers. If all their recommendations were implemented, they would have a high impact on customer satisfaction by ensuring that orders were delivered within three days and that they were complete on the first shipment, but lesser impact on completing calls within two minutes. Reviewing the column totals revealed the degree of overall customer satisfaction that would be derived from implementing each of the recommendations. The team members used this information to update their cost and time ranking (Exhibit 7.8) by adding a "Customer Impact" column. The result is shown as Exhibit 7.10. This shows that of the three low cost/low time improvements, only one has any significant impact on the customer, namely separating orders by widget size.

Although team members recognized that developing a self-service order entry system would provide the greatest overall benefits to the customers, and although they planned to recommend that as their ultimate solution, they knew that this was a high cost/high time project and looked for some "low hanging fruit" to pick while the new system was being developed.

Moving the fax machine was a no-brainer, because it cost virtually nothing and would improve customer satisfaction in one area, namely, faster answering of calls.

The team then focused on low cost changes that would have high impact on reducing delivery time. Because eliminating the manual verification of large orders was a no cost/no time change, the team explored the reasons for the policy and the risks associated with eliminating that step. When team members discovered that only one order in a thousand was found to be erroneous in this step, they believed that the risk of eliminating the step was minimal. They were pleased because this meant that they could eliminate a non-value-added step and shorten overall cycle time.

Irene Technowiz, who had analyzed the existing computer system, suggested that modifying the system to create separate packing orders for large and small widgets be one of the first wave of process improvements. The result of this change would be that when there were inventory shortages, customers would receive at least a portion of their orders within the designated time. The team agreed that this was a good change to pursue.

Because shipping by air would eliminate the problem of long-distance truck delivery delays and would have a positive effect on customer satisfaction, the team decided to recommend further investigation. Although there was concern that this might result in additional costs, the

Exhibit 7.10   Cost, Time, and Customer Impact Ranking of Proposed Process Improvements

Improvement	Cost	Time	Customer Impact
Move fax machine	Low	Low	Low
Develop self-service web-based system	High	High	High
Link existing system to inventory records	Medium	Medium	Medium
Eliminate verification of large orders	Low	Low	Low
Develop system to track partial shipments	Medium	High	Medium
Separate multi-sized widget orders into two orders	Low	Low	Medium
Ship by air instead of truck	Unknown	Medium	Medium

team believed that the benefits were great enough that the change should be considered. They also believed that if GWC was willing to give a single supplier all shipping business, rather than dividing shipments among four suppliers as was the current policy, they might be able to negotiate air shipment rates that did not exceed the current costs of truck deliveries. This, in fact, proved to be the case.

Step 4: Develop Proposed Process Map

The team's next step was to develop a process map for the revised process. Because the "quick hit" or "low hanging fruit" changes made no substantial modifications to the process maps they had drawn for the current process, they did not update the map for those changes but developed a map for the ultimate process, the one that incorporated the Web-based, self-service order entry system.

Before they finalized it, the team evaluated the map to determine where non-value-added steps still occurred and how they could eliminate them. The result is shown as Exhibit 7.11.

Exhibit 7.11   Functional Process Map: Proposed Process

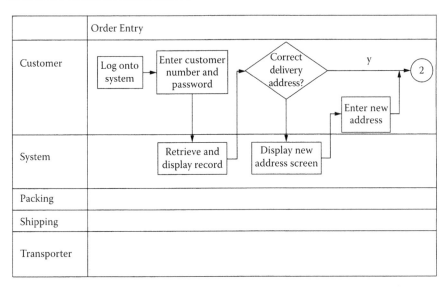

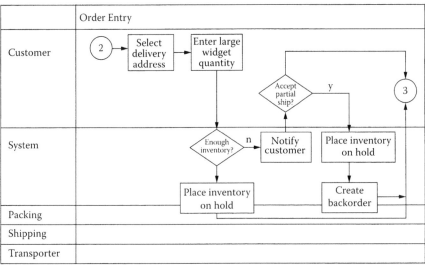

Exhibit 7.11   Functional Process Map: Proposed Process (continued)

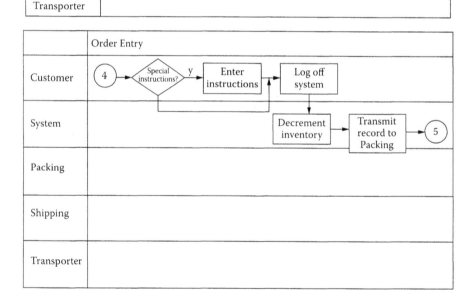

Step 5: Assess Risks Associated with Revised Process

Although they were anxious to present their recommendations to Oscar Early, the project champion, team members knew that their proposal would not be complete unless they assessed the risks associated with the revised process. To perform the risk analysis, they used a tool called the Failure Modes and Effects Analysis (FMEA).

Exhibit 7.11   Functional Process Map: Proposed Process (continued)

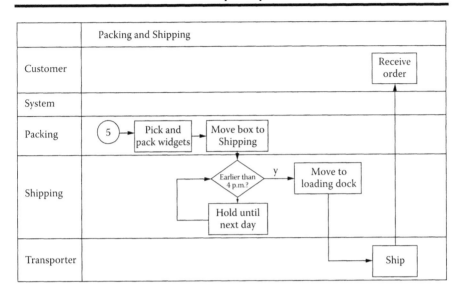

The objectives of an FMEA, which originated in NASA, are to:

■ Identify ways in which a process might fail to meet customer requirements (the failure mode).
■ Determine which potential failures would have the greatest effect on the customer.
■ Evaluate current controls that are designed to prevent the failure.
■ Develop a corrective action plan to prevent the failure and document its results.

Appendix D provides detailed instructions for the development of an FMEA. Exhibit 7.12 shows the beginning of the FMEA that the team developed. For each of the potential failure modes, team members:

■ Identified the effect of that failure and rated the severity of the effect using their standard 1-4-7-10 scale
■ Determined possible causes and ranked the likelihood of the cause occurring, using the same scale
■ Identified any existing controls that would prevent the failure from occurring and the probability that those controls would fail

Like the other analyses that the team had performed, the FMEA provides an importance ranking for each potential failure mode. This is called the risk priority number (RPN). The system calculates the risk priority number

Exhibit 7.12   Failure Modes and Effects Analysis

Failure Modes and Effects Analysis (FMEA)

| Process Name: | Revised order entry | | Date Prepared: 8/20/01 | Revision Number: 0 |
| Prepared By: | George Greenbelt | | Revised By: | Revision Date: |

	What Could Happen?			Why and How Often?		How do We Prevent It?			Action Plan				Results of Actions			
Process Step	Potential Failure Mode	Potential Failure Effects	SEV	Potential Causes	OCC	Current Controls	FAILB	RPON	Actions Recommended	Resp.	Target Date	Actions Taken	SEV	OCC	FAILB	RPON
Customer Order Entry	Web site is not available	Customer unable to place order, buys widgets from competitor	10	Server down	4	Alert sent to computer center	7	280	Establish server mirroring	IT	12/01/2001					0
	Customer's computers are down	Customer unable to place order	10	Internal to customer	7	Keep skeletal OE staff in place to accept telephone orders; continue to accept faxed orders	1	70								0
								0								0
								0								0
								0								0
								0								0
								0								0
								0								0
								0								0
								0								0
								0								0

by multiplying the severity, likelihood of occurrence, and failure probability. The higher the RPN, the more serious the impact of the failure. Items with high RPNs normally have corrective action plans developed to mitigate the risks.

After identifying all possible failure modes, the team reviewed the RPNs to determine which failures would have the greatest impact and should be the focus of corrective action plans. As shown in Exhibit 7.12, because the unavailability of the Web site had an RPN of 280 compared to the customers' computer downtime (RPN of 70), the first planned action was to mitigate the risk of server unavailability. Irene Technowiz explained that they could accomplish that by mirroring the server.

Their analysis was now complete. Team members knew what had caused variation in their process. They had identified possible process changes and had weighed those against customer requirements to select the ones that would have the greatest impact on customers. They had assessed and mitigated risks. They were now ready to enter the improvement phase.

Chapter 8

The Improvement Phase

The fourth phase of the DMAIC model, Improvement, is the one in which all the planning and analysis of the previous phases come to fruition. The fact-based decisions have been made. Now the resulting process improvements can be implemented.

Team members approached this phase with renewed enthusiasm because they were anxious to see how well their recommended changes would resolve the problems they had identified.

Like the previous three phases, the improvement phase consists of a number of steps. Betty outlined them as follows:

1. Gain approval for the proposed changes.
2. Finalize the implementation plan.
3. Implement the approved changes.

Step 1: Gain Approval for the Proposed Changes

As they prepared their recommendations for approval by Oscar Early and the other executives, the team expanded its explanation of the proposed changes. Although they knew that a self-service (Web-based) order entry system would resolve many of the problems, they were concerned about the time required to implement it. Accordingly, in keeping with the philosophy of picking low-hanging fruit first and to maximize benefits and minimize risk, they decided to propose a multi-phase improvement project, implementing the "quick hits" first.

The steps that they planned were:

1. Implement procedural changes (move the fax machine, eliminate large order verification).
2. Modify the current computer system to separate orders by widget size.
3. Negotiate a new transporter agreement.
4. Develop a self-service order entry system.

These could all be worked on concurrently because there were no dependencies among them.

Because developing the new system was a lengthy project, the team decided to implement it in phases. This would allow some of the benefits to be achieved early in the process. Phased implementation was also a proof-of-concept approach, allowing the team to evaluate the benefits without incurring the complete cost.

The phases that they proposed were:

1. *Develop a Web front end for order entry.* This would be a shell that allowed customers to enter the same information they had given over the phone or faxed to GWC. Although there was no new functionality, the system would be available 24/7 and would eliminate call answering delays. The new system would have no links to existing systems but would generate a paper order that would be entered into the current order entry system. Customer data would be extracted from existing databases and refreshed nightly.
2. *Add the ability for customers to update their records*, adding new locations, etc. This would help reduce the incidence of shipments to the wrong customer address.
3. *Add a product information database*, giving customers the ability to query it and ensuring consistency of information.
4. *Link the order entry system to the packing system*, eliminating the need for rekeying of information as it passed from one department to the next. Although not visible to the customer, this step would eliminate non-value-added steps, reduce cycle time, reduce internal costs, and increase accuracy.
5. *Link the order entry system to inventory records*, giving customers the ability to authorize partial shipments. To do this, it would be necessary to update inventory in real-time, rather than the periodic refresh that was currently occurring. When fully implemented, this step would ensure that customers knew at the time they placed an order exactly how many widgets they would receive and when to expect delivery.

Irene Technowiz confirmed that Phase One of the new system could be implemented quickly, giving the customers the 24/7 service they had requested and eliminating the need for most telephone calls.

The entire team recognized that the proposed improvements, if approved, would result in dramatic changes to the Order Entry department. These included the fact that many of the existing jobs would be eliminated by the time the new system was fully implemented, with remaining jobs substantially restructured. Although not so widespread, there would be staffing changes within the Packing department as well.

Recognizing the impact that change has on employees and the different ways that individuals react to it, Harold Resourceful advised that they implement a comprehensive communication and counseling program for the employees. Chapter 3 discusses change and outlines ways to help mitigate its negative effects.

The Impact Assessment

As part of the package that they planned to present to Oscar Early, the team created an impact assessment. As shown in Exhibit 8.1, this document summarizes the effects — both positive and negative — that the proposed process improvements will have. In developing the impact assessment, the team documented the projected cost and time to implement each suggestion, along with expected benefits. These benefits were classified as:

■ Cost reduction
■ Cost avoidance
■ Improved sigma level
■ Improved customer satisfaction
■ Cycle time reduction
■ Reduced cost of poor quality (COPQ)

As shown in Exhibit 8.1, although team members believed they would be able to reduce COPQ and improve the sigma level of the order entry process, because they were unable to quantify those improvements at this stage of the project, they did not include them on the impact assessment. They wanted the approval decision to be based on facts, not intuition.

The team also assessed the impact on employees, customers, policies, procedures, training programs, and computer systems. Although they did not quantify those effects, their chart indicates areas that would be affected. Costs of revised training programs and modifications to computer systems are included in the "Cost to Implement" column.

At the same time that they were developing the impact assessment, the team developed an approval checklist. As shown in Exhibit 8.2, the

Exhibit 8.1   Impact Assessment

| Action | Costs | | Benefits | | | | | |
	Cost to Implement	Time to Implement	Cost Reduction	Cost Avoidance	Sigma Level	Customer Sat	Cycle Time	COPQ
Move fax machine	0	1 day				x	5 minutes	
Eliminate large order verification	0	1 week				x	4 hours	
Separate orders by widget size	8,000	2 weeks	9,000/year				1 day	
Negotiate new transporter agreement	15,000	3 months	20,000/year			x	2 days	
Develop web front end	32,000	8 weeks	50,000/year	2,000/year, beginning second year		x	1 minute	
Add customer record update	16,000	4 weeks				x		
Create product info database	50,000	8 weeks	50,000/year	2,000/year, beginning second year		x		
Link to packing system	150,000	4 months	150,000/year	6,000/year, beginning second year			5 minutes	
Link to inventory records	200,000	6 months	50,000/year	8,000/year, beginning second year		x		
Totals	471,000		329,000/year	18,000/year, beginning second year				

Exhibit 8.1 Impact Assessment (continued)

Action	Impact					
	Employees	Customers	Policies	Procedures	Training Programs	Computer Systems
Move fax machine				x		
Eliminate large order verification			x	x		
Separate orders by widget size		x				x
Negotiate new transporter agreement		x	x	x		
Develop web front end	x	x		x	x	x
Add customer record update		x		x	x	x
Create product info database	x	x		x	x	x
Link to packing system	x			x	x	x
Link to inventory records	x	x	x	x	x	x
Totals						

Exhibit 8.2 Approval Checklist

Department	Person	Approval Needed	Date Needed	Responsible Team Member	Meeting Date and Time	Further Actions Needed	Approved	Approval Date
Order entry	Oscar Early	Overall project	8/31/01	BB	8/27/01 10:00			
Human resources	Harriet Rouge	Staff reduction	9/14/01	HR	9/4/01 2:00			
Procurement	Pat Cure	Negotiate new contract	9/7/01	GG	8/30/01 8:30			
Information technology	Irwin Tex	Develop new system	9/14/01	IT	9/4/01 10:30			
Packing	Peter Pack	Staffing changes	9/21/01	CS	9/4/01 1:00			

checklist is designed to ensure that all necessary approvals are documented on a single form. When Charlie Satiz asked how this form differed from the approval section of the project charter (see Exhibit 5.5), Betty explained that the checklist was a record of various approvals and how they were gained, whereas the project charter contained actual signatures. The initial version of the approval checklist showed only the approvals to be obtained and the first steps. It would be updated at subsequent meetings to include actions taken and those still remaining.

Because team members knew that the staffing changes would be the most difficult part of the project and because they wanted all of the affected department managers to learn about their proposal at the same time, they scheduled a briefing session for the day after Oscar Early's expected approval of the project. At that time, they planned to review the project's goals and their recommendations. This briefing session was one of the first steps that the team included in its formal communication plan. Exhibit 3.1 shows a sample communication plan.

As the team members had hoped, they had little difficulty in obtaining approval to proceed with their recommendations. They were ready for the second step in the improvement phase.

Step 2: Finalize the Implementation Plan

Although George Greenbelt had begun developing an overall project plan using common project management software, Harold Resourceful suggested that they publish a simplified version of the plan that would present the "35,000 foot" view. This could be used as part of the ongoing communications that they would share with all stakeholders, including the affected departments. Exhibit 8.3 shows the first draft of the summary implementation plan.

Step 3: Implement the Approved Changes

As team members began to develop and implement their solutions, they knew that although they would be focused on the details of turning their recommendations into reality, it was essential that everyone affected understand what was happening. Oscar Early agreed that honest communication was the key to success and committed to ensuring that it occurred.

Working with GWC's Communications department, the team developed an overall communication plan that included the following components:

- *Weekly team meetings*, key results of which were summarized and published on the project's Web site.
- *Weekly "rumor control" meetings* run by Oscar Early. These gave employees a chance to ask questions and have rumors either confirmed or denied. Informal in nature, these became one of the primary vehicles for keeping employees motivated.
- *Monthly "lunch and learn" sessions* conducted by a member of the project team. These workshops, which began after the prototype of the Web front end was available, were designed to introduce employees to the new system in an informal setting.
- *Bi-monthly letter to customers.* This was designed to explain the coming changes and the implementation schedule.
- *"Progress map."* Charlie Satiz suggested that the team develop a visual representation of its progress. After brainstorming, the team decided to use a journey analogy and announced that, in keeping with GWC's global presence, the project would be portrayed as a round-the-world airplane trip. The team took a map of the world, replacing major cities with key milestones on the project. Each week, the map — a large version of which was posted outside the team's

meeting room — was updated to show how far they had progressed. Reception of the map was so positive that the team included a small version as a logo on all project communications.

Exhibit 8.3   Summary Implementation Plan

Task	Steps	Responsibility	Target Completion	Actual Completion	Results
Gain approval	• Meet with champion • Meet with department managers • Conduct individual meetings	BB, GG, IT, HR, CS			
Communicate progress	• Develop communications plan • Deliver	HR			
Implement "quick hit" changes	• Move fax machine • Eliminate large order verification • Separate orders by widget size	GB, BB, IT			
Change to air shipments	• Negotiate new transporter agreement • Implement new plan	CS, procurement			
Develop new system–Phase I		IT			
Develop new system–Phase II					
Develop new system–Phase III		IT			
Develop new system–Phase IV		IT			
Develop new system–Phase V		IT			
Develop new system–Phase VI		IT			
Revise policies and procedures		CS			
Train	• Develop training materials • Schedule sessions • Conduct training	GG			

Actual development and implementation of the new system followed the IT department's Six Sigma version of its system development methodology. Subsequent sections of this book discuss the ways in which Six Sigma tools and concepts can be adapted to improve standard methodologies.

The new system was not the only change the team implemented. George Greenbelt served as a member of the sub-team that developed and evaluated a Request for Proposal (RFP) to potential transporters.

As it had throughout the project, this team wanted to ensure that the decisions it made were based on facts and that they were ones that best met customers' requirements. Accordingly, when the team had narrowed the potential suppliers to three, George suggested that they document their assessment using a decision matrix. As shown in Exhibit 8.4, the decision matrix presents key selection criteria and the degree to which each supplier meets them. Because First-to-Deliver was the only company that met all criteria, they were awarded the contract.

In the past, decisions might have been made based solely based on price. Like the cost, time, and customer impact ranking they had developed previously (Exhibit 7.10), the decision matrix allowed the team to evaluate and rank all criteria and make a fully informed decision.

As expected, developing and implementing the new system was the longest step in the improvement phase. When it was completed, the team entered the final DMAIC phase: control.

Exhibit 8.4   Decision Matrix

Supplier	Selection Criteria			
	Cost (Goal: < or = $10/pkg)	% Guaranteed 2 day Delivery (Goal: 98%)	Confidence in Contingency Plan (Goal: 95%)	Current Customer Satisfaction (Goal: 4.8)
RapidityTran	9.75	97.75	95	4.6
SpeedieTruck	9.99	99.00	90	4.8
First-to-deliver	10.00	98.50	95	4.8

Chapter 9

The Control Phase

Unlike some prior quality initiatives, which stop at the point that solutions are implemented, Six Sigma recognizes the need for an additional phase, one that is designed to ensure that the gains that were achieved in the previous phases are not lost. This phase is called Control.

The objectives of the control phase are to:

- Institutionalize the process improvements so that the changes are permanent and gains are sustained.
- Develop and communicate metrics that continue to reinforce the value of the improvements.
- Establish mechanisms for dealing with out-of-control situations.

As she had for previous phases, Betty Blackbelt guided the team through the process. She identified the steps of the control phase as:

1. Establish key metrics.
2. Develop the control strategy.
3. Celebrate and communicate success.
4. Implement the control plan.
5. Measure and communicate improvements.

Step 1: Establish Key Metrics

Although team members had conducted measurements in the second phase, Betty told them that they had not developed metrics. When Charlie Satiz appeared confused by Betty's statement, she explained the difference. The distinction is that a measurement is a single dimension, capacity, or quantity, whereas a metric is a value calculated from multiple measurements. As an example, during the measurement phase, the team measured the number of days it took for a shipment to arrive at the customer's address as well as the number of shipments that were made. Each of those (number of days and number of shipments) is a measurement. The average number of days in transit is a metric derived from those two measurements. It is calculated as the sum of all days in transit divided by the total number of shipments.

When establishing metrics, the team knew that it was important to develop meaningful ones. As the first step, the team decided to apply the RAVE principles that it had used for measurements. (Chapter 6 explains RAVE.) In addition, as part of its deployment of Six Sigma, GWC had developed the following guidelines for metrics:

- *Less is more.* Company policy suggested no more than six meaningful metrics, believing that the value of individual metrics would be diluted if there were too many.
- *Balance internal with external perspectives.* In addition to measuring internal performance, GWC stressed the importance of including the customers' view of their performance.
- *Communicate.* To avoid the "black hole" syndrome where employees conducted measurements only because they were instructed to but had no understanding of why, GWC policy stated that there be a clear definition of why each measurement was being made and how the resulting metric would be used. GWC also insisted that metrics be distributed not just to senior management, but also to the data collectors so that those who were taking the measurements could see the value of their efforts.

The team believed that the following metrics were relevant and that they provided the appropriate balance between external and internal perspectives:

1. Average length of time for a customer to enter an order
2. Average delivery time for a shipment
3. Percentage of shipments with returned items
4. Average customer satisfaction

The first two metrics addressed the customer requirements shown in Exhibit 5.15. The last two metrics provided internal measures of quality and satisfaction.

Betty reminded team members of the risks of measurement systems (see Exhibit 6.5) and stressed that because these metrics would be used to determine the success of the project, it was essential that they use only reliable measurements. GWC had developed a metric reliability assessment spreadsheet to help determine which metrics would be most valid. It includes an evaluation of both the data and the person who will collect the data, because the goal is to have repeatable, reproducible, objective measurements. Appendix E details the use of the assessment matrix. A portion of the one that the team developed for the order entry project is shown as Exhibit 9.1.

When reviewing the Total Reliability column, which is the overall rating for a metric, calculated by summing the individual components of reliability, the team was not surprised that the least reliable metric was the one that required manual counting. They decided that they would place the least emphasis on this metric. They also noted that, by general GWC guidelines, which said that data should be collected immediately, their metrics had collection delays. However, because the team planned to generate and publish metrics on a monthly basis, the delays would have no negative impact on them, and would not compromise the integrity of the metric.

Step 2: Develop the Control Strategy

Metrics provide a way to measure success. The team's next step, Betty explained, was to help guarantee that success. The team would do that by developing a control strategy. The first step would be the creation of a formal control plan to ensure that the project's improvements are sustained. Like all control plans, this one's objectives included.

- Eliminating the need for manual controls *and*
- Minimizing process tweaking

Because it undesirable to react to special causes of variation (see Exhibit 7.1), the control plan seeks to prevent that from occurring.

As shown in Exhibit 9.2, the control plan identifies key inputs and outputs of the process, specification levels, measurement techniques, current controls, and a reaction plan, should the process fail to meet specifications. In this case, because the system — rather than the person — is performing the measurement, it is possible to perform continuous sampling. Other, less automated processes may require manual controls and measurements that are performed less frequently.

Exhibit 9.1   Metric Reliability Assessment Spreadsheet

Process:	Web-Based Order Entry								
Prepared By:	Betty Blackbelt								
Date Prepared:	Nov 2 2001								
Metric	Measurement	Collector	Data Reliability	Data Repeatability	Collection Delays	Collector Availability	Total metric Reliability	Comments
Average length of time to enter an order	Time customer logs on	System	10	10	10	10	40	Measurements are generated in real time.
	Time customer logs off	System	10	10	10	10	40	Measurements are generated in real time.
Percentage of orders with returns	Count of orders placed	System	10	10	4	10	34	Measurements are generated daily
	Count of orders placed	System	10	10	4	10	34	Measurements are generated daily
	Count of orders with returned items	Customer service department	7	7	7	4	25	Requires manual counts; month end processing can cause delays in recording returns.
Averages			9.4	9.4	7.0	8.8	35	

Exhibit 9.2   Control Plan

Process								
			Revised Order Entry					
	What's Being Measured?		**What Are the Expected Results?**			**How Are We Measuring?**		**What if There's a Problem?**
Process step	Input	Output	Specification	Capability Index	Measurement/ Control Technique	Sample Size	Sample Frequency	Reaction Plan
Online order entry	Customer keystrokes	Order	USL (max call length) = 2 minutes		System calculates elapsed time, flags if 80% of calls within a 10 minute interval exceed USL	n/a; all orders are measured	Continuous	IT–408

Exhibit 9.3   Reaction Plan

Procedure Number	IT-408		Revision Number: 0
Procedure name	Reaction to order entry system excessive call length alert		
Date issued	12/01/01		
Date revised	N/A		
Primary responsibility	IT control group		
Out of spec condition	> 80% of calls within 10 minutes exceeded the 2 minute USL for call length		
Identified by	Order entry system		
Probable Cause	*What to Check*		*Corrective Action*
Excessive firewall traffic	Screen FW3705 shows firewall traffic.		If red alert, • Control group has been notified and will resolve. • Post warning message OE-336. If yellow alert, • Notify control group of potential problem. • Post warning message OE-337.
Local carrier problems	Run test (see procedure IT-116).		If test indicates problem, • Notify carrier. • Post warning message OE-337.

Team members were pleased that the first control they developed met both goals. This eliminated the need for manual recording and measuring, and it helped avoid overreacting to variation. As noted in the Measurement/Control Technique column, the system will not send an alert if only a few calls exceed the two-minute limit, because those variations could be caused by the customer's being distracted, not understanding the system, or simply working slowly. However, if a pattern of lengthy calls develops and is sustained, the system will trigger the reaction plan. That plan is documented as Exhibit 9.3 and shows the steps to follow to diagnose and correct the causes of variation.

The control plan is only one part of the control strategy. The overall strategy included monthly post-implementation project reviews for the first quarter, followed by three quarterly audits of the control plan. During the second and subsequent years, audits would be performed semi-annually. All of these were documented on the TMAP and added to the implementation plan.

Step 3: Celebrate and Communicate Success

As a company, GWC believed strongly in the importance of recognizing the accomplishments that its Six Sigma teams achieved. When the company began its Six Sigma initiative, GWC's CEO told employees that the "C" in DMAIC stood for two things: control and celebrate. He might have added a third "C" — communicate — because the company emphasized communication of team successes.

Although most projects were designed to last no more than six months, when they exceeded that time, teams were encouraged to celebrate not just the conclusion of the project, but also major milestones. Celebratory events included team lunches and trips to sporting or cultural events. Because one of the objectives was to foster teamwork, all such events were designed for the team as a whole.

At the conclusion of projects, the sponsoring department normally held a departmental meeting to recognize the team's accomplishments. Depending on the size and cost savings generated by the project, team members might receive a plaque or a certificate citing their accomplishments. Large-scale projects frequently included monetary awards as part of their celebration step. In all cases, the project's conclusion was highlighted in the company's quarterly newsletter and on its Six Sigma Web site.

Step 4: Implement the Control Plan

Team members knew that, like all plans, their control plan would be only as good as its use, which was why they had established a monitoring schedule. George Greenbelt volunteered to be responsible for implementing and auditing the control plan and providing quarterly reports to the rest of the team.

Step 5: Measure and Communicate Improvements

The team's final step to ensure that gains were sustained was to develop a system for monthly metrics reporting. Because they had established four key metrics, they decided to display the results on a single page with each metric in a quadrant as shown on Exhibit 9.4. Because each chart contained the goal, this provided an easy way to measure improvements. Like other project communications, the scorecard was posted within the Order Entry, Packing, and Shipping departments and on the project's Web site.

Before the project was considered complete, the team made a final update to the project charter, showing the actual benefits it had achieved.

Exhibit 9.4 Monthly Scorecard

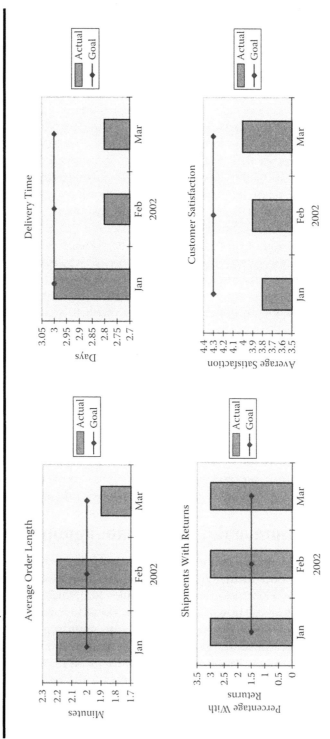

The project charter then became part of the company's Six Sigma data repository and was available for other teams to reference. The repository was designed to foster communication among project teams. In addition to providing information about individual projects' goals, schedules, and accomplishments, the fact that the charters listed all team members had the added benefit of identifying subject matter experts (SMEs) whose experiences and knowledge could assist future teams.

Although the team was officially disbanded three months after the new system was implemented, the members continued to receive monthly metrics and agreed that they would meet annually to discuss ways in which the new system and processes could be improved. After all, they knew that DMAIC was an iterative process and that this first project set the stage for future improvements.

Exhibit 9.5 provides a summary of the steps that the GWC OE team followed in each of the five Six Sigma phases.

Exhibit 9.5 Summary of DMAIC Phases and Steps

Phase	Steps
Define	1. Define the problem. 2. Form a team. 3. Establish a project charter. 4. Develop a project plan. 5. Identify the customers. 6. Identify key outputs. 7. Identify and prioritize customer requirements. 8. Document the current process.
Measure	1. Determine what to measure. 2. Conduct the measurements. 3. Calculate current sigma level. 4. Determine process capability. 5. Benchmark process leaders.
Analyze	1. Determine what caused the variation. 2. Brainstorm ideas for process improvements. 3. Determine which improvements would have the greatest impact on meeting customer requirements. 4. Develop proposed process map. 5. Assess the risks associated with the revised process.
Improve	1. Gain approval for the proposed changes. 2. Finalize the implementation plan. 3. Implement the approved changes.
Control	1. Establish key metrics. 2. Develop the control strategy. 3. Celebrate and communicate success. 4. Implement the control plan. 5. Measure and communicate improvements.

III

DESIGN FOR SIX SIGMA

Although a powerful strategy, Six Sigma has limitations; and after a few years of dramatic quality improvements, companies may find themselves faced with decreasing returns on their quality improvement efforts. The problem is not Six Sigma itself but the fact that effort is being expended to perfect flawed processes and products. Design For Six Sigma (DFSS) takes a different approach and helps companies build in quality from the beginning.

Using another case study of the fictitious Global Widget Company (GWC), Section III illustrates the use of DFSS tools and techniques in the creation of a totally new widget.

Chapter 10 provides an introduction to DFSS, explaining the differences between it and classic Six Sigma. Similar to classic Six Sigma, DFSS is normally divided into phases; however, unlike Six Sigma's DMAIC, those phases are not consistently named or defined. Chapter 10 introduces the IDDOV methodology and the background for the new case study.

The "I" in IDDOV represents the Identification of Opportunities phase and is discussed in Chapter 11. In addition to the steps associated with classic Six Sigma's Define phase, Identification includes the use of a critical new tool: the Quality Function Deployment (QFD) matrix.

During the Definition of Initial Design phase (Chapter 12), the reader is introduced to a second new technique, the Pugh Concept Selection, as the team quantifies the benefits of several potential solutions and selects the most suitable. In the Development of Concept phase (Chapter 13), the team models its proposed design and uses the classic Six Sigma tool FMEA to identify and mitigate potential risks in that design. Optimization (Chapter 14) demonstrates methods for ensuring that the project achieves the highest possible quality at the lowest possible cost by introducing the reader to parameter and tolerance design. During the final phase, Verification (Chapter 15), the team uses prototypes and pilots to demonstrate that its design is a robust one and that the product will meet all customer requirements.

Chapter 10

Introduction to DFSS

As discussed in Chapter 1, although classic Six Sigma is powerful, it has limitations.

The Need for DFSS

Many companies have discovered that once they identify key processes and reduce variation in those processes, it becomes increasingly difficult to continue improving quality. For the first few years after they implement Six Sigma techniques, the companies achieve tangible benefits, and those benefits are substantial. Not only has the quality of their products and processes improved, but the corporate culture has also changed. Employees of Six Sigma companies have a common vocabulary, clearly focused priorities, and an appreciation of the power of teamwork. The companies are stronger, and so too are their bottom lines.

Quality continues to improve as the companies continue to refine their processes and reduce variation. Unfortunately, the reality is that the upward spiral cannot continue indefinitely. Although companies have accepted the iterative nature of Six Sigma and the need for continuous improvement as shown in Exhibit 1.3, the fact is that they hit barriers, frequently after they reach the 4.5 sigma level. They have picked all the "low hanging fruit." That is, they have fixed the largest and most egregious problems. They have increased quality but they have not yet achieved the goal of five sigma. At some point, typically before they reach five sigma, the effort required to increase quality becomes cost-prohibitive.

Writing about classic Six Sigma, Harry and Schroeder aptly entitled their book *Six Sigma: The Breakthrough Management Strategy Revolutionizing the World's Top Corporations.*[1] They were not exaggerating. Six Sigma has provided significant breakthroughs and it was revolutionary; but as time passed, it was apparent to Six Sigma veterans that another breakthrough was needed. Enter Design For Six Sigma (DFSS).

The premise of DFSS is simple: begin earlier in the process and design in quality rather than add it after the design has been implemented. This concept has its roots in ancient history. Archimedes[2] claimed that if he had a long enough lever (and, of course, a place from which to wield that lever), he could move the earth. While companies are not trying to move the earth, they do want to break through the 4.5 sigma barrier, and they can. Archimedes' statement was based on the fact that the effect of a lever is directly proportional to the distance between the fulcrum and the force applied. When it is not possible to increase the force, lengthen the lever. By increasing the length of the lever and the distance from the fulcrum, it is possible to achieve the desired results with less effort.

Because they had hit a barrier and could no longer afford to expend increasing effort to improve quality, Six Sigma companies needed a longer lever. As shown on Exhibit 10.1, DFSS is that longer lever. By its very nature, being employed at the beginning of the process, DFSS places the would-be earth mover further from the problem. The result is that less force is required to achieve the desired change, and what was not cost-effective becomes feasible. This is no surprise to IT professionals, who know that the earlier in the system development life cycle that a problem is detected, the less it costs to correct it. DFSS, however, is concerned with more than correcting problems — it seeks to prevent them.

Defining DFSS

As its name suggests, Design For Six Sigma (DFSS) has as its core the *design* of a product, process, or — for IT — a piece of software. The objective is to create a design that can be produced at the six sigma level. Consider the effect that such a design would have. If the resulting product, process, or software module operated at the six sigma level, it would have virtually no defects. The cost of support, which IT professionals know is the largest portion of a software product's life cycle, would be minimized. Similarly, the rework and redesign that often occur during the development process would be reduced, if not totally eliminated.

That is, the goal of DFSS is to start at the beginning and do everything right the first time, thus eliminating the all-too-frequent iterations in the design and production process, as well as substantially reducing support

Exhibit 10.1   The Effect of the DFSS Lever

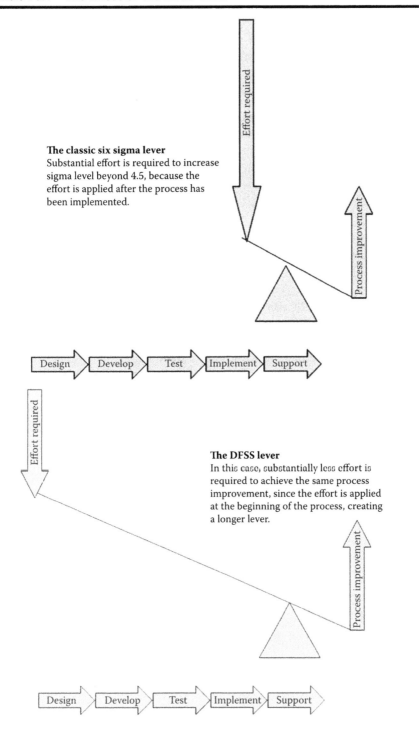

The classic six sigma lever
Substantial effort is required to increase sigma level beyond 4.5, because the effort is applied after the process has been implemented.

Effort required

Process improvement

Design   Develop   Test   Implement   Support

Effort required

The DFSS lever
In this case, substantially less effort is required to achieve the same process improvement, since the effort is applied at the beginning of the process, creating a longer lever.

Process improvement

Design   Develop   Test   Implement   Support

Exhibit 10.2   Forces Affecting Design

and warranty costs once the product is in production. Although the concept is simple, implementation requires rigorous attention to details and a consistent focus on what is most important.

As Exhibit 10.2 shows, there are two forces that drive a design: (1) the customer and (2) the process. For a design to be successful, it must accomplish two things. It must:

1. Meet the customer's expectations *and*
2. Define a process or product that can be produced at the six sigma level.

Although these might sometimes be opposing requirements, the combination of the two is what distinguishes a Six Sigma design from others. A design that satisfies every customer requirement but cannot be produced effectively is one that will require constant tweaking and improvement and one that will not be profitable for the company. Conversely, a process that produces defect-free products that are not what the customer wants or needs is of little value. It also will not be profitable for the company.

Six Sigma companies are well aware of the importance of building the right product the right way and ensuring that customer requirements are satisfied. They are also well-versed in the need to reduce variation and in techniques to do that. DFSS has the same goals. It can be viewed as an add-on or a front end to classic Six Sigma, because it provides a set of tools and techniques that helps reduce variation in the design process at the same time that they work to ensure that both the voice of the customer (the functional requirements) and the voice of the process (the capability to manufacture at the desired quality level) are fully understood and are in sync.

Phases of DFSS

Classic Six Sigma is a mature strategy. As such, it has been standardized to the extent that any Six Sigma practitioner recognizes the acronym DMAIC and knows it stands for the five phases of Six Sigma. DFSS is younger. While companies have been using Six Sigma techniques since the mid-1990s, Chowdhury's book, entitled *Design For Six Sigma*, which he explains was the first book on the subject,[3] was first copyrighted in 2002. As might be explained by that relative immaturity, although the goals of DFSS are consistent, the way it is implemented is not. Most DFSS training courses and textbooks divide the process into between four and six phases. The names vary, as do the steps included within each one.

Chowdhury[4] uses the five-letter acronym IDDOV but divides it into four phases:

1. ID: Identify the opportunity and Define the requirements
2. D: Develop the concept
3. O: Optimize the design
4. V: Verify the design

Stamatis, author of the seven-volume *Six Sigma and Beyond* series,[5] prefers a five-phase process that he calls RDCOV:

1. R: Recognize
2. D: Define
3. C: Characterize
4. O: Optimize
5. V: Verify

Honeywell International DFSS training features six phases with the acronym UDMOVC:[6]

1. U: Understand customer needs
2. D: Define initial solution
3. M: Model design performance
4. O: Optimize design
5. V: Verify design
6. C: Control

A search of the Web uncovers yet another variation: five phases named DMADV:[7]

1. D: Define
2. M: Measure
3. A: Analyze
4. D: Design
5. V: Verify

A casual study reveals the similarities among the phase names. Rather than create a new acronym, this book uses Chowdhury's acronym of

IDDOV. It should, however, be noted that IDDOV will be treated as five different phases, and that the steps described in the following chapters do not necessarily coincide with those of Chowdhury.

Distinguishing between Six Sigma and DFSS

As Chapter 1 pointed out, although classic Six Sigma and DFSS are complementary strategies and employ some of the same tools and techniques, there are differences between them. Exhibit 10.3 outlines those differences. It is important to note that the two strategies are neither mutually exclusive nor dependent on each other. Each has its strengths and its most effective uses. Although it is important to consider each of the factors shown in Exhibit 10.3 when deciding whether to use DFSS techniques or to treat the project as a traditional Six Sigma initiative, the critical question is often whether the project involves a new product (or process) or an existing one. DFSS's strengths are best employed on new products, while classic Six Sigma is used to improve existing products or processes.

The remainder of Section III uses a case study to illustrate the IDDOV process and the use of DFSS tools and techniques.

Exhibit 10.3   Differences between Classic Six Sigma and DFSS

Element	Six Sigma	DFSS
Focus	Existing process	New process
Goal	Reduce variation	Reduce variation and optimize performance
Time required to implement improvements	Shorter	Longer
Potential financial results	Lower	Higher
Payback period	Shorter	Longer
Disruption to internal organization	Lower	Higher
Best suited for	Maximizing current process	Developing new products or reengineering existing processes
Major effect is on	C_p (reducing variation)	C_{pk} (centering within customer requirements)
One word description	Reactive	Predictive

Background to the Case Study

GWC manufactures one product, metal alloy widgets, in two sizes. Large widgets have an interior diameter of $1\frac{1}{4}$ inches, while the diameter of small ones is $\frac{1}{8}$ inch. Although they are the market leader with a 40 percent market share, GWC is concerned about increasing competition from Consolidated Asian Widgets (CAW), which has a reputation for producing widgets of equal or better quality than GWC's but at a lower cost.

The CEO of GWC was playing golf with two of GWC's major customers, Great Auto and Little Telecom, both of whom expressed their frustration because their businesses were changing, and neither of GWC's current widgets would meet their new requirements. They needed medium-sized widgets.

Recognizing both the opportunity and the risk if GWC did nothing, the CEO convened a special meeting of the Executive Committee. His staff confirmed that the current production lines were running at full capacity but there was unused space in the factory, which meant that it would be possible to add a new production line. They could get that new production line up and running in a relatively short time if they duplicated their current manufacturing process, changing nothing other than the widget's size.

Although that was a possibility that GWC might have considered seriously several years earlier, the Executive Committee was vocal in insisting that there had to be a better way. The VP of Marketing was concerned that the medium-sized widget would be too expensive for Great Auto and Little Telecom, while the VP of Customer Relations feared that the existing quality level might not satisfy the customers' new needs.

The answer, the Executive Champion of Six Sigma said, was a DFSS project. The Committee, all of whom had been trained in DFSS concepts, recognized that there were risks associated with making this a DFSS project. There would be a longer implementation time because of the front-end planning involved in DFSS. Furthermore, there was a potential for disruption to the organization because the design selected through DFSS might be fundamentally different from the current manufacturing process and might demand different skills or fewer employees. The rewards, however, could be substantially higher than GWC would achieve with a replication of the current process.

The Committee balanced the risks against the rewards and decided that this would be a DFSS project. Because her department would be the most heavily impacted, Veronica Major, the VP of Manufacturing, was asked to serve as the champion.

GWC's first major DFSS project had begun.

References

1. Harry, Mikel, Ph.D., and Richard Schroeder, Six Sigma: The Breakthrough Management Strategy Revolutionizing the World's Top Corporations. New York: Doubleday, 2000.
2. Archimedes, Pappus of Alexandria Collection, bk. VIII, prop. 10, sec. 11 from Bartlett's Familiar Quotations. Boston: Little, Brown and Company, 1980, p. 93.
3. Chowdhury, Subir, Design For Six Sigma. Chicago: Dearborn Trade, 2005, p. 177.
4. Chowdhury, Subir, Design For Six Sigma. Chicago: Dearborn Trade, 2005, p. 18.
5. Stamatis, D.H., Six Sigma and Beyond: Design For Six Sigma. Boca Raton, FL: St. Lucie Press, 2003, Preface.
6. Honeywell International, Inc., 2002.
7. www.iSixSigma.com

Chapter 11

The Identification of Opportunities Phase

The first phase of a DFSS project is similar to the first phase of DMAIC. As was true of the Definition phase of DMAIC, the Identification phase has as its goal understanding the problem to be solved, or, in DFSS terminology, the opportunity to be addressed. Many of the steps are the same as those outlined in Chapter 5. In some cases, there is a slightly different focus, and new tools are employed. These differences are caused by the fact that instead of improving the existing process, the goal of DFSS is to create a new one that both meets the customers' requirements and is capable of producing defect-free products.

As noted in the previous chapter, there are many different flavors of DFSS. Even when companies adopt an existing acronym and the phases have the same names as ones identified in Chapter 10, the steps within each phase may vary. GWC had established eight steps for its Identification of Opportunities phase:

1. Define the problem.
2. Form a team.
3. Establish a project charter.
4. Develop a project plan.
5. Identify the customers, suppliers, and stakeholders.
6. Identify customer requirements.
7. Identify CTQs.
8. Begin to develop the QFD matrix.

Step 1: Define the Problem

Before she assembled the team, Veronica Major developed a draft problem statement. Based on everything she had heard during the executive staff meeting, that problem statement became "GWC may lose up to 10 percent of its market share unless it has a medium-sized widget available for sale by calendar year-end 2007." She evaluated the statement using the SMART criteria that everyone at GWC had learned as part of their Six Sigma training and believed that it met four of the five criteria. It was:

1. *Specific.* The loss of market share was quantified.
2. *Measurable.* Because GWC knew its current market share, it would be possible to measure gain, loss, or retention of market share.
3. *Relevant.* No one would doubt that retaining market share was relevant to GWC's continued existence.
4. *Timebound.* The problem statement clearly specified the timeframe within which the changes were required.

That left one characteristic in question: *attainability.* At this point in the project, no one could determine whether or not meeting the year-end 2007 goal was realistic. Answering that question would be one of the project team's major objectives.

Although all that GWC required was a problem statement, Veronica went one step further and drafted a mission statement for the team: "By year-end 2007, create a six sigma quality level manufacturing process that will result in the production of 1000 medium-sized widgets per day. The process must have scalability up to 10,000 widgets per day."

With both the problem and the mission statement in hand, she was ready for the next step — assembling the team.

Step 2: Form a Team

Although it is always important to have the right people on a team, the high visibility of this project made Veronica determined to select the best team members possible. Drawing on her Six Sigma training, she weighed the characteristics of effective team members (see Exhibit 5.2) and the list of support functions to be considered for team membership (see Exhibit 5.1) as she began to invite employees to serve on the team.

Her first decision was to select Daniel First as the team leader. A DFSS Black Belt, he was one of Veronica's direct reports and a key player in the Manufacturing organization. With Daniel's assistance, the following employees became part of the team:

- Mary Frances Glidden, another member of the Manufacturing department. As a group leader on the plant floor, Mary Frances provided a different perspective from Daniel.
- Susan Chain, representing Supply Chain, the new name for the Procurement department. Both Veronica and Daniel recognized that without effective suppliers, the project would have little chance of success.
- Harold Resourceful, the operational development expert from Human Resources. Veronica and Daniel knew of Harold's contributions to the Order Entry project and wanted him to be part of this team because they thought it likely that organizational changes would result from the project.
- Irene Technowiz from Information Technology. Although she was not directly involved with the manufacturing systems, both Veronica and Daniel respected her analytical skills and her ability to manage IT projects. While they hoped that existing computer systems would need no modifications, Veronica and Daniel suspected that would not be the case.
- George Greenbelt from Order Entry. Not only was Order Entry a part of the overall process that would be impacted, but George's experiences with the previous project had given him an excellent understanding of the packing and shipping processes, both of which would be affected by the new project.

The team held their first meeting on May 30, 2006. Although normally they would have started drafting their project charter, they realized that there were still too many open questions. As a result, they created an initial thought process map (TMAP), listing their questions and the immediate actions they would take. Exhibit 11.1 shows the TMAP at the end of the first meeting.

Exhibit 11.1 Initial Thought Process Map

ENTRY DATE: May 30, 2006

What facts do we know about the project?

1. Two major customers have expressed a need for medium-sized widgets.
2. The customers would prefer to use GWC's products but must be assured that they will have the new widgets by YE 2007.
3. Current production lines are running at capacity.
4. There is unused space in the factory (approximately $1/4$ of the total floor space).
5. GWC's senior management is concerned about a potential loss of market share if we cannot produce medium-sized widgets.

Questions:

What questions do we have at this point in the project?

1. What is the scope of our project?

Exhibit 11.1   Initial Thought Process Map (continued)

2. Will GWC's smaller customers also buy medium-sized widgets?
3. How big is "medium-sized?"
4. How will customers use the new widgets?
5. Do they have any other requirements?
6. What name should we give our project?
7. Can our existing suppliers provide the raw materials we'll need?
8. What skills will be needed for the new production line?
9. What lean techniques can we incorporate into the new process?
10. Will the unused factory space be adequate?
11. Is there enough room in the warehouse to store the new raw materials?
12. Can packing and shipping accommodate additional product?
13. Are there any new regulatory requirements that must be addressed?
14. What changes will be needed to existing information systems?

What tools or methods will we apply to answer the questions? (Include action items, due dates, and responsible person.)

Question #	Action/Tool	Responsibility	Target Date
1	Meeting with champion	DF	6/2/06
2–5	Customer focus group sessions	All	6/30/06
7, 8, 10–12, 14	TBD as project progresses		
9	Meeting with lean master	GG	6/2/06
13	Meetings with chief counsel and Health, Safety, and Environmental	SC (legal) and HR (HSE)	6/2/06

Answers:

What were the answers to the questions? (Include reference to actual tools used.)

Question #	Date Answered	Answer	Tool Used
6	5/30/06	Just right widget	Brainstorming

One of the things the team decided to do during this meeting was give the project a name. Although it could have remained the "medium-sized widget project," team members wanted something with a little more pizzazz to it. As they brainstormed ideas, Mary Frances suggested they call it the "Goldilocks Project," reminding the team of Goldilocks' tasting the three bears' oatmeal. One bowl was too hot, the next too cold, the final one just right. She pointed out that the team's charge was to create a widget that was not too big, not too small, but just right. The team liked the analogy and decided to call the project the "Just Right Widget Project."

Step 3: Establish a Project Charter

When team members met three days later, they reviewed the actions that had been taken to resolve some of their initial questions. Daniel reported that their scope would not include the negotiation of new contracts with suppliers or labor unions but would focus strictly on the manufacturing process. Separate projects would be chartered to handle the contracts, if needed. This answered question #1 from the TMAP.

In response to question #9, George met with the Lean Master, who suggested that the team remember to design in simplicity; that is, the team should strive to reduce the number of parts involved and, wherever possible, to specify parts that were being used in existing processes. They should also attempt to reduce wait time, perhaps by replacing the current system of batch production with constant flow processing.

Although the first set of suggestions related to the product and process, the Lean Master told George there were ways the team itself could be more effective. Team members recognized the value of the Lean Master's recommendation that they have contiguous workspaces for the duration of the project and requested that that workspace be located near the manufacturing floor. The objective of the move was twofold: (1) communication within the team would be facilitated by their proximity; (2) being near the plant floor would place the team as close as possible to the employees and processes that would be impacted. By being there, the team could observe daily interactions and, as much as feasible, become part of the operation. This would enable them to observe problems with the existing process and ensure that they were not repeated in the new one.

Susan's meeting with the Law department and Harold's meeting with Health, Safety, and Environmental revealed that there were several cases where GWC's existing process had been grandfathered and was not required to comply with more-stringent new regulations. If a new production line was created, all regulations would apply, resulting in more governmental reporting. This answered question #13.

The team was now ready to begin drafting the project charter. As was true of all project charters, they recognized that it, like the TMAP, would be a work-in-progress, being refined as the project progressed. Exhibit 11.2 shows the initial charter.

Exhibit 11.2 Initial Project Charter

Project Charter
The Just Right Widget Project

Summary			
Process Impacted	Manufacturing	Total financial Impact	
Team leader	Daniel First	Champion	Veronica Major
Start date	May 30, 2006	Target completion date	December 30, 2007
Project description	Design and develop a medium-sized widget that can be produced with six sigma quality, preventing a projected 10% erosion of market share.		

Benefits					
	Units	Current	Goal	Actual Achieved	Projected Date
Sigma level		4.5 (for large and small)	6		
COPQ					
Customer sat	Scale of 1 to 5	4.6	4.8		
Other customer benefits					
Market share	Percentage	40.1	40.1		

Team membership				
Name	Role	Department	% time	GB and DFSS Trained?
Daniel First	Leader	Manufacturing	100	Both; BB
Mary Frances Glidden	Team member	Manufacturing	50	Both
Irene Technowiz	Team member	Information Technology	30	Both
Harold Resourceful	Team member	Human Resources	30	Both
Susan Chain	Team member	Supply Chain	25	Both
George Greenbelt	Team member	Order Entry	20	Both

Support required	
Training Required	
Other support required	Team members will need work space contiguous to the manufacturing floor.

Schedule				
Milestone/ Deliverable	Target Date	Owner	Estimated Cost	Comments
Identify	7/30/06			
Define	9/15/06			
Develop	10/30/06			
Optimize	11/30/06			
Verify	12/31/06			

Critical success factors and risks	
Critical Success Factors	Ability to obtain accurate and complete customer requirements.
Risks	A competitor may introduce a similar product prior to GWC.

Exhibit 11.2   Initial Project Charter (continued)

Approvals		
Role	Name	Date

Revision History		
Revision Number	Authors	Date
0	G. Greenbelt	6/3/06

Step 4: Develop a Project Plan

As the Order Entry team had, the Just Right Widget team created a formal project plan using GWC's standard work breakdown structure and PC-based project management software. Although only the milestones were shown on the project charter, the plan was created with "inchstones." Following GWC's policy, which had been implemented after the successful completion of the Order Entry project, no task had a duration exceeding one week. These were what they referred to as inchstones.

Establishing a maximum length for a task had two benefits: (1) it ensured that slippages would be detected early enough to correct them without major impact to the entire schedule, and (2) it provided team members with a sense of accomplishment and a reason to celebrate when individual inchstones were met.

Step 5: Identify the Customers, Suppliers, and Stakeholders

When team members began their initial identification of customers, they developed a chart that looked remarkably like the one the Order Entry team had created several years earlier (see Exhibit 5.7). Although that was a list of the groups traditionally considered to be customers, Daniel asked the team members to expand their chart to include suppliers and stakeholders, that is, every group that contributed to or was impacted by the manufacturing process. The list, as expected, grew substantially longer.

The Order Entry department became a supplier, because they provided the orders that triggered the manufacturing process. When the team asked who Order Entry's primary supplier was, the answer was simple: the external customer shown in Exhibit 5.7. At that point, the team knew it had reached the beginning of the chain because the customer was both the start and the end of the process. In DFSS, as in classic Six Sigma, everything begins and ends with the customer.

George Greenbelt, who had recently completed Black Belt training, suggested that although this list appeared comprehensive, there might be other groups to consider. To help identify those groups, he recommended using a value chain map, which would list the suppliers, customers, and influencers related to one particular customer: Great Auto. The purpose of a value chain map is to show the interactions between suppliers and customers and how value flows all the way to the ultimate customer.

The concept of value was not a new one to GWC's employees. They knew that value — like quality — was defined by the customer and that unless they provided value, they would lose their customers and ultimately their jobs. As Thomas Berry states, value "includes not only the actual product or service purchased, but also the customer's entire experience during the duration of its use."[1] That was one of the reasons why reliability needed to be built into the widget. GWC was not selling a single-use, disposable product but, rather, one that was expected to have a long life span.

The team knew that Great Auto planned to use the Just Right Widgets on a new navigation system designed to be installed on their top-of-the-line vehicles. That navigation system would be manufactured and supplied by EZ-Nav, Inc. While the widget would not be visible to the ultimate customer, if it failed, the entire navigation system would be inoperative, because the widget was the key component connecting the navigation system to the car's dashboard.

The ultimate customer might not know that the failure was caused by GWC's widget; but as complaints traveled up the value chain, Great Auto would recognize the cause of the problem and, if the defects were serious enough, might seek a different widget supplier. The goal of the Just Right project was to ensure that the new widgets had no defects when they left the GWC factory and that they did not develop any during the life of the navigation systems. The team was determined that they would not be the weakest link in any chain.

As they developed the value chain map shown on Exhibit 11.3, the team began asking questions about Great Auto's navigation system. Those questions included:

- Did EZ-Nav have any requirements that were not documented?
- Could the design of the Just Right Widget influence EZ-Nav's design and possibly reduce the cost?
- Was there a way the Just Right Widget could enhance the ultimate customer's perceived value of the navigation system?

Exhibit 11.3   Value Chain Map

Suppliers	GWC process	Direct customer	Customer	Customer
Ready-to-serve raw materials	Just right widget manufacturing	Great Auto	Car dealer	Car buyer
Key activities	Key activities	Key activities	Key activities	Key activities
	Manufacture widget for use in navigation system	Manufacture car with widget in navigation system	Sell car	Use navigation system to arrive at correct destination

Influencers	Other suppliers	Other suppliers	Other suppliers
Governmental agencies (federal, state, county)	Labor unions	EZ-Nav	A-1 Advertising Agency
Key activities	Key activities	Key activities	Key activities
Define acceptable practices and reporting requirements	Provide rules relating to work force	Provide nav system for installation in car	Develop ad campaign to convince customer to buy car

Exhibit 11.4 Suppliers and Customers of the Just Right Widget Manufacturing Process

Upstream Supplier	Immediate Supplier	Process	Customer	Ultimate Customer
	Ready-to-serve	Just right widget manufacturing	Great Auto	Car buyer
Great Auto and Little Telecom	Order Entry		Little Telecom	Telephone buyer
Labor unions	Manufacturing workforce		Packing department	Shipping department
	Governmental agencies		Auditing department	
	GWC executive committee		Customer service department	Great Auto, etc.
			Law department	Governmental agencies
			Health, safety, and environmental department	Governmental agencies
			GWC board of directors	GWC shareholders

Developing the value chain map also reminded team members that any product they designed would need to consider not just customers' requirements, but also those of the external influencers, the governmental agencies that regulate widget producers. When Harold Resourceful pointed out that they had other requirements to consider, namely the company's profit goals and shareholder expectations, the team updated the list of suppliers and customers as shown in Exhibit 11.4.

Step 6: Identify Customer Requirements

Although team members suspected that they would continue to refine the list of customers and suppliers, they were ready to begin capturing customer requirements or, as they now referred to them, the Voice of the Customer (VOC).

As they decided how to obtain customer needs, they reviewed the techniques shown in Exhibit 5.8 and decided to concentrate on customer surveys and focus group meetings. Although they believed that returned items and complaints were of minimal relevance to their project, because they were developing a new process, Susan Chain agreed to review the record of returns and complaints to determine what elements in the current manufacturing process were creating defects in the customers' view. The team would work to ensure that the new design eliminated those defects.

Prior to creating the customer surveys and conducting the focus groups, the team developed a SIPOC (an acronym for Supplier, Input, Process, Output, Customer). This chart, which can be considered an extension of the list of suppliers and customers shown on Exhibit 11.4, has as its goal to create a basic understanding of the process and the factors that impact it. For simplicity's sake, the team used generic terms rather than specific names for both suppliers and customers when they created the SIPOC.

When reading the SIPOC, it is important to note that the process, which is shown in the middle of the chart, serves as a break between inputs and outputs. Although there is a direct relation between suppliers and inputs and also between outputs and customers, SIPOC rows do not provide a correlation between specific inputs and the outputs listed on the same row and should not be read as such. For example, on the preliminary SIPOC shown as Exhibit 11.5, the first entry in both the supplier and the customer column is "Customers." While it might appear that the customer order results in the creation of a widget, which it does, that is only part of the equation. All suppliers and their inputs form part of the process that produces a Just Right Widget as well as the other outputs: profits and the procedures for returns and refunds.

As the team had expected, the list of suppliers and customers continued to grow as it developed the SIPOC. When Irene Technowiz pointed out that the manufacturing process depended on computer systems, including the company's ERP (enterprise resource planning) system, and that the process

Exhibit 11.5 Preliminary SIPOC

Supplier	Input	Process	Output	Customer
Customers	Order		Just right widget	Customers
	Returned widgets		Reshipped widgets	
	Compliments and complaints		Refunds	
Internal systems	Data feeds		Data feeds	Internal systems (including law and HSE)
		Just right widget manufacturing		
Outside suppliers	Raw materials		Unpacked just right widget	Packing department
Governmental agencies	Regulations and reporting requirements		Profit	GWC shareholders
Labor unions	Work rules			
GWC executive committee	Required profit margin			
	Policies and procedures			

would provide information back to that system and to others, the team added Internal Systems as both a supplier and a customer of the process.

The team conducted its first round of focus group meetings with the two customers who had requested the Just Right Widgets (Great Auto and Little Telecom). Although some teams preferred to simply obtain requirements in general terms at this stage of the project, the Just Right team knew that it would need specificity as part of a later step and decided to ask for it during these focus group meetings. Accordingly, each time that the customers listed a requirement in general terms, the team asked them to quantify their requirement. As the Order Entry team had, the Just Right team also asked customers to provide an importance ranking for each requirement using GWC's standard 1-4-7-10 scale and, when appropriate, to rate their satisfaction with the current product. The results of the focus group meetings are shown in Exhibit 11.6.

The team was concerned by the fact that these meetings revealed several potential problems:

- Although Veronica Major's mission statement specified the production of 1000 Just Right Widgets per day, that quantity would not be sufficient to meet Great Auto's requirements and would leave none for Little Telecom.
- Great Auto and Little Telecom's definition of "medium size" varied. Although a $\frac{1}{2}$-inch diameter would meet both companies' requirements, because this was the maximum size Little Telecom could use and the minimum for Great Auto, the team was concerned that any variation would result in a product that did not meet the customers' requirements.
- Little Telecom's projected use of the widget meant that, for the first time, a GWC widget would be visible to the ultimate customer. This triggered Little Telecom's requirements for an attractive appearance and durable finish, neither of which had been a consideration in the design of the current large and small widgets.

Because of these concerns, the team expanded its membership by inviting Ernest Engineer from the Engineering department to join the team. Ernest echoed the team's concerns, confirming that the current manufacturing process would not be able to guarantee a perfect $\frac{1}{2}$-inch diameter. He also did not believe that any finish applied to the metal alloy that GWC currently used for its widgets would be durable, although it would be attractive initially. It was good, he told the other team members, that this was a DFSS project, because it appeared that they would need a radically different process to meet their customers' requirements.

Exhibit 11.6   Customer Requirements Matrix after Focus Group Meetings

Customer: Great Auto

Requirement	Importance to Customer*	Satisfaction with Current Products**
Medium size (between ½ and ¾ inch inside diameter)	10	NA
Affordable cost (less than 10 cents per unit)	7	4
Long life (10 years)	7	7
Adequate supply (1250 per day for first year; then up to 1500 per day)	7	4
Smooth exterior	1	4
Timely shipment (same day as ordered)	7	7
Made in USA	10	10
Timely replacement of defectives (shipped same day problem reported)	4	7
Rapid credit of refunds (same billing cycle)	1	4

Customer: Little Telecom

Requirement	Importance to Customer*	Satisfaction with Current Products**
Medium size (between ¼ and ½ inch inside diameter)	10	NA
Affordable cost (less than 8 cents per unit)	10	4
Long life (3 years)	7	4
Adequate supply (200 per day for first six months; then up to 500 per day)	10	7
Timely shipment (same day as ordered)	4	7
Distinctive packaging	4	1
Attractive appearance	7	1
Durable finish	10	4
Less frequent billing (monthly rather than weekly)	4	1

*Importance ranking scale:
1 = not very important
4 = moderately important
7 = very important
10 = extremely important

**Satisfaction ranking scale:
1 = not very satisfied
4 = moderately satisfied
7 = very satisfied
10 = completely satisfied

When the team had completed the focus group meetings with internal customers as well as the external ones and had tallied the results of the customer surveys that they had sent out, Daniel indicated that the next step would be to transcribe requirements from those documents onto their SIPOC. Although a basic SIPOC does not include requirements, Daniel pointed out that the addition of requirements provides a more complete understanding of the Voice of the Customer and would be helpful in subsequent steps. Exhibit 11.7 shows the expanded SIPOC.

Daniel explained that the expanded SIPOC consisted of two major sections, each of which when read from right to left answers the question, "Who needs what from whom?" The first section, which consists of the four rightmost columns, expresses the customers' needs:

- Who — the various customers
- Needs — requirements
- What — outputs
- From whom — the process

It should be noted that although there may be multiple customers (the "who") in this section, there is a sole supplier ("from whom"). That sole supplier is the process.

The second section (the four leftmost columns) recognizes that the process itself is a customer and describes the process's requirements.

- Who — the process
- Needs — requirements
- What — inputs
- From whom — suppliers

In this case, although there is a sole customer (the "who"), there are multiple suppliers ("from whom").

While team members believed that they had captured the customers' requirements, Harold was concerned that they were missing several categories of requirements. His Black Belt training had taught him that there were three forms of needs and that some were typically not expressed. The unspoken requirements, he knew, could be the most important. He suggested they use the Kano model, developed by Dr. Noriaki Kano, to categorize the requirements they had received and to brainstorm the unspoken ones.

The Kano model, as shown in Exhibit 11.8, depicts three forms of requirements and the effect that fulfillment of those needs through product functionality has on customer satisfaction. The three categories of requirements are:

Exhibit 11.7 Expanded SIPOC

Supplier	Input	Requirements	Process	Output	Requirements	Customer
Customers	Order	Complete data	Just right widget manufacturing	Just right widget	Medium size	Customers
					Affordable cost	
					Long life	
					Adequate supply	
					Timely shipment	
					Made in USA	
					Attractive appearance	
					Durable finish	
					Less frequent billing	
	Returned widgets	Traceable to customer		Reshipped widgets	Timely replacement	
					Shipped to correct address	
				Refunds	Rapid credit	
	Compliments and complaints	Traceable to customer			Accurate amount	
		Traceable to specific order				

Exhibit 11.7 Expanded SIPOC (continued)

Supplier	Input	Requirements	Process	Output	Requirements	Customer
Internal systems	Data feeds	Timely		Data feeds	Timely	Internal systems (including law and HSE)
		Accurate			Accurate	
Outside suppliers	Raw materials	Timely delivery		Unpacked just right widget	Defect-free	Packing department
		Correct quantity Defect-free			Correct quantity Timely	
Governmental agencies	Regulations and reporting requirements	Appropriate lead-time		Profit	Expected amount	GWC shareholders
		Comprehensible				
Labor unions	Work rules	Appropriate lead-time				
		Comprehensible				
GWC executive committee	Required profit margin	Appropriate lead-time				
	Policies and procedures	Appropriate lead-time				

Exhibit 11.8   The Kano Model

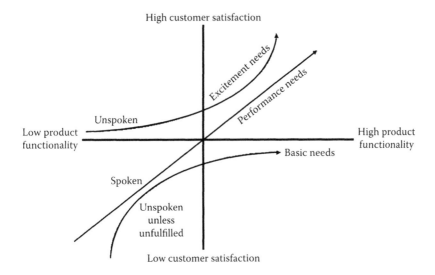

1. *Basic.* These are fundamental characteristics of the product and are often not expressed as requirements because customers expect them to be present. As shown by the fact that the arrow does not rise above the central axis into the high customer satisfaction quadrants, fully meeting these requirements will not raise customer satisfaction. On the other hand, absence of the basic needs will create dissatisfaction.

2. *Performance.* These are the characteristics that are most likely to be identified by traditional requirements gathering activities. As shown on the chart, there is a linear relationship between fulfillment of these needs and customer satisfaction.

3. *Excitement.* Like basic needs, these are normally unspoken, but for a different reason. In this case, the customer does not recognize the need. The ability to understand what Stamatis calls the customer's latent needs[2] is what distinguishes one product from another and what transforms the customer from satisfied to delighted. As Chowdhury points out, filling excitement needs "will gain the company the leadership position in the marketplace."[3]

Because delighting customers and achieving market leadership are key goals for Six Sigma companies and for GWC in particular, team members recognized that it was important to discover ways to excite and delight their customers. Recognizing that their list of requirements might not include the customers' unspoken basic needs, they brainstormed to develop a list of basic requirements as well as ways to surprise and delight their customers.

As a result of the first brainstorming session, which was designed to identify basic needs, the team added the following requirements to their SIPOC:

1. Online ordering
2. Exterior diameter within 1/100 inch of specification
3. Interior diameter within 1/1000 inch of specification
4. Smooth exterior
5. Delivered within three working days of order
6. Delivered to correct address
7. Just Right Widgets packed separately from large and small widgets

As they discussed excitement factors, team members considered Little Telecom's request for an attractive exterior finish and realized that if they could create a widget that was both attractive and extremely durable, they could transform GWC's utilitarian product into one with pizzazz, thus delighting both customers and shareholders and creating a new market niche. The new niche might do more than prevent erosion of market share. It might actually increase GWC's piece of the pie.

Although they themselves were excited, the team recognized that it might not have the full perspective on customer needs and scheduled a second brainstorming session to include representatives from the Customer Service and Marketing departments.

Step 7: Identify CTQs

The team's next step was to determine which of the customers' requirements were the most important, or — in DFSS terms — which were critical to quality (CTQ).

Before they did that, the team members, several of whom described their requirements gathering sessions as "drinking from a fire hose," were concerned that their project scope was too large. They knew from their experiences with previous Six Sigma projects that their success would depend on having a manageable scope.

To understand what appeared to be involved, they began by creating a process map (PMAP) similar to the one shown as Exhibit 5.11. The purpose of the PMAP was to understand *what* the process needed to accomplish. *How* that would be accomplished would be determined in subsequent phases of the project.

Exhibit 11.9   Preliminary PMAP

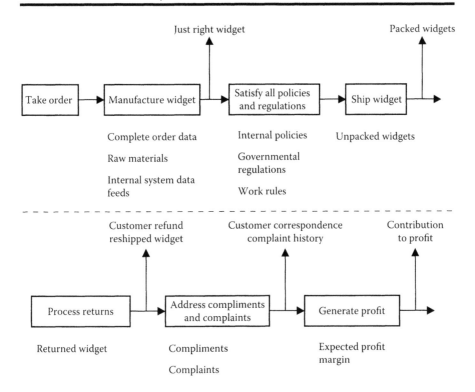

Although the team began with a basic high-level process map, because they also wanted to understand how the elements on their expanded SIPOC related to the process, they added inputs and outputs to the PMAP. As shown on Exhibit 11.9, inputs are shown below the process steps. The vertical arrows point to the outputs from each step.

When they completed this step, the team met with Veronica and presented the PMAP along with their concerns. She agreed that the project scope should be narrowed and decided that the only steps to be included were the manufacturing of the widget and the satisfaction of all internal policies and external regulations related to the manufacturing process.

Relieved, the team returned to the identification of CTQs. There are two reasons for identifying CTQs. The first is that, although the team might want to satisfy every customer requirement, that desire is unlikely to be consistent with completing the project in a reasonable amount of time at a reasonable cost. The second reason is to avoid generating the first form of waste shown in Exhibit 6.3, namely overprocessing. There is no point in doing work that does not increase customer satisfaction. In

Kano terms, overprocessing could be considered all work that is expended in perfecting those characteristics that satisfy the customers' basic needs beyond their minimum expectations. As shown on Exhibit 11.8, once the minimum threshold of needs is satisfied, adding functionality to basic needs generates no additional customer satisfaction.

To determine which requirements were most critical to the customer, the team members reviewed the matrix they had created after their focus group meetings (Exhibit 11.6). They were able to eliminate the requirements that were no longer inside the project scope (replacement of defectives, rapid crediting of refunds, and less frequent billing). As their next step, anything with an importance rating of 4 or less was considered a candidate for elimination. That included smooth exterior, distinctive packaging, and timely shipments. However, because Great Auto had assigned timely shipment an importance rating of 7, the team realized that it was a CTQ, at least for that customer. Although they would do further analysis in the next step, they were ready to begin constructing the QFD.

Step 8: Begin to Develop the QFD Matrix

Quality Function Deployment (QFD) is not new to DFSS or even to classic Six Sigma. Similar to many of the quality tools, it was developed in Japan and became part of the American business lexicon during the quality movements of the 1980s. The objective of a QFD is to provide a tool that translates customer needs ("what") into product features ("how"), ensuring that the project focuses on the right things, namely the CTQs.

Reduced to its simplest form, a QFD is a cause-and-effects matrix (C&E matrix) similar to the process improvement ranking shown as Exhibit 7.9. The "hows" in the QFD are the causes in a C&E matrix; the "whats" are the effects.

There are several reasons for using a QFD, including:

- *Consistency.* Similar to the use of standard templates for project charters, the QFD provides a consistent way of recording key information about a project. This facilitates communication with other project teams and contributes to the common vocabulary that helps unite a company.
- *Objectivity.* By using weighting factors and standard formulas, QFD removes subjectivity from the analysis of the relationship between needs and features. In short, it helps teams make fact-based decisions.

In its full form, QFD is anything but simple. It is, however, a powerful tool, in part because it includes so much information on one spreadsheet.

Exhibit 11.10   House of Quality

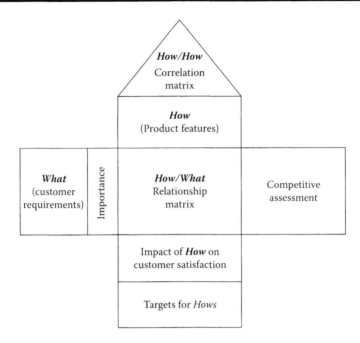

Because there are numerous components or "rooms," QFD is frequently called the House of Quality (HOQ). Exhibit 11.10 provides a pictorial representation of a House of Quality. Although Appendix F provides detailed instructions on the use of QFD, a brief explanation of the components is helpful in understanding the functions included in the matrix. Exhibit 11.11 provides that explanation.

The power and the complexity of QFD lie in the fact that, not only are there multiple "rooms" within a single QFD, but there also are up to four QFDs to be used in any one project. Although some people consider QFD and HOQ synonymous, software quality engineer Richard Biehl of DOQS (Data-Oriented Quality Solutions) makes a distinction between the two terms, using HOQ to refer to a single complex matrix that constitutes one layer of the QFD. The interlinking of multiple layers of HOQ creates a QFD.[1]

As shown in Exhibit 11.12, each level of the QFD identifies the characteristics that are critical to quality at that stage. Those CTQs become the input to the next QFD level. The key "hows" of QFD1 become the "whats" of QFD2 as the project "drills down" to increasingly greater levels of detail to answer the question, "How can we best accomplish this?" This cascading process ensures that each stage of the project focuses on the right things.

Exhibit 11.11   Explanation of House of Quality Rooms

Room	Contents
What (Customer Requirements)	Each row lists a single customer CTQ requirement.
Importance	The customer-determined importance ranking is shown next to the requirement.
How (Product Features)	Each column represents a potential feature or function of the product.
How/What Relationship Matrix	Each cell represents the effect that the product feature above it will have on the customer requirement in that row. Each of these effect rankings is multiplied by the importance and becomes part of the row and column totals. The row totals indicate the degree to which the customer requirement will be satisfied if all features are implemented.
Impact of **How** on Customer Satisfaction	The column totals (the sum of each how/what relationship) represent the overall impact that the individual product feature will have on customer satisfaction. These totals identify CTQs for the next step of the QFD.
Target for **Hows**	To further quantify requirements, each CTQ is assigned target quality measures such as the upper and lower specification limits (USL and LSL).
Competitive Assessment	Each row indicates how well competitive products meet each of the customers' requirements.
How/How Correlation Matrix	The "roof" of the house provides an assessment of how much of an impact each product feature will have on the other features. The objective of the correlation matrix is to determine whether features are in support of or in conflict with each other.

Exhibit 11.12   The Four Levels of QFD

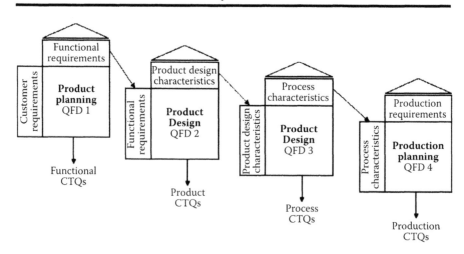

Pande and Holpp[5] recommend that all projects be selected based on the criteria they call the Two Ms: meaningful and manageable. This is excellent advice, but it is not limited to project selection. Those Two Ms are equally relevant when considering individual requirements. Creating a QFD helps identify meaningful requirements, namely the CTQs, and assists teams in determining what is manageable.

Because the full QFD can be overwhelming in its apparent complexity, especially at the early stages of a project, Biehl has divided the HOQ into a series of individual spreadsheets within a single workbook.[6] Each spreadsheet addresses one section of the HOQ, while links between them ensure that key information flows to the next sheet, creating a full QFD. Biehl's workbook has four levels of spreadsheets to accommodate the four levels of QFD. Each level contains individual sheets for planning (identification of customer requirements and competitive assessment), requirements relationships, and measurements. He also includes a separate sheet for Pugh Concept Selection, a topic discussed in Chapter 12.

The team adopted Biehl's approach and created an initial customer requirements QFD as shown on Exhibit 11.13. At this stage of the project, they were able to complete only a portion of the first QFD, because they had not yet performed a competitive analysis. However, this section of the QFD confirmed the importance of creating a medium-sized widget. The team was now ready to proceed to the second phase of DFSS: defining the initial design.

References

1. Berry, Thomas H., *Managing the Total Quality Transformation*. New York: McGraw-Hill, Inc., 1991, p. 217.
2. Stamatis, D.H., *Six Sigma and Beyond: Design for Six Sigma*. Boca Raton: St. Lucie Press, 2003, p. 71.
3. Chowdhury, Subir, *Design for Six Sigma*. Chicago: Dearborn Trade, 2005, p. 92.
4. Biehl, Richard, Data-Oriented Quality Solutions, personal communication, 2006.
5. Pande, Pete and Holpp, Larry, *What is Six Sigma?* New York: McGraw-Hill, 2002, p. 28.
6. Biehl, Richard, Data-Oriented Quality Solutions, QFD.XLS, 2006. Available at www.doqs.com.

Exhibit 11.13   Initial QFD

	Requirements	Importance	Satisfaction with Current solution	Satisfaction with Available Alternatives				Satisfaction Goal for New Solution	Improvement Required (Negative Values Are Converted to 0)	Impact Multiplier	Development Priority	Normalized Priority
				A	B	C	D					
1	Medium size	10	0					10	10	5.0	500.0	0.67
2	Affordable cost	7	4					10	6	1.0	42.0	0.06
3	Long life	7	7					7	0	1.0	0.0	
4	Adequate supply	7	4					7	3	1.0	21.0	0.03
5	Timely shipment	7	7					7	0	1.0	0.0	
6	Made in USA	10	10					10	0	1.0	0.0	
7	Attractive appearance	7	1					7	6	1.0	42.0	0.06
8	Durable finish	10	4					7	3	1.0	30.0	0.04
9	Stable market share	10	1					10	9	1.0	90.0	0.12
10	Stable profit margin	7	7					10	3	1.0	21.0	0.03
	Weighted overall performance		360					706			746.0	

Copyright Data-Oriented Quality Solutions, 2006.

Chapter 12

The Definition of the Initial Design Phase

The Just Right Widget team members were excited about the possibilities that their first steps had revealed; however, they had three major questions:

1. Were their ideas feasible? That is, could they be accomplished within a reasonable amount of time and at a reasonable cost?
2. Were there any better ideas?
3. What were GWC's competitors doing?

The objective of the next phase of DFSS is to answer the second and third questions and begin to answer the first. To do this, the team would follow a four-step process:

1. Identify potential designs.
2. Evaluate those potential designs using Pugh Concept Selection techniques.
3. Identify potential failure modes of the most feasible design.
4. Expand the QFD with the results of the analyses.

Step 1: Identify Potential Designs

While it was tempting to begin brainstorming solutions, team members knew that there was one step they had to take before they did that. They needed to determine what competition existed and how well that competition satisfied the customers' requirements. Not only would this help them complete the first section of the QFD, but — more importantly — they knew that understanding what was currently available on the market had the possibility of generating other ideas for the design of the Just Right Widget.

The team took two approaches toward identifying competitive designs: (1) purchased and examined every product that they believed could be a competitor, and (2) benchmarked the other industry leaders. The latter effort was similar to the traditional benchmarking described as Step 5 in Chapter 6.

Before evaluating the competitive products, team members reviewed Stamatis' characteristics of quality to develop a checklist they would use with each product. Stamatis' characteristics are:[1]

- *Function:* how well the product fulfills its primary purpose.
- *Features:* the presence and performance of secondary functionality.
- *Conformance:* the degree to which product specifications have been met.
- *Reliability:* performance measured over time.
- *Serviceability:* the ability to repair the product quickly, inexpensively, and effectively.
- *Aesthetics:* overall sensual experience (for the Just Right Widget, this translated into appearance).
- *Perception:* reputation of both the product and the company.

In addition, the team tracked the cost of competitive products and whether or not each product was part of the competitor's core business. Non-core products, the team knew, could be eliminated at any point and would be less likely to be long-term alternatives to the Just Right Widget.

What the team discovered was that, although there were no direct competitors to the projected Just Right Widget, three companies had products that were closer to meeting the customer's requirements than either of GWC's current widgets.

- Consolidated Asian Widgets (CAW) produced a medium-large widget with an inside diameter of $7/8$ inch. Although larger than Great Auto's maximum specification, it was possible that it could be retooled to meet their needs. It did not, however, meet Great Auto's requirement for a product made in the United States, and it was not suitable for Little Telecom.
- Rubber Industries (RI) had a flexible connector that could expand from $1/8$ to $3/8$ inch. While this would not meet Great Auto's size

specifications, it might be adaptable for Little Telecom. It did, however, have an unattractive appearance, which would not satisfy Little Telecom.

- Major Conglomerate (MC) offered a plastic connector that it calls its All-in-One (AIO). This product boasted a flexible expansion joint that allowed it to vary its inside diameter from $\frac{3}{8}$ to $\frac{5}{8}$ inches. Although the size met both Great Auto and Little Telecom's specifications, MC was experiencing heavier than normal warranty claims on the AIO and had scaled back production. The team believed these quality issues prevented the AIO from being a viable alternative.

The team expanded the QFD that it had begun in the identification phase, adding the three competitive products and their assessment. As they had for all rankings, they used a 1-4-7-10 scale, with 0 reserved for features that were completely unmet. The results are shown as Exhibit 12.1. It should be noted that the team did not evaluate competitive products against the last two requirements, because GWC management, not external customers, generated those.

The presence of at least one 0 in each product's ratings confirmed what the team had believed: that there were no products currently available that would fully meet GWC's customers' needs.

The team was now ready to brainstorm ideas for the new product. The brainstorming was made easier by the competitive assessment the team had just completed. Although team members did not like the appearance of either RI's connector or MC's AIO, they were intrigued by the flexibility that both products offered. An expandable widget would meet both Great Auto and Little Telecom's size requirements and have the potential of being used by other customers. It would, however, involve radically new production methods.

Team members continued brainstorming. When they finished, they had four alternatives:

1. Rigid metal, similar to the current GWC widgets
2. Metal with a flexible section, a variation of MC's AIO
3. Elastic polymer, similar to RI's Connector but using a more durable and attractive material
4. Rigid polymer with a flexible interior

The last one was unlike anything currently on the market. While team members believed that it had the most potential, they were also concerned about it being the highest risk alternative, because GWC's only experience with the materials and the production methods was in its test labs. Ernest

Exhibit 12.1 QFD with Competitive Product Assessment

	Requirements	Importance	Satisfaction With Current Solution	Satisfaction With Available Alternatives[*]				Satisfaction Goal for New Solution	Improvement Required (Negative Values are Converted to 0)	Impact Multiplier	Development Priority	Normalized Priority
				A	B	C	D					
1	Medium size	10	0	4	4	10		10	10	5.0	500.0	0.67
2	Affordable cost	7	4	10	4	7		10	6	1.0	42.0	0.06
3	Long life	7	7	7	7	0		7	0	1.0	0.0	
4	Adequate supply	7	4	7	10	4		7	3	1.0	21.0	0.03
5	Timely shipment	7	7	1	7	10		7	0	1.0	0.0	
6	Made in USA	10	10	0	10	10		10	0	1.0	0.0	
7	Attractive appearance	7	1	4	0	4		7	6	1.0	42.0	0.06
8	Durable finish	10	4	7	1	4		7	3	1.0	30.0	0.04
9	Stable market share	10	1					10	9	1.0	90.0	0.12
10	Stable profit margin	7	7					10	3	1.0	21.0	0.03
	Weighted overall performance		360	313	346	415		706			746.0	

[*]Competitive products
A – CAW's medium-large widget
B – RI's connector
C – MC's plastic AIO

Engineer told the team that the research scientists had been experimenting with rigid polymer and were pleased with the test results but had not envisioned bringing a polymer-based product to market this quickly.

At the same time that they were brainstorming concepts for the widget itself, the team considered production alternatives and identified three possibilities:

1. *In-house:* build a third production line within the existing GWC factory.
2. *Partner:* develop a partnership relationship with another company and produce the widgets at one of the partner's facilities.
3. *Outsource:* provide the specifications to a third-party manufacturer that would produce the widgets under the GWC label.

Having identified the concepts, the team was ready for the next step: evaluating them.

Step 2: Evaluate the Potential Designs Using Pugh Concept Selection Techniques

There are a number of techniques that can be used to evaluate multiple choices, including developing a C&E matrix of solutions and requirements and assigning weighting factors to each intersection as the team had done with the competitive products. While this is a highly effective method, the team decided to use a standard Six Sigma tool, the Pugh Concept Selection matrix.

The primary difference between the Pugh matrix and the evaluations the team had already conducted was that, instead of ranking each alternative using the 1-4-7-10 scale, Pugh uses a simpler scale to indicate whether each solution is better, worse, or the same as the baseline. Typically, the scale is plus, minus, and zero, although some companies replace the zero with an "S" for "same." Others use color coding, with red being worse, green better, and white neutral.

The Just Right team members used the standard plus, minus, zero scale. They then tallied the number of pluses, minuses and zeros for each solution. This simplicity translated into a fast, easy to complete, and understandable approach. While it lacks the precision of the 1-4-7-10 rankings in a standard C&E, at this point the team did not need precision. Their goal was to quickly identify the strengths and weaknesses of potential solutions. Pugh is ideal for that.

As noted in Chapter 11, Richard Biehl's QFD workbook includes a Pugh spreadsheet for each level of the QFD. He points out that the Pugh process provides an objective analysis regarding what should ultimately be included in the columns (the features or functions) of the next sheet.[2]

It is important to note that in each case as they created their Pugh evaluation, the team was ranking each of the alternatives against a baseline rather than against each other. Although it was not a direct competitor, the team selected the current GWC widgets as the baseline. That product is reflected in the Current Solution column. The numbers in that column correspond to the Satisfaction with Current Solution column on the QFD (Exhibit 12.1). Exhibit 12.2 shows the team's evaluation of the product alternatives, using Pugh Concept Selection techniques.

When they completed the Pugh matrix, team members believed that they had a clear winner in alternative D, the rigid polymer widget with a flexible interior. Although they could have stopped at this point, one of the reasons for using Pugh techniques is to clearly identify each potential solution's strengths and weaknesses so that teams can attempt to combine strengths from different alternatives, minimizing the weaknesses of the selected concept.

The two weaknesses identified for alternative D were its cost and potentially negative effect on profit margin. In contrast, the cost of the

Exhibit 12.2 Pugh Concept Selection Matrix

	Requirements	Current Solution	Possible Product Solutions[*]			
			A	B	C	D
1	Medium size	0	+	+	+	+
2	Affordable cost	4	0	−	+	−
3	Long life	7	0	−	−	+
4	Adequate supply	4	0	0	0	0
5	Timely shipment	7	0	0	0	0
6	Made in USA	10	0	0	0	0
7	Attractive appearance	1	0	−	−	+
8	Durable finish	4	−	−	−	+
9	Stable market share	1	0	0	+	+
10	Stable profit margin	7	0	−	0	−
	Totals	**Plus**	1	1	3	5
		Minus	1	5	3	2
		Neutral	8	4	4	3

[*]Solutions:
A – Rigid metal
B – Metal with flexible section
C – Elastic polymer
D – Rigid polymer with flexible interior

elastic polymer shown as alternative C was one of its strengths. Team members brainstormed ways to use elastic polymer for alternative D; but when they were unable to find any, they recognized that cost might be the deciding factor and could prevent implementation of alternative D.

They performed a similar Pugh analysis of production alternatives. In this case, although the second alternative, using a partner's manufacturing facility, had the lowest cost and start-up time, making it an attractive solution, the team was concerned about the loss of quality control that GWC would have had if the manufacturing were done on a partner's premises. They identified two ways to mitigate that risk: (1) having GWC quality staff located at the partner's site, overseeing the process; and (2) acquiring the partner company, making it a part of GWC and thus subjecting it to the same quality standards. Although the team was not empowered to make those decisions, they presented them to Veronica Major, who addressed them with the Executive Committee.

Step 3: Identify Potential Failure Modes of the Most Feasible Design

Before they could consider this phase of the project complete, team members knew they had to complete the first draft of QFD1. This meant identifying the "hows" (product requirements or features), determining the relationship between those "hows" and the customers' requirements (the "whats"), identifying any negative or positive interactions among the "hows" (the "how/how correlation matrix"), and establishing targets for each of the "hows."

The key was identifying product requirements, as all the other sections of the QFD hinged on them. Because of the work it had done in identifying potential designs, the team already had some ideas of possible product features. These included:

■ Rigid exterior material
■ Flexible interior material
■ Inexpensive materials
■ Regulation-compliant materials
■ Extrusion molding
■ High-capacity manufacturing line

Recognizing that they could modify this list later, the team's next step was to create a Failure Modes and Effects Analysis (FMEA).

Although the FMEA is a key tool in classic Six Sigma, it is not normally employed until the third phase, Analysis. Because DFSS has as its goal preventing defects, the FMEA is used earlier in the process. As Chowdhury says, "You need to do it right the first time. That means *planning* for perfection from the very beginning, instead of looking for good enough and then fixing things after the fact."[3]

One method of planning for perfection is to identify everything that could go wrong with a process, and then ensure that the design prevents those failures.

The team members brainstormed, answering the question, "What could we do to make the process worse?" as they identified ways in which the Just Right Widget manufacturing process could fail. They then continued brainstorming to determine ways to prevent the failures with the greatest risk priority number (RPN). They documented the prevention methods and action plans on the FMEA. In a classic Six Sigma project, when the team develops a corrective action plan, they are normally constrained by thoughts of costs and practicality. In this case, because they were at the beginning of a project and wanted to consider all possibilities, they indulged in "blue sky" thinking. No suggestion was eliminated because it might be too costly or too difficult to implement. The results of the brainstorming are shown on Exhibit 12.3.

Step 4: Expand the QFD with the Results of the Analyses

The team was now ready to enter product requirements and features into the QFD. As shown in Exhibit 12.4, the two action items that were identified as part of the FMEA — just in time (JIT) supply of raw materials and automated measuring and calibration — were added to the list of product requirements. Note: to avoid confusion with customer requirements, product requirements will be referred to as "features" for this discussion.

Once the team had entered the product features into the matrix, the next step was to assess the degree to which each of these features would impact customer satisfaction. This was done using the normal 1-4-7-10 scale to rank each feature against each requirement. The column totals form the Impact section of the QFD and reflect the weighted impact each feature would have on overall customer satisfaction.

It should be noted that there are two options when calculating the degree of satisfaction. The individual feature ranking can be multiplied by either the original importance rating that the customers assigned or by the normalized priority calculated as part of the initial QFD entry (see Exhibit 11.13). The advantage of using the normalized priority is that it factors in current customer satisfaction, highlighting the changes that will create the greatest improvement in customer satisfaction.

Exhibit 12.3 Preliminary FMEA

| Process Name: | Just Right Widget manufacturing | | | Date prepared: 06/26/06 | | | | Revision Number: 0 | | | | | | | |
| Prepared By: | George Greenbelt | | | Revised by: | | | | Revision Date: | | | | | | | |

Failure modes and effects analysis (FMEA)

What Could Happen?				Why And How Often?		How Do We Prevent It?			Action Plan				Results of Actions			
Process Step	Potential Failure Mode	Potential Failure Effects	SEV	Potential Causes	OCC	Current Controls	DET	RPN	Actions Recommended	Resp.	Target Date	Actions Taken	SEV	OCC	DET	RPN
Manufacturing	Raw materials are not available	GWC unable to manufacture widgets	10	ERP system did not order materials	1		7	70								0
			10	Delays in transporting materials from supplier to GWC	7	Supplier or transporter phones GWC if delays occur	7	490	Establish JIT deliveries with supplier co-located at GWC site	TBD						0
	Orders are not received	GWC unable to manufacture widgets; customer dissatisfied	7	Order entry system not available	4	Alert sent to computer center	4	112								0
	Interior diameter of widget does not meet specification	Customer unable to use	10	Forming machine improperly calibrated	4	Manual measurement at beginning of each shift	7	280	Build in automated measurement and calibration	Eng						0
	Exterior of widget is not smooth	Customer unable to use	10	Polishing machine improperly calibrated	1	Manual adjustment at beginning of each shift	7	70								0
								0								0
								0								0
								0								0
								0								0
								0								0
								0								0
								0								0

Exhibit 12.4   QFD with Product Requirements

Product Requirement/Feature Correlation

Product Requirement	Flexible interior material	Inexpensive materials	High capacity manufacturing line	JIT supply of raw materials	Extrusion molding	Translucent material	Reg-compliant raw materials	Automatic measuring and calibration
Rigid exterior material	−	0	0	0	++	+	+	+
Flexible interior material		0	0	0	++	0	+	+
Inexpensive materials			0	0	−	−	−	0
High capacity manufacturing line				0	+	0	0	+
JIT supply of raw materials					0	0	0	0
Extrusion molding						+	+	0
Translucent material							++	+
Reg-compliant raw materials								0
Automatic measuring and calibration								

Product Requirements/Features

Customer Requirements — Requirement	Importance to customer	Rigid exterior material	Flexible interior material	Inexpensive materials	High capacity manufacturing line	JIT supply of raw materials	Extrusion molding	Translucent material	Reg-compliant raw materials	Automatic measuring and calibration
1 Medium size	10	7	10	1	0	0	4	0	0	7
2 Affordable cost	7	4	1	10	0	0	7	1	0	4
3 Long life	7	7	4	1	0	0	10	4	0	0
4 Adequate supply	7	0	0	0	10	10	4	0	0	7
5 Timely shipment	7	0	0	0	10	10	7	0	0	10
6 Made in USA	10	0	0	0	7	0	0	0	0	0
7 Attractive appearance	7	10	0	1	0	0	7	10	0	4
8 Durable finish	10	7	0	1	0	0	4	1	0	0
9 Stable market share	10	4	10	1	7	7	0	4	7	4
10 Stable profit margin	7	0	0	10	4	7	0	0	0	0

Exhibit 12.4   QFD with Product Requirements (continued)

Impacts On Customer Satisfaction

	Exterior Diameter	Interior Diameter	Final unit Cost	Number of Units Per Day	Number of Units Per Day	Number of Burrs in Exterior	Customer Sat	Compliance With Govt Regs	Exterior Diameter
Impact on customer sat	6.29	7.96	1.79	1.26	1.35	3.8	1.18	0.84	5.86
Ranked impact	2	1	5	7	6	4	8	9	3

Targets

How measured	Exterior Diameter	Interior Diameter	Final unit Cost	Number of Units Per Day	Number of Units Per Day	Number of Burrs in Exterior	Customer Sat	Compliance With Govt Regs	Exterior Diameter
Direction of goodness	LSL	USL	LSL	USL	LSL	LSL	USL	USL	USL
Upper spec limit (USL)	1.1 inch	3/4 inch	$0.10	2000	2000	10 DPMO	5	100%	1.1 inch
Lower spec limit (LSL)	1.0 inch	1/4 inch	$0.08	1450	1450	4 DPMO	4.5	95%	1.0 inch

Exhibit 12.4 QFD with Product Requirements (continued)

					Competitive Assessment/Development Priorities				
Impact of all features on customer req	Current performance/cust sat	Competitive product 1	Competitive product 2	Competitive product 3	Performance/satisfaction goal	Improvement required	Impact multiplier	Development priority	Normalized priority
19.43	0	4	4	10	10	10	5.0	500	0.67
1.62	4	10	4	7	10	6	1.0	42	0.06
0	7	7	7	0	7	0	1.0	0	0.00
0.93	4	7	10	4	7	3	1.0	21	0.03
0	7	1	7	10	7	0	1.0	0	0.00
0	10	0	10	10	10	0	1.0	0	0.00
1.92	1	4	0	4	7	6	1.0	42	0.06
0.52	4	7	1	4	7	4	1.0	30	0.04
5.28	1				10	9	1.0	90	0.12
0.63	7				10	3	1.0	21	0.03
	360	313	346	415	706	**Totals**		746	1.00

After entering the feature rankings, the team analyzed the results. Although they were not surprised that the flexible interior material had the greatest impact on overall customer satisfaction, they were surprised at how important automatic measuring and calibration was.

The team's next step was to determine the correlations among the product features. As they completed the "roof" of the House of Quality, they used a five-point scale as follows:

- ■ – – Implementing this feature will have a strong negative effect on the other.
- ■ – Implementing this feature will have a mild negative effect on the other.
- ■ 0 Neither feature will have an impact on the other.
- ■ + Implementing this feature will have a mild positive effect on the other.
- ■ ++ Implementing this feature will have a strong positive effect on the other.

As they expected, the greatest negative correlation was between the use of inexpensive materials and the other features.

The final section of the QFD that the team needed to complete was the one showing targets. The objective of this section is to translate customer requirements into actionable product requirements; that is, requirements that are quantified and that meet the SMART criteria.

Because they had attempted to quantify customer requirements during their focus group meetings, the team had already obtained most of that specificity from the customer view. They knew, for example, that the customers considered "medium size" to be a widget with an interior diameter between $\frac{1}{4}$ and $\frac{3}{4}$ inch. The team agreed that the requirements they had recorded in Exhibit 11.6 were Specific, Measurable, and Relevant. Timebound could be inferred. Whether or not they were achievable would be determined in future steps as they analyzed the process.

By establishing the quality requirements of each feature, the team was setting the stage for developing a product and process that would meet customer requirements consistently. They believed they were ready for the third phase of DFSS: the development of the concept. But first they met with Mary McMaster, the Master Black Belt who was advising them.

When Mary reviewed the QFD, she noted that many of the items the team had designated as product features were actually product design or process characteristics and belonged in different levels of the QFD (see Exhibit 11.12). This is a common problem, Richard Biehl explains, when teams brainstorm features rather than engineer them.[1] It is also the reason that companies like GWC involve Master Black Belts in their major projects and insist on reviews at the completion of each project phase.

Under Mary's guidance, the team rethought its list of features. The relevant sections from the resulting QFDs are shown on Exhibit 12.5. Armed with the improved QFD, the team was ready to begin developing its concept.

References

1. Stamatis, D.H., *Six Sigma and Beyond: Design For Six Sigma*. Boca Raton, FL: St. Lucie Press, 2003, p. 113.
2. Biehl, Richard, Data-Oriented Quality Solutions, personal communication, 2006.
3. Chowdhury, Subir, *The Ice Cream Maker*. New York: Doubleday Currency, 2005, p. 79.
4. Biehl, Richard, Data-Oriented Quality Solutions, personal communication, 2006.

Exhibit 12.5 Four Levels of QFD Requirements

QFD1

Customer Requirements		Functional Requirements					
Requirement	Importance to Customer	Interior That Accepts Parts with 1/4 to 3/4 Inch Diameter	Exterior Color That Blends with a Variety of Colors and Materials	Smooth Exterior	All materials Reg-compliant	Unit Price < 0.08	Impact of All Features on Req
1 Medium size	10	7	10	1	0	0	180
2 Affordable cost	7	4	1	10	0	0	105
3 Long life	7	7	4	1	0	0	84
4 Adequate supply	7	0	0	0	10	10	140
5 Timely shipment	7	0	0	0	10	10	140
6 Made in USA	10	0	0	0	7	0	70
7 Attractive appearance	7	10	0	1	0	0	77
8 Durable finish	10	7	0	1	0	0	80
9 Stable market share	10	4	10	1	7	7	290
10 Stable profit margin	7	0	0	10	4	7	147
Total impact of each feature		327	235	184	308	259	

QFD2

Functional Requirements		Product Design Characteristics					
Requirement	Importance to Customer	Rigid Exterior Material	Flexible Interior Material	Inexpensive Materials	Transparent Materials		Impact of All Features on Req
1 Interior that accepts parts with 1/4 to 3/4 inch diameter	10	7	10	1	0		180
2 Exterior color that blends with a variety of colors and materials	7	1	0	7	10		126
3 Smooth exterior	4	7	0	4	0		44
4 All materials reg-compliant	10	7	7	7	7		280
5 Unit price < 0.08	7	4	1	10	7		154
Total impact of each feature		203	177	215	189		

Exhibit 12.5 Four Levels of QFD Requirements (continued)

QFD3

Product Design Characteristics		Process Caharacteristics					
Requirement	Importance to Customer	High Capacity Manufacturing Line	JIT Supply of Raw Materials	Extrusion Molding	Automated Measuring and Calibration		Impact of All Features on Req
1 Rigid exterior material	10	7	4	10	10		310
2 Flexible interior material	7	7	4	10	10		217
3 Inexpensive materials	10	1	4	4	0		90
4 Transparent materials	7	7	4	4	0		105
Total Impact of Each Feature		178	136	238	170		

QFD4

Process Characteristics		Production Requirements					
Requirement	Importance to Customer	24/7 Supplier Access to Plant	New Power Supply				Impact of All Features on Req
1 High capacity manufacturing line	7	10	10				140
2 JIT supply of raw materials	4	10	0				40
3 Extrusion molding	10	1	10				110
4 Automated measuring and calibration	7	1	10				77
Total Impact of Each Feature		127	240				

Chapter 13

The Development of Concept Phase

With its initial design completed, the team proceeded to the next phase: the development of the concept. The objective of this phase is simple: to determine whether the proposed design is capable of satisfying the customers' CTQs. To meet that objective, the team needed to formalize its concept, and then apply modeling techniques to quantify the capabilities of the proposed design. The process that the team followed included five steps:

1. Define the proposed product and process.
2. Identify possible causes of variation in the process.
3. Model the design.
4. Identify potential risks and mitigation plans.
5. Develop quality measures for the process.

Step 1: Define the Proposed Product and Process

Although the team members had been talking enthusiastically about the revolutionary Just Right Widget and its potential impact on the company's future, they had not drafted a formal definition of the product. They knew they needed to do that to ensure there was no confusion over what they were proposing. The formal definition would become part of the project communication plan along with other key documents, including the project charter.

At their next meeting, after they updated their thought process map with the answers to the questions they had obtained, the team created the following explanation of their proposed product:

> The Just Right Widget, which is designed to fill the gap between GWC's existing large and small widgets, will be constructed of a rigid translucent exterior material with an exterior diameter of 1.0 inch. Its interior will consist of a flexible material that can contract or expand as needed to create a widget with an interior diameter between $\frac{1}{4}$ and $\frac{3}{4}$ inch. The translucency of the materials will result in a widget that assumes the color of the customer's product, making it suitable for applications where the widget will be exposed. Its flexible interior dimensions will expand the potential uses and make the Just Right Widget applicable to a wide range of customers. It is believed that the combination of the smooth, translucent exterior and the flexible interior will delight customers and will be the "excitement" factor that will increase GWC's market share.

After joking that they deserved jobs in the Marketing Department, the team members proceeded to the next step in defining the product and created a high-level process map for the manufacturing of Just Right Widgets. This, too, would be used in communicating the project's objectives to all levels of GWC staff. Because they knew that it was likely to undergo changes, they titled this an "interim process map," as shown on Exhibit 13.1. For ease of understanding, they referred to the exterior of the widget as the casing and the interior as the core.

Exhibit 13.1   Interim PMAP

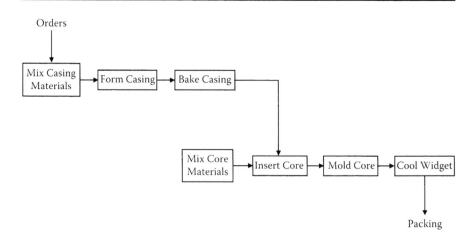

Although they had shown inputs on the first PMAP they had drafted (see Exhibit 11.9), they deliberately omitted them from this map. Because the audience for this PMAP would include people who had little familiarity with GWC's existing manufacturing process, the team decided to employ the KISS principle (keep it simple, stupid). They did, however, create a second PMAP that listed the inputs to each step (Exhibit 13.2). This second PMAP was expanded to include the two inspection steps that had been omitted from the first one for the sake of simplicity. It also highlighted the two batch steps in the process, the two mixing operations, because the team knew that there could be delays in the overall process if the batches were not ready on time.

In addition to helping the team to explain the process, the addition of inputs was important for the next task, identifying the variables that could impact the desired output; that is, the satisfaction of the customers' CTQs.

In their quest to make fact-based decisions and to eliminate variation, Six Sigma companies know that they must first understand what can cause variation. Once all potential variables are identified, the next step is to quantify the variation that each causes. By knowing which variables have the greatest effect, the team can focus on them and develop methods to reduce that variation. Like the identification of CTQs, the quantification of variation helps the team avoid spending time on items of minimal importance.

Step 2: Identify Possible Causes of Variation in the Process

Although inputs are a common cause of variation, team members knew they were not the only sources. As Exhibit 6.1 shows, there are six easily recognized types of variation, often referred to as the Six Ms. The team brainstormed ways in which each of these types of variation might apply to their process. Exhibit 13.3 shows the results of their discussion of the most complex process step, the insertion of the core into the baked casing. As noted in the exhibit, the team believed that the only M that did not apply was method. Because this step of the process was automated, there would be only one method.

The next source of variation that the team considered was noise variables. As discussed in Chapter 7, when teams are optimizing existing processes, noise variables are typically considered special causes of variation and no attempt is made to control them. The situation is different for DFSS projects. Because the team is designing a new process with a goal of building in reliability and ensuring minimal variation, all variables — including noise — are considered candidates for control.

Exhibit 13.2 Interim PMAP with Inputs

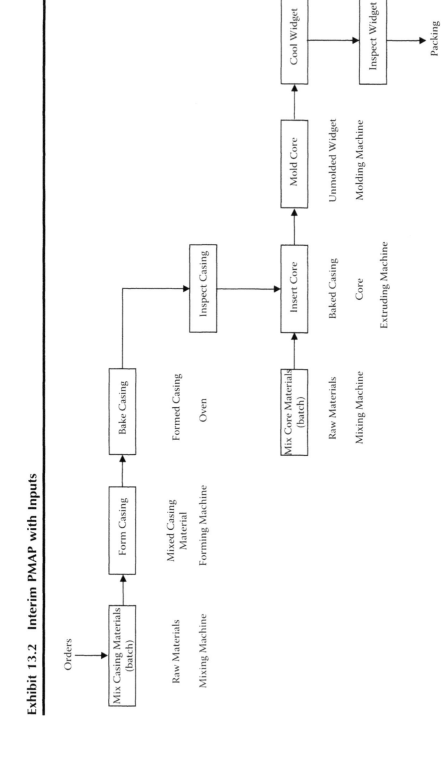

Exhibit 13.3   The Six Ms in the Insertion Process

Six M Element	Insertion Process Variable
Man	Extrusion machine operator
Machine	Extrusion machine, conveyor belt (transporting baked casing to the extrusion machine), core mixing machine
Material	Baked casing, mixed core material
Method	
Measurement	Automated calibration system
Mother Nature	Temperature and humidity on factory floor

Chapter 7 explains that noise variables are often divided into three categories: (1) positional, (2) sequential, and (3) temporal. In exploring the possible noise variables for the Just Right Widget manufacturing, the team believed that the most significant ones would be temporal. Because the plant operated 24/7, they were concerned about the differences in environmental conditions throughout the day. They had identified these as Mother Nature variables in Exhibit 13.3. The team knew that the extrusion and calibration processes, which were critical to satisfying the customers' CTQ of correct size, were sensitive to changes in heat and humidity. What the team did not know at this point was how sensitive the machines were and how much impact environmental variation would have on the output. To determine that, the team proceeded to the next step.

Step 3: Model the Design

The team was at a critical point in the project. Although they believed that the Just Right Widget would be a breakthrough product for GWC, they did not have enough information to change "we believe" to "we know." Although other companies might have proceeded with the project at this point, as a Six Sigma company, GWC would not. They did not yet have enough information to know whether the Just Right Widget would actually meet customers' requirements and whether it would be cost-effective for GWC to produce it.

To answer those questions, they used a computer simulation program to model the process. In Six Sigma terms, this is referred to as design of experiments (DOE). The objective of DOE is to vary multiple parameters (variables) at the same time, determining the optimum combination.

A simple example that is frequently used to explain DOE is evaluating the conditions that produce maximum fuel economy in a car. Variables include fuel octane, tire pressure, speed of the automobile, outside temperature, and presence or absence of head winds. In this case, the outside temperature and head winds are noise variables and cannot be controlled, because it is unlikely a driver will choose not to take a trip simply because it is a hot, windy day. Octane, tire pressure, and speed are, however, controllable variables. To determine the optimum combination of those three variables, the team takes sample measurements at a number of combinations and enters them into the simulation program. The program then uses these parameters as starting points and varies them to create all possible combinations. The output shows the fuel mileage at each combination of variables, making it possible to select the optimum combination.

Simulated sampling is commonly referred to as Monte Carlo simulation, because — similar to the games of chance in the Monte Carlo casinos — it is based on the concept of random numbers. The simulation programs use random number generators to determine the value of each unknown variable, repeating the exercise multiple times to provide multiple scenarios. Simulation programs are available as part of some statistical software packages and as purchased add-ins to Excel. Stamatis points out that Excel's built-in tool, Solver, can also be used for simulation.[1]

In addition to providing information about optimum values for a specific combination of variables, some simulation programs can produce control charts similar to the ones shown in Chapters 6 and 7. The team used such a software product and generated a number of reports, including a process capability (see Exhibit 6.22) and an I and MR control chart (see Exhibit 7.2), as they attempted to answer the following questions:

- Which inputs (Xs) have the greatest effect on the output (Y)?
- What is the capability of the process? Is it centered within the USL and LSL? What are its C_p and C_{pk}?
- How reliable is the process? Are there variations over time?
- Where are the potential wait states and what effect will they have on the output?

After completing the analysis, the team had learned that the process could produce the required number of widgets at the desired quality level and that the primary environmental variable to control was humidity.

Because excessive humidity, which was common on the GWC manufacturing floor during the summer months, would have an adverse effect on the extruding process, the team proposed separating the Just Right Widget line from the rest of the plant and installing dehumidifiers. They included the additional costs of the new wall and the dehumidifiers and reran their simulation to determine whether or not they could meet the cost and profit targets. Because the model showed a payback period of 59 months, which was within GWC's maximum of 60 months for capital projects, the team believed that its project would be approved.

They presented their findings to Veronica Major, who concurred that the project was a valuable one. However, because the expenditures were beyond her approval level, the team needed to obtain the concurrence of the Executive Committee. They prepared a brief presentation, summarizing their work and their recommendations, and delivered it to the Executive Committee. Although they met the expected resistance to the length of the payback period, the team had run simulations, showing the effects of not including the environmental controls.

Because they suspected that they would be asked to reduce costs in other ways, they had prepared additional simulations, showing the effects of creating a thinner casing. While that would reduce costs and create a shorter payback period, the team could demonstrate that the reliability of the Just Right Widget would be compromised by that change. The expected life span of the widget decreased from ten years to five with a thinner casing.

Ultimately, the Executive Committee approved funding for the next phase of the DFSS project, and also challenged the team with finding a way to reduce costs and thus shorten the payback period.

Step 4: Identify Potential Risks and Mitigation Plans

Although the team members had passed the first hurdle, they were not finished developing their concept. They still needed to mistake-proof the Just Right Widget manufacturing process. To do that, they knew they needed to identify potential risks and develop mitigation plans for those risks. That is, they would develop another FMEA. As they had for the FMEA that they created in the previous phase (see Exhibit 12.3), they brainstormed ways in which the process could fail, then found ways to either prevent the failure or identify it early enough in the process that it would not create a major problem. Because they had already identified variables (Exhibit 13.3), they used those as the starting point for their brainstorming of failure modes.

The portion of the FMEA that deals with the insertion process is shown as Exhibit 13.4.

Exhibit 13.4 FMEA for the Insertion Process

Failure Modes and Effects Analysis (FMEA)

| Process Name: | Just Right Widget Manufacturing | | Date Prepared: 07/06/06 | Revision Number: 0 |
| Prepared By: | George Greenbelt | | Revised By: | Revision Date: |

What Could Happen?				Why and How Often?		How Do We Prevent It?			Action Plan				Results of Actions		
Process Step	Potential Failure Mode	Potential Failure Effects	S E V	Potential Causes	O C C	Current Controls	F A R I P O L N B	R P N	Actions Recommended	Resp.	Target Date	Actions Taken	S E V	O C C	F A R I P O L N B
Insertion	Extrusion operator halts process	Assembly line stops; widgets cannot be completed	10	Inability to read control dials; incorrectly believed an error condition exists	1	Operator training	7	280	Increase size of readout on controls	Eng					0
	Conveyor belt halts	Assembly line stops; widgets cannot be completed	10	Mechanical failure	1	None	10	100							0
	Core mixing machine halts	Assembly line stops; widgets cannot be completed	10	Humidity exceeds limits	4	Alerts when humidity begins to increase	1	40							0
	Casing diameter is wrong size	Finished widget does not meet customer's specs	7	Automated calibration system failed	4	Readout showing current condition	4	112							0
	Mixed core material is wrong consistency	Core does not mold properly; finished widget does not meet customer's specs	7	Excessive humidity	1	Alerts when humidity begins to increase	1	7							0

Step 5: Develop Quality Measures for the Process

The final step in the concept development phase is the creation of quality measurements for the new process. This involves using several of the tools and techniques that are part of the Control phase of classic Six Sigma. As the Order Entry team had, the Just Right Widget team identified key metrics and assessed the reliability of those metrics using the Metric Reliability Assessment spreadsheet (Appendix E). Because they knew they would use those metrics when they developed a project scorecard similar to the one the Order Entry team had created (see Exhibit 9.4), they limited their key metrics to four:

- Total widgets shipped that month
- Number of widgets returned
- Total minutes of process outage
- Percent market share

The returned widget metric reflected customer-detected defects, while the process outage statistic indicated lost opportunities, because every minute of outage translated into 1.4 fewer widgets produced. Although the market share metric was not obtained directly from the Just Right Widget manufacturing process, because it was the primary impetus for the project, team members believed it should be included on their scorecard.

Exhibit 13.5 provides a sample of the scorecard they designed. When displayed on the Web site or in formal presentations, the scorecard is color-coded. All unfavorable actuals are shown in red, while favorable ones are shown in green. For the scorecard shown in Exhibit 13.5, the following columns are red:

- Widgets Shipped — January and February
- Widgets Returned — All
- Minutes of Process Outage — All
- Percentage Market Share — January through April

George Greenbelt, who had been reading a book on lean manufacturing and knew the importance of visual controls, suggested that the team also create a dashboard. The dashboard, he explained, was not a substitute for a scorecard but, rather, a complementary set of measurements. Although both communicate essential information, the dashboard — which takes its name from the dials on an automobile's dashboard — can be considered a tactical tool, while the scorecard is strategic. Using a family's vacation as an example, the scorecard would reflect how well they met their goals of visiting ten national parks and spending no more

Exhibit 13.5   Just Right Widget Scorecard

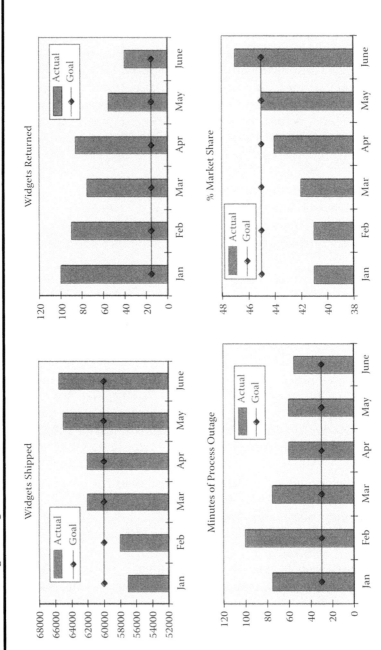

Exhibit 13.6   A Comparison of Dashboards and Scorecards

Question	Dashboard	Scorecard
Who is the target audience?	Employees closest to the process	Management and customers of the process
What is displayed?	Current key data about the process	Historical measurements showing how well targets were met
Where is it displayed?	As close to the affected employees as possible	In formal presentations, hard copy or web-based
Where is it generated?	Continuously during the process	Periodically
Why is it produced?	To enable employees to monitor the process, making changes when required to prevent problems	To provide stakeholders with a report of whether the function has produced the desired results

than half their budget on gasoline, while the dashboard indicates current speed, fuel consumption, and (although not literally displayed on the car's dashboard) the day's expenditures. Exhibit 13.6 uses the Five Ws to provide a comparison of scorecards and dashboards.

After brainstorming elements for their dashboard, the team selected eight, which were designed for three different audiences:

1. All employees on the manufacturing floor:
   - Number of widgets produced during that shift
   - Total defects by shift
2. Employees involved in the casing production process:
   - Number of batches of casing material produced during that shift
   - Maximum humidity in the casing mixing area during that shift
   - Number of casing defects detected during that shift
3. Employees involved in the core mixing and insertion processes:
   - Number of batches of core material produced during that shift
   - Maximum humidity in the core mixing area during that shift
   - Number of finished widget defects detected during that shift

In each case, the dashboard would indicate the goal, the actual, and the difference.

Although it was possible to have continuous updating of the dashboard, the team did not want to distract the workers with data overload. Instead, they decided that the dashboards — which would be displayed on large electronic screens visible from all parts of the plant floor — would be updated once a minute. Exhibit 13.7 shows the design of the dashboard.

With their measurements complete, the team was ready to proceed to the next phase: optimization of the design.

References

1. Stamatis, D.H., *Six Sigma and Beyond: Design For Six Sigma*. Boca Raton FL: St. Lucie Press, 2003, p. 182.

Exhibit 13.7   Just Right Widget Dashboard

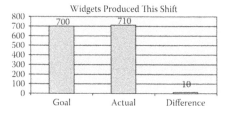
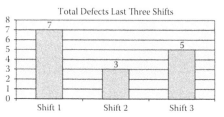

Exhibit 13.7   Just Right Widget Dashboard (continued)

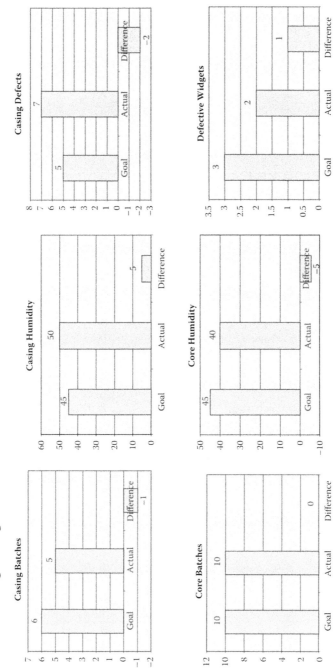

Chapter 14

The Optimization Phase

Although team members were excited by the potential of the Just Right Widget, they were also mindful of the CFO's concerns about costs. The models they ran as they developed their concept proved that the design could meet the customers' CTQs.

The Challenge

The problem was that if they wanted to fully satisfy their internal customer, the CFO, and the company's shareholders, costs had to be lower. Unless they could find a way to reduce costs, they faced the possibility that the project would never get past the planning and analysis stages and that the Just Right Widget would not become a real product.

Mary McMaster tried to encourage the team, reminding them that the objective of the fourth phase of DFSS is to optimize the design and that balancing cost with features is a part of optimization.

When discussing optimization, Mary stated that it is important to make a clear distinction between it and maximization. A quick look at a dictionary reveals that maximization is concerned with reaching the *greatest* possible value, whereas optimization is the pursuit of the *most favorable* condition. The most favorable condition, that is, the optimum, may or may not be the one with the maximum value.

Optimization begins with what is commonly referred to as robust design. Developed by Dr. Genichi Taguchi, robust design has as its objective creating products or processes that exhibit the same behavior regardless of the operator, environment, or passage of time. In discussing this definition, the team noted that the variables listed all fit into the category of noise. This is not coincidental. As the team had learned when developing their concept, a DFSS design does not ignore noise. It seeks to understand it and to, whenever possible, control it. The objective is to produce products that are insensitive to noise. Robustness is one of the desired characteristics of the optimum product.

There are two major steps in designing for robustness: (1) parameter design and (2) tolerance design. The first seeks to maximize the design, to create what is sometimes called the *ideal function*. The second is the true optimization step, tightening — or loosening — tolerances to obtain the maximum quality possible at the minimum cost. This is the balancing act Mary McMaster described.

Parameter Design

As is true of all aspects of Six Sigma projects, the first goal of parameter design is to obtain facts so that decisions can be based on them. In the case of parameter design, those facts include:

- The identification of all the variables (parameters) involved in a process *and*
- Obtaining an understanding of the variables' effect on each other

This is a continuation of the exploration of the transfer functions in the process. A transfer function, Daniel explained, is the official term for the $Y = f(x_1, x_2, x_3, \ldots)$ equation discussed in Chapter 6.

The objective of this first step is to understand all the x values in the equation and to quantify their relative importance. This is similar to the process the team had followed when analyzing CTQs and features using the QFD. In both cases, the goal is to identify and focus on the factors that will have the greatest effect on the output.

The team began with a pictorial representation of the variables. Although there are numerous ways to display variables, the technique the team used is called a parameter diagram or, in some cases, a P-Diagram. Exhibit 14.1 shows the format of a generic parameter diagram. Although the terms "signal" and "response" were not ones the team had used in this project, they recognized them as input and output, particularly when they saw their position on the diagram. The team was also familiar with noise variables. Control variables, however, were a new concept. Daniel explained that controls were parameters that could be varied deliberately to affect the output or response.

Exhibit 14.1 Parameter Diagram

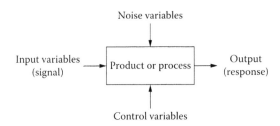

Exhibit 14.2 Parameter Diagram for the Insertion Process

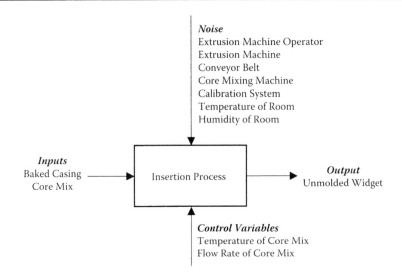

As the first step, team members applied the results of the brainstorming they had done in the previous phase to create a parameter diagram for each step in the Just Right Widget manufacturing process. Using the information shown in Exhibits 13.2 and 13.3, they were able to list the inputs, outputs, and noise variables. With this complete, they turned their attention to possible control factors. What could they design into the process that would affect the output? Would there be settings on the machines that could be adjusted as needed? Would the mixture of materials vary based on environmental conditions? Could they place additional controls on the environment?

Exhibit 14.2 reflects the P-Diagram for the insertion process, showing the addition of two control factors: (1) the temperature and (2) the flow rate of the core mix. At this point, the team did not know how great an effect modifying those control factors would have on the output. That would be determined by the tests they planned to conduct.

Using statistical modeling software, the team ran a series of tests, varying the parameters they had identified. Although the statistical software provided a wealth of data, the primary metric that they analyzed initially was the signal-to-noise ratio (S/N). At this point, their objective was to maximize the S/N ratio as part of the effort to develop the ideal function. For them, the ideal function was a perfect Just Right Widget.

The team was particularly interested in the effect the two control variables had on the quality of the widget. Their experiments demonstrated that, although the flow rate of the core mix had no effect on the output, varying the temperature of the core mix did. A higher temperature resulted in less variation in the finished widget, although it required additional costs to heat the core mix and to cool the molded widget.

Using their new set of variables, the team reran the simulations they had conducted during the previous phase to confirm that the results still met the customers' CTQs. As expected, the sigma level rose, and the external customers' CTQs were satisfied. This was clearly a better widget than they had had before. However, there was still the question of cost.

Having maximized the process through parameter design and created the ideal widget, team members were now ready for the next step — tolerance design — which they began to call The Great Balancing Act.

Tolerance Design

As stated above, the objective of tolerance design is to adjust parameters to provide the maximum quality possible at the minimum cost. Having defined the ideal widget, the team would experiment to learn whether some variables could be set at less than their maximum value without reducing quality below the customers' expectations. Mindful of the Kano model (see Exhibit 11.8), team members wanted to ensure that they did not reduce the excitement or performance needs, but also that they did not expend unnecessary resources attempting to perfect basic requirements. As Chowdhury says, "Tolerance design is all about balancing cost against performance and quality."[1] Although the CFO and GWC's shareholders wanted the team to minimize costs, because that would increase profit margins, the team members knew they could not do that if it meant sacrificing the quality that the ultimate customer expected. They needed to balance both groups' requirements.

Because there was a potential for a reduction in quality as they reduced costs, the team members needed a method of quantifying the cost of that quality reduction. While in the past companies determined the cost of poor quality by calculating the cost of returns, Taguchi postulated that there are other costs to consider. Those costs include possible lost future

Exhibit 14.3 The Quality Loss Function

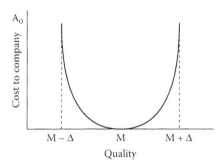

sales. While a customer might not return a product, dissatisfaction with that product could result in the customer's refusing to buy anything more from the company. This is what Taguchi refers to as the quality loss function (QLF).

The fundamental concept of QLF is that customers expect products to be manufactured at a specific quality level, the target. Furthermore, the level of satisfaction customers have with products is not binary; they are not simply satisfied or dissatisfied. Instead, customer satisfaction decreases with the amount quality varies from their expectation. Exhibit 14.3 provides a pictorial representation of QLF. M is the target specification and A_0 is the cost to the company of each defective product.

Taguchi postulates that QLF makes it possible to calculate the total cost of loss of quality, including the cost of customer dissatisfaction. The formula for calculating QLF is:

$$L = K(X - M)^2$$

where L is the loss, X is the value of the product, M is the target level of quality, and K is the cost of a defective product (A_0) divided by the deviation (Δ) from the target squared or, in quadratic equation format, $K = (A_0 / \Delta^2)$.

Once team members had identified the values needed to calculate the QLF, they were ready to begin adjusting tolerances on the key variables they had identified during parameter design. The adjustments were done by running a series of simulations, using standard design of experiments (DOE) statistical software, to determine which variables could be adjusted without reducing quality to the extent that it would create a QLF.

As they modified the values of the key variables, the simulation software allowed the team to identify the costs (or cost savings) associated with each tolerance adjustment. This was the balancing act, as the team sought ways to reduce costs without creating a negative impact on quality. They wanted their widgets to remain centered on the quality target (M on Exhibit 14.3).

By conducting the DOE, the team learned that the core mixture temperature, which the team had identified as a control variable, was critical. Any reduction created a reduction in quality. However, the team members discovered that keeping the temperature of the core mix at the maximum they had identified meant they could substitute a raw material with a lower cost in the core material mixing step. This was the breakthrough they had hoped to achieve. The lower cost of the raw material more than compensated for the higher energy costs they had incurred by increasing the temperature. The result was a reduction in the total cost of the widget without a reduction in quality. Parameter design followed by tolerance design had produced the desired result: a high-quality product that could be manufactured at a reasonable cost.

Team members were delighted that they would be able to meet the CFO and shareholders' expectations without compromising customer satisfaction. This was their goal, and it meant they had a high probability of project approval. However, before they declared this phase of DFSS complete, they ran one more simulation to satisfy themselves that the revised parameters would have the effect they expected. They also reviewed the FMEA they had created in the Development of Concept phase to determine whether they had introduced any new risks. When both steps confirmed that the Just Right Widget design appeared to be robust, they were ready for the final phase of DFSS: verification.

Reference

1. Chowdhury, Subir, *Design For Six Sigma*. Chicago: Dearborn Trade, 2005, p. 143.

Chapter 15

The Verification Phase

The team finally reached the step "where the rubber meets the road." Team members were ready to create actual widgets. Until this point, they had been working with pieces of paper and computer screens. They had been planning, designing, modeling, and analyzing. They knew what the Just Right Widget would look like; they knew how much it would weigh; and they knew how long it would take to produce one — in theory. It was now time to translate theory into reality and to prove that their simulations were correct and that they could produce Just Right Widgets that met the customers' needs.

Ten years earlier, GWC might have begun full production at this stage in the project. But now, as a company committed to Six Sigma and — more importantly — to DFSS, they knew they were not yet ready. Although everything looked promising, the team needed to demonstrate that its design would produce the desired results. In DFSS terms, the team needed to verify.

Chapter 10 pointed out that there are a number of definitions of the phases of a DFSS project, each with a different acronym. It is perhaps not accidental that although the other phases have little naming consistency, each definition includes a phase called "verify." The consensus is clear: verification is an important part of DFSS.

Verification, which is a specialized form of testing, consists of two major steps: (1) prototyping and (2) piloting. Although there are similarities between them, they have different objectives. Prototyping tests the product itself, while piloting focuses on the process used to create that product. Both prototyping and piloting can be viewed as continuations of the modeling and analysis that the team had already conducted, and — as was true of those earlier steps — each one includes a major go/no-go decision. After all, the goal of DFSS is to produce a product that meets the customers' needs and that can be manufactured without defects. If any step in the process demonstrates that the product will not satisfy those requirements, the project should either be terminated or reworked until it does meet the CTQs. If a less-than-perfect product is placed in full production, eventually the company will find itself in a reactive mode, trying to correct errors at the most costly stage of the process. They will have lost the advantage of the DFSS lever (see Exhibit 10.1).

The Prototype

A prototype, according to *Webster's Dictionary*, is "a first full-scale and usually functional form of a new type or design of a construction."[1] The key words in this definition are "full-scale" and "functional." Anything else is a model; and although models have important places in product development, they are not adequate for a prototype. The prototype should be as close to the final product as possible.

The reason companies produce prototypes is to assess the viability of their design and to prove that the product will meet customer requirements, typically by using the prototype in real-world situations. The object is to observe the product's performance first under normal and then under distinctly abnormal conditions. In the case of a DFSS company, this verification follows a formal process and typically employs statistical tools as well as manual inspection to analyze the results.

Like most manufacturers, GWC had a test facility that they used to generate and then test prototypes of new products. As part of the Just Right project, the prototype engineers along with the project team created a small batch of the new widgets. Rather than conduct random tests, the team developed a formal test plan, outlining what tests would be performed, how often, for how long, and with what expected results. This process resulted in a document with contents similar to those shown on Exhibit 21.2. The team knew that it was important to have a fully documented test plan to ensure that all conditions were tested and that anomalies in the results were identified quickly. For the team, this was another example of the Five Ps (Prior Planning Prevents Poor Performance).

The objectives of the prototype testing were twofold:

1. To verify that the product performed as expected
2. To determine under what conditions the product would break

For the initial testing, the team evaluated the output of the prototype production, ensuring that all widgets met the targets specified on the QFD (see Exhibit 12.4) for exterior and interior diameter and burrs in the exterior. At this point, because the widgets were being produced in a test facility, they could not measure unit cost or the daily production rate. Those tests would be made during the piloting step.

To verify that the product would perform as expected, the team members had obtained prototypes of Great Auto's navigation system components and Little Telecom's new mobile phone. They installed the Just Right Widgets on those products to ensure that the fit and functionality were as specified.

Once they were convinced that the widgets met the basic requirements, the team began to test reliability. The objective of this step was to determine the product's life span and mean time between failure (MTBF). At the same time, the team sought to understand the causes of product failure and to correct them, if feasible.

Although there are a number of methods that companies use to stress test their products, GWC's standard is accelerated stress testing (AST). The goal of AST is to subject a product to increasingly higher levels of stress until it fails. While the stresses involved typically exceed those that would occur in normal use, they help to identify extreme conditions and to understand the effects that time and normal wear will have on a product.

Once the stress tests were completed, the team plotted the results, specifically the time to failure, using a Weibull probability chart. Weibull charts, which are plotted on special graph paper, are used to estimate the percentage of a product that will have failed at a specific time in the product's life span. In addition, the slope of the curve on the graph is used to classify failures into one of three categories based on the failure rate:

- Decreasing failure rate signifies infant mortality; that is, products that fail excessively during their early use.
- A constant rate of failure is normally considered as the result of random events.
- Increasing failure rate is associated with product wear-out; that is, the product fails over time.

It is also possible to determine the Weibull probability distribution using Excel's Weibull function. In that case, rather than considering the slope of the line, failures are categorized based on the result of the function:

- <1 = infant mortality
- ~1 = constant rate
- >1 = product wear-out

The team recognized the value of prototyping when the first tests revealed high infant mortality because of cracks in the rigid casing. Because this was unacceptable, the team conducted another series of tests to determine the cause of the cracking. When it proved to be an instability in the polymer they had used for the casing, they adjusted the formula. Although everyone was anxious to run another prototype, before they committed to that time and expense, the team members reran the model simulations they had conducted in the Development of Concept phase to ensure that the formula change would not have a negative impact on quality. Only when they were confident that quality would not be compromised did they rerun both the parameter and tolerance design simulations from Optimization.

All models confirmed that the change would have no ripple effect and that costs would not be increased. At that point, the team was ready for the second prototype. Stress testing that prototype produced the results the team had expected, namely failure rates centered after the end of the projected life span of ten years.

Having proven that the prototype widget would meet the customer's requirements, the team received approval and funding to proceed to the next step of verification: the pilot.

The Pilot

As noted above, while the prototype focuses on the *product*, the pilot seeks to verify that the *process* is robust. The objective is to test the final production process, identify any defects, and correct them prior to beginning full-scale production. The pilot was the last hurdle to be crossed before the Just Right Widgets were released to customers.

While engineers and the project team developed the prototype in a test facility, the pilot would take place on the production floor and be run by the same employees who would be responsible for full production. The only differences between the pilot run and production would be the scale and the timeframe. Instead of producing the target 2000 widgets per day, running all three shifts, the pilot would encompass a single shift and would seek to produce only 200 widgets during the first running. Only after the team had verified that there were no problems producing at this scale, would the pilot increase its production until it had met the shift target of 700 widgets.

Because it was necessary to construct the new assembly line prior to running the pilot, there was a time delay between the completion of the prototype and the commencement of the pilot. The team was not idle during this period. In addition to developing a test plan for the pilot, they developed and conducted training for the operators. One of the things they would be testing during the pilot was the efficacy of that training, because — for the production process to work efficiently — it was necessary that both the machinery and the employees who would operate it were fully prepared. (Training techniques are discussed in more detail in Chapter 22.)

Many of the tasks that the team performed during the pilot were similar to those in the Improvement and Control phases of classic Six Sigma's DMAIC model. They developed a full implementation plan and created the final set of metrics that they proposed to use for the monthly scorecard and the continuous-read dashboard. After reviewing the initial scorecard (see Exhibit 13.5) with Veronica Major, the team decided to change the "widgets returned" metric to a percentage rather than a count of returned items. They also changed one dashboard measurement (see Exhibit 13.7) from "core humidity" to "core temperature," because that variable had a substantially greater impact on the output.

At the same time, the team decided to color-code the dashboard. The team recognized that colors would aid in instant recognition of problem areas and would reduce the amount of time anyone had to spend looking at the display. All goals would be shown as black columns, but the actuals would use stoplight color-coding. Any actuals that met or exceeded the goal would be displayed in green. Those that were within 3 percent below the goal would be yellow, and any actuals that failed to meet the goal by more than 3 percent would be color-coded red.

Before completing their review and revisions of the metrics, the team members once again evaluated their metrics using the metric reliability assessment worksheet. Although little had changed, they were taking nothing for granted.

Prior to actually running the pilot, the team developed an initial control plan using the format shown in Exhibit 9.2. This control plan, they knew, would be an essential part of sustaining the quality that they had designed into the process. It also formed part of the team's training materials.

When the pilot began, all members of the team served as observers and recorders, noting the ease — or lack thereof — with which the assembly line team operated. They kept copious records of every problem encountered and subjected each of the finished widgets to stringent inspection. The pilot, Daniel pointed out, could be considered a classic Six Sigma DMAIC project by itself, starting with the measurement phase.

The team measured each of the outputs as well as the time required for each step and entered the information into their statistical software package so that they could generate process capability charts similar to Exhibit 6.22. As they had hoped, their C_p and C_{pk} measurements were 2.1 and 1.6, respectively, telling them that they had a six sigma process. They also generated an I and MR control chart similar to Exhibit 7.2 to identify types of variation and were pleased when the moving range indicated they were within specifications.

Although the pilot met the expectations of output quality that the project required, the team noted that two operators wasted steps as they moved from their workstations to look at the dashboard displays. In response, the team repositioned the dashboard to eliminate that form of waste and reran the first limited pilot. When they were satisfied that there were no additional problems to resolve, they increased the speed of the production line to its normal capacity and proceeded with the pilot, once again observing all aspects of the process.

Full-speed production identified a delay in getting casing materials mixed and into the forming machine. Although the instinctive reaction was to increase the speed of the mixing process, the team realized that would introduce new defects by stressing the mixer. Instead, the team experimented with smaller batches and discovered that smaller, more frequent batches resolved the problem. Rerunning the pilot at full speed confirmed that the delay had been eliminated.

Team members ran pilot production for a week and noted no additional problems. They were now ready for full production and their favorite part of every project: celebration. Although the project would continue for another six months as the team monitored the quality and calculated the financial return, the majority of the work was complete.

One year later, GWC's market share had risen from 40 to 43 percent, and per-share earnings had increased by $0.01, thanks to the Just Right Widget project and DFSS. Designing in quality at the beginning and listening to both the voice of the customer and the voice of the process had achieved the desired result: a robust process producing a product that satisfied customers and met internal cost targets.

Exhibit 15.1 provides a summary of the steps the team followed during the project.

Reference

1. *Merriam Webster's Collegiate Dictionary*, tenth edition. Springfield, 1993, p. 939.

Exhibit 15.1 Summary of IDDOV Phases and Steps

Phase	Steps
Identification of Opportunities	1. Define the problem
	2. Form a team
	3. Establish a project charter
	4. Develop a project plan
	5. Identify the customers, suppliers and stakeholders
	6. Identify customer requirements
	7. Identify CTQs
	8. Begin to develop the QFD matrix
Definition of the Initial Design	1. Identify potential designs
	2. Evaluate those designs using Pugh Concept Selection techniques
	3. Identify potential failure modes of the selected design
	4. Expand the QFD
Development of Concept	1. Define the proposed product and process
	2. Identify possible causes of variation in the process
	3. Model the design
	4. Identify potential risks and mitigation plans
	5. Develop quality measures for the process
Optimization	1. Conduct parameter design analysis
	2. Conduct tolerance design analysis
Verification	1. Prototype the product
	2. Pilot the process
	3. Develop the control plan

IV

SIX SIGMA AND THE TRADITIONAL SDLC

Sometimes referred to as the "waterfall" methodology, the traditional system development life cycle (SDLC) was the IT industry's first attempt to bring structure to previously ad hoc methods of developing systems. Although it has shortcomings, including excessive rigidity and lack of customer involvement, the waterfall approach can help organizations deliver successful systems. The probability of success is increased for those organizations that incorporate Six Sigma tools and techniques into the SDLC. Although there are no Six Sigma tools designed specifically for system development, some have direct applicability. In other cases, basic Six Sigma concepts can be used and the tools adapted for the SDLC.

Chapter 16 provides an overview of the traditional SDLC, outlines the advantages and disadvantages of the waterfall approach, and maps the six phases of the traditional life cycle to Six Sigma's DMAIC model. It also shows how DFSS tools and techniques can be used to improve the quality of the SDLC.

Chapters 17 through 22 explore each of the traditional life-cycle phases, showing how Six Sigma and DFSS tools can be employed within them. Each of the chapters includes forms that are part of a typical methodology but that have been given Six Sigma attributes, where appropriate. In addition, where the DMAIC model has steps that are not included in the traditional SDLC, the chapters point out the value of adding new tasks.

Project Initiation (Chapter 17), which corresponds most closely to the Definition phase of DMAIC, is the stage in which a project is identified and a feasibility study developed. Assuming approval, the project proceeds to System Analysis (Chapter 18), where the requirements definition is completed. Although apparently simple, this is one of the most difficult phases of system development.

Analysis is followed by System Design (Chapter 19), in which three design documents are created: (1) functional, (2) technical, and (3) program. Construction (Chapter 20) has as its goal the development of executable code. Once complete, the project proceeds to Testing (Chapter 21). As was true of design, there are multiple types of testing to perform, including unit, system, integration, and acceptance.

Only when testing is complete and all bugs resolved is the project ready for Implementation. Although this is the final step in a traditional SDLC, a Six Sigma project would include metrics design and reporting, and the development and implementation of a control strategy. All of these are outlined in Chapter 22.

Chapter 16

Introduction to the Traditional SDLC

As is expected of any profession that is still relatively young, IT has evolved — and is still continuing to evolve — from highly individual seat-of-the-pants techniques for developing and maintaining systems to formal, well-documented methodologies. In the early days, when what is now called information technology (IT) was referred to as data processing, there were no methodologies or formal guidelines for developing systems. Systems were developed under what IT now knows was the mistaken belief that their life span would never exceed five years, and thus long-term maintainability was not considered a major concern.

Data processing was an art rather than a science, with no two systems being developed in the same way. As a result, it was difficult to predict the length of a project, its cost, and the degree to which it would solve the problem that had initiated it.

If the process was an art, the practitioners were definitely artists. Two separate departments frequently performed systems analysis and programming with only minimal communication between them. The systems analysts gathered customer requirements and gave them to the programming staff, who then worked their black magic to translate those requirements into computer systems. Because there were few common processes and because programmers were frequently unwilling to share the secrets of their success, individual programmers were viewed as creative beings who were essential to the continued running of the systems they had developed. In SEI CMM terms, the industry was at Level 1. (Exhibit 2.1 outlines the five levels of the CMM maturity path.)

As business applications expanded beyond the Finance department, it became obvious that there must a better way to manage data processing and, in particular, a better way to develop systems. The result was the creation of formal methodologies centered around what was commonly referred to as a system development life cycle (SDLC). The objective of these methodologies was to document and institutionalize the best practices of system development. Although Six Sigma had not become part of the business vocabulary, the goal of an SDLC was one of the Six Sigma tenets: the desire to reduce variation.

In its simplest form, an SDLC divides the software development process into a number of clearly defined phases, each of which is further divided into steps. Progress through the steps is measured by the completion of forms and checklists. Because the phases were viewed as sequential steps, with the output from one phase becoming the input to the next, a traditional SDLC was often called "a waterfall." And, like water flowing over a precipice, the underlying premise of the waterfall approach to system development was that all motion was forward. Once a phase was completed, there was no returning to it. Exhibit 16.1 shows the phases in a typical traditional SDLC.

Although a number of industry experts and major consulting firms developed their own versions of the methodology, each with forms for every step of the process, there were many common elements. The forms

Exhibit 16.1   Traditional SDLC (The Waterfall)

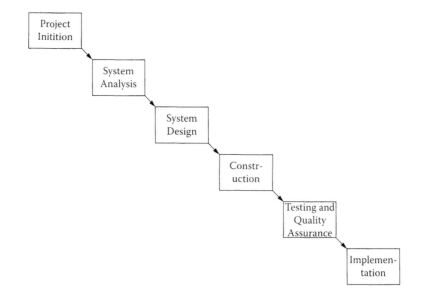

varied; the philosophy did not. Use of an SDLC, the proponents claimed, would ensure that system development followed a common, sequential process with all critical information being properly documented.

Although there were shortcomings, with the development of a life cycle, the data processing industry had made a major step in transforming itself from seat-of-the-pants programming to software engineering. SDLC can be viewed as the foundation of the modern IT department. In SEI terms, it was an attempt to reach Level 2 and have repeatable processes.

Advantages of the Traditional SDLC

Although sometimes criticized for its rigidity, a traditional SDLC provided and continues to provide benefits for many organizations. In addition to the reason it was initiated — namely, adding structure to a previously unstructured process — the waterfall approach to system development has two primary advantages:

1. The explicit guidelines allow the use of less-experienced staff for system development, as all steps are clearly outlined. Even junior staff members who have never managed a project can follow the "recipes" in the SDLC "cookbook" to produce adequate systems. Reliance on individual expertise is reduced. Use of an SDLC can have the added benefit of providing training for junior staff, again because the sequence of steps and the tasks to be performed in each step are clearly defined.

2. The methodology promotes consistency among projects, which can reduce the cost of ongoing support and allow staff to be transferred from one project to another. Although coding techniques are not specified in a typical SDLC, the extensive documentation that is an inherent part of most methodologies simplifies ongoing maintenance by reducing reliance on the original developers for explanations of why the system was constructed as it was and which functions are included in which program modules.

SDLC Disadvantages

While there is no doubt that the waterfall approach to system development is superior to a totally unstructured environment, there are some known disadvantages:

1. If followed slavishly, it can result in the generation of unnecessary documents. Many methodologies have forms for every possible

scenario. Inexperienced staff may believe that all are required and may, for example, insist on three levels of customer sign-off when only one is needed. This can have the effect of complicating the process and extending the project schedule unnecessarily. To prevent this from occurring, most organizations view an SDLC as a set of guidelines and use only the steps and forms that apply to the specific size and type of project under development. Many even provide templates for their staff, outlining which steps are required for specific types and sizes of projects. An 18-month mainframe development project might require different processes than a two-week Web front end.

2. It is difficult for the customer to identify all requirements early in the project; however, the sequential "river of no return" approach dictates this. The philosophy of the SDLC means that there are no easy ways to mitigate this problem and still remain true to the methodology.

3. The customer is involved only periodically, rather than being an active participant throughout the project. This can result in misunderstandings on both sides: IT and the customer.

4. As a corollary to the previous two points, the waterfall approach is usually applied to large projects with long development cycles. The combination of incomplete specifications, infrequent communication, and long elapsed time increases the probability that the system will be "off track" when it is finally delivered. As highway engineers know, an error of only a few degrees, if left uncorrected for thousands of miles, will result in the road going to the wrong destination.

5. Similarly, the long development cycle increases the possibility that by the time the system is delivered, business changes may have invalidated the initial design or that the project champions may have left the company or been reassigned, taking with them the impetus for the project.

How Six Sigma Can Help

Just as Six Sigma helps companies eliminate defects, reduce costs, and improve customer satisfaction in their manufacturing processes, it can increase the effectiveness of the traditional system development process. While not all Six Sigma tools are applicable to all projects, the judicious use of some tools and strict adherence to the concepts of customer focus and fact-based decisions can increase the probability of successful implementation of waterfall projects by:

- Keeping the customer involved throughout the process
- Identifying a manageable scope for the project
- Ensuring continued commitment to the project, even if key players leave the organization

Just as the definition phase of the DMAIC model seeks to identify customers and to understand the current process before making any changes, the first step in applying Six Sigma to traditional system development is to understand what constitutes the waterfall approach and who is typically involved in each phase.

Although phases and their names may vary between different SDLC methodologies, this book describes a six-phase life cycle:

1. Project Initiation
2. System Analysis
3. System Design
4. Construction
5. Testing and Quality Assurance
6. Implementation

Each of these phases is described in detail in subsequent chapters.

The concepts discussed in this section can be applied to all traditional life cycles, regardless of the names given to the phases or the individual steps included in each phase.

Before a process can be improved, a Six Sigma company knows that it is important to understand which departments and functions are normally involved in that process so that workflow and dependencies are clearly delineated. As the GWC Order Entry team learned, a functional process map provides a pictorial outline of major steps and responsibilities. Exhibit 16.2 presents a functional process map for the traditional life cycle, showing the departments that are normally involved in each phase of the life cycle. Although some individuals may perform multiple roles (e.g., systems analyst and programmer analyst) because the functions differ, they are shown as separate rows on the process map.

A review of the process map confirms the third disadvantage of the waterfall approach, the fact that customers are involved only periodically. This presents the first challenge of adapting Six Sigma concepts to the traditional SDLC — that of maintaining a focus on customers.

Exhibit 16.3 shows how the Six Sigma DMAIC phases map to the traditional SDLC. It should be noted that although the waterfall SDLC is considered a sequential process, its first two phases are a combination of Define, Measure, and Analyze, with functions being repeated at different levels of detail in later phases.

Exhibit 16.2   Traditional SDLC Functional Process Map

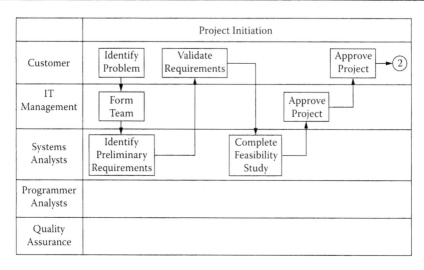

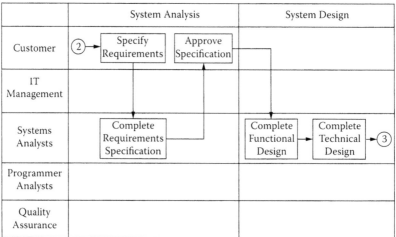

Exhibit 16.3   Traditional SDLC Functional Process Map (continued)

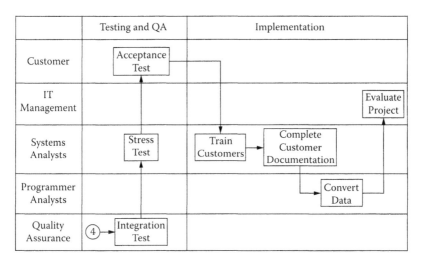

Exhibit 16.4   Mapping Traditional SDLC Phases to Six Sigma's DMAIC

SDLC Phase	Six Sigma (DMAIC)
Project Initiation	Define, Measure, Analyze
System Analysis	Define, Measure, Analyze
System Design	Analyze
Construction	Improve
Testing and Quality Assurance	Improve
Implementation	Improve and Control

Exhibit 16.5   Mapping Traditional SDLC Phases to DFSS's IDDOV

SDLC Phase	DFSS (IDDOV)
Project Initiation	Identification, Definition
System Analysis	Definition, Development
System Design	Development
Construction	Development
Testing and Quality Assurance	Verification
Implementation	Verification

The Role of DFSS

As discussed in Chapter 10, although classic Six Sigma can be employed at any stage of the life cycle, the greatest benefits of DFSS are achieved if the techniques are applied to new products or processes. The traditional SDLC is an excellent candidate for DFSS improvement. Judicious use of several DFSS tools, notably the value chain map and QFD, can help mitigate the disadvantages of the waterfall SDLC by more clearly identifying customers and their requirements and ensuring that key requirements, the customers' CTQs, are satisfied by the resulting system.

It can also be argued that the traditional SDLC phases have a more exact correspondence to the DFSS phases than they do to DMAIC. Exhibit 16.4 provides a map of the waterfall phases to IDDOV. That increased correlation is logical because both methodologies are designed to be employed from the earliest stages of a product or system's creation, rather than being applied after the product or system has been implemented. It is, however, significant that no phase of the traditional SDLC corresponds to DFSS's Optimization. This is one of the shortcomings of the waterfall approach to system development.

The remainder of Section IV outlines each of the six system development life-cycle phases, showing the tasks normally completed in each and how the use of Six Sigma and DFSS can contribute to a more successful project.

Chapter 17

Project Initiation

The first phase of the waterfall SDLC is Project Initiation. Some methodologies refer to this phase as Project Planning. This is a misnomer because it encompasses far more than planning. The overall objectives of the Project Initiation phase are to clearly define the problem, scope the project, propose a solution, determine the costs and benefits of that solution, creating what is often called a "business case," and obtain approval. For many companies, these steps equate to the development of a feasibility study. An outline of a sample feasibility study is included as Exhibit 17.1. The individual elements of the feasibility study are discussed in detail later in this chapter.

A typical Project Initiation phase consists of six steps:

1. Identify the problem.
2. Form the team.
3. Identify preliminary requirements.
4. Validate the requirements.
5. Develop a feasibility study.
6. Obtain project approval.

While some of these steps appear to be the same as those included in the Six Sigma Definition phase, comparing them to Exhibit 9.5 reveals that some Definition steps are missing and that Project Initiation includes steps from Analysis and, although not explicitly, from Measurement. As shown below, incorporating all the steps from the DMAIC Definition phase helps increase the likelihood of a successful system development process,

Exhibit 17.1 Feasibility Study Outline

1. Project Overview

    (a) Problem Statement

    (b) Scope of Project

    (c) Objectives

    (d) Critical Success Factors

    (e) Assumptions

    (f) Recommended Approach

    (g) Alternative Approaches and Reasons for not Selecting Them

    (h) Risks and Recommended Mitigating Actions

    (i) Resource Requirements

2. High Level Project Plan

3. Cost/Benefit Analysis

as does the inclusion of several steps from the DFSS Identification and Definition phases.

Step 1: Identify the Problem

As is true of a Six Sigma process improvement initiative or a DFSS project, information technology (IT) projects begin with a problem or an opportunity. Either something is not working properly or the company realizes that it can benefit from the implementation of a new process or the development of a new product.

Although requests are sometimes received informally, most companies have a standard form for requesting IT services. Exhibit 17.2 illustrates a request for services (RFS) that can be used to initiate a new project or to request a change or enhancement to an existing system. This form may include enough information for IT to begin work on small maintenance projects, particularly nondiscretionary ones, such as those that are required by a regulatory body. However, for major development projects that would be implemented using an SDLC, it serves only as preliminary notification that a customer would like a new system. The information on the RFS form is used to place the work in the queue and, for companies with customer steering committees that prioritize projects, to obtain approval to proceed

Exhibit 17.2   Request for IT Services

Request for IT Services			
		Request Number	
		Date Received	
To be Completed by Customer			
Customer Name		Date	
Department		Phone Number	
System Name (if known)			
What would you like done?			
Why? (check all that apply)	■ System doesn't work properly ■ Required by regulatory authority ■ New feature will provide 　■ Cost savings 　■ Cost avoidance 　■ Increased revenue 　■ Other (specify) ■ Other (specify)		
When do you need the work completed?			
Customer Signature			
Approval Signature			
To be Completed by Information Technology			
Project Name		Project Number	
Manager		Phone Number	
Project Leader		Phone Number	
Target Start Date		Actual Start	
Target Completion Date		Actual Completion	

to the next step: full project initiation. Note that the term "customer," when used in this context, typically means an internal customer.

Although some companies might consider an RFS sufficient authorization to initiate a system development project, a Six Sigma company would insist on several interim steps. In Six Sigma software development, before agreeing to a project, the IT manager would:

- *Ensure that there is a project champion in the customer department.* Traditional system development projects have project managers — typically from IT — but do not require a champion. As discussed in Chapter 5, the champion's commitment is essential to a project's overall success. Furthermore, it is important that all projects have sponsorship from the customers — not IT. If projects are to be truly customer focused, their impetus must come from the customer department. Vision and commitment must be set by the customer.
- *Ensure that the champion will make key members of her department available to serve on the project team.* Although the traditional SDLC calls for periodic review and approval of documents by customers, one of its weaknesses is the lack of continuous involvement from the customer departments. Having customers serve as active members of the project team increases the probability of success by fostering true teamwork and reducing communication gaps. In addition, having customers on the team demonstrates the champion's commitment to the project.
- *Review the project goals with the champion, applying the SMART criteria to them.* In addition to providing clarity for the team, this step helps to set expectations, not simply for the project's deliverables, but also for the level of communication and teamwork that will be required throughout the project's life cycle.

Only when these steps are complete would the IT manager commit to staffing a team.

Step 2: Form the Team

Traditional system development projects were viewed as IT projects with teams comprised of IT staff. Six Sigma projects, on the other hand, are chartered by the department that wants to improve its processes, and the team includes members from various functions, depending on the nature of the project.

A Six Sigma system development project should be considered like any other Six Sigma project. That is:

- The champion is a member of the requesting (customer) department.
- The champion forms the team, with the IT manager providing necessary resources.
- Other departments are invited to join the team, as required. Exhibit 5.1 lists support functions that may be part of a team.
- The team leader is at least a Green Belt.
- Roles of team members and the amount of time each is expected to devote to the project are clearly defined.

The actual size and composition of the team will vary, depending on the size and complexity of the project. From an IT view, although there may be dozens of staff members working on the project at various stages, it is important that the person who will serve as the IT project leader and a representative from Quality Assurance be members of the core team, participating in all phases of the project and being part of key decisions. Exhibit 5.2 provides a list of key characteristics for team members.

Step 3: Identify Preliminary Requirements

The next step in the traditional SDLC is to obtain customer requirements. In Six Sigma system development, a number of different tasks would be undertaken at this point, including:

- Begin to develop a thought process map.
- Develop the initial project charter.
- Define the problem statement and project goals.
- Identify the customers.
- Identify key outputs.
- Document the current process.
- Define high-level requirements.

Although the first six of these may not be performed as part of a traditional SDLC, they are important in improving the likelihood of success. They help form the team, increase the focus on customers, and drive toward fact-based decision making.

The steps and the reasons for their inclusion in an SDLC are detailed below.

Begin to Develop a Thought Process Map

As the GWC Order Entry team learned, a good thought process map (TMAP) serves as a repository for project knowledge. If, as is frequently done, the TMAP includes links to all documents produced during the project, it can provide a single source of information about the project.

The TMAP can also be viewed as an audit trail of decisions because it documents both the team's choices and the reasons why they were made. It is significant that although traditional SDLCs emphasize documentation and tend to produce pounds of paper, what is documented is typically the result of a decision, not the reason for it. This is a critical difference.

On short projects, the absence of a written rationale may cause no problems, because the team remains intact from inception to completion. A long project can be quite different. Not only can team members or the project's sponsor change, but it is also possible that business conditions may alter enough during the development process that the project may be reevaluated.

Although a TMAP is valuable on any project, it is particularly useful on a long system development project because it provides tribal memory. In the past, it was accepted that some project knowledge would be lost as a result of staff rotation or loss. Although a TMAP does not guarantee that nothing will be forgotten, it does minimize the probability. The TMAP is also helpful in reconstructing the project's key decision points, should it be necessary to brief a new champion or to justify the project a second time, and it provides value to future system development project teams that may want to review it for lessons learned.

Develop the Initial Project Charter

Whether it is called a project charter, a project initiation form, or something else, traditional SDLCs typically have a form to document the beginning of the project. Unlike the Request for Services (RFS) (Exhibit 17.2), which contains only minimal information, a project charter should provide details about costs, benefits, milestones and deliverables, team members, critical success factors, and risks. Its objective is to clearly define the project scope, helping to ensure common expectations.

Regardless of the presence of a project charter form in its methodology, if the entire company has adopted Six Sigma, it is preferable for IT to use the company's standard Six Sigma project charter. (A sample is included in Appendix A, along with instructions on how to complete it.) Using the same form for IT projects as for all other projects has three benefits:

1. It helps reinforce the fact that IT is part of the company and that its projects are initiated for the benefit of customer departments.
2. It reduces communication gaps, because customers and all team members should be familiar with the standard form.
3. It reduces variation throughout the company.

If the company has not adopted Six Sigma, IT may still want to use a Six Sigma project charter similar to the one shown in Appendix A if it includes more information than the standard methodology charter's.

In either case, the project charter should be dynamic, not the static document that is typical of a waterfall methodology. Similar to the TMAP, it should be updated when changes occur so that it always reflects the current state of the project.

Define the Problem Statement and Project Goals

While this may appear to be a duplication of the first step (i.e., Identify the Problem), it is not. Problem definition provides clarity and specificity that were not present in the earlier step. As part of the "Project Description" section of the charter, the team should clearly identify the problem that it is trying to resolve as well as overall goals. Problems should be quantified, and goals should be developed using the SMART criteria as described in Chapter 5. These goals will normally be an extension or refinement of the goals set by the champion when the project was initiated.

Without applying the SMART criteria, a project description might have been:

> "Replace four separate General Ledger packages with a consolidated reporting system."

This statement explains *what* is to be done but not *why*. Because there is no link to customer requirements, it is theoretically possible to complete the project and declare success, while decreasing customer satisfaction.

Using Six Sigma principles, the problem goal statement would be:

> "The company currently has four separate General Ledger systems with a combined annual support cost of $150K. Manual consolidation of financial results costs $40K per year, and results are not available until the third working day of the month. The project's goals are to reduce annual support costs by $100K, to eliminate manual consolidation and the related costs of $40K per year, and to have consolidated financial results available on the second working day of the month. These goals will be achieved by replacing the current General Ledger systems with a single consolidated reporting system."

The specificity and measurability of this project description help avoid the problem of developing and delivering a solution that does not meet customer requirements.

Having clear, measurable goals helps the team maintain its focus. The goals also serve as key criteria when evaluating requirements, giving a framework for determining whether a system enhancement should be implemented and helping to control scope creep. Once goals are identified and quantified, the team can ask, "How does this feature contribute to achieving the project goals?" and can make fact-based decisions.

Identify the Customers

Traditional IT projects do not identify customers but, instead, assume that the department that requested the system is the customer. While it is true that that department is *a* customer and maybe the primary customer, it is frequently not the only one. If the customer is the pivot around which a project is focused — and Six Sigma companies know this to be true — then it is essential to identify all customers and to ensure that their requirements are considered when developing the system. As discussed in Chapter 5, there are customer groups beyond external or ultimate. This is equally true of IT projects. In addition to the department that requested the project, customers may include the data center staff, who will be required to run the new system; internal audit, who will validate the results; and the help desk staff, who will assist system users.

A brainstorming session is normally helpful in identifying customers. The Value Chain Map, a tool used in the Identification phase of DFSS, provides an effective method of documenting customers. As shown in Exhibit 11.3, the Value Chain Map includes influencers as well as suppliers to each of the customer groups. The identification of key activities associated with each customer helps clarify the role that the new system will play and can be useful in identifying interdependencies.

Identify Key Outputs

While it is important to have identified all categories of customers, at this stage of the project it is not essential to be able to identify all outputs of the process. Because the objective of this first phase is to scope the project and to determine at a high level its size, cost, and length, what is needed is an understanding of the primary outputs. For the GL consolidation project, these outputs might be: consolidated balance sheets and income and expense statements. The preliminary SIPOC shown as Exhibit 11.5 can be used to document the outputs and provide a very high-level understanding of the process. For the GL consolidation project, the SIPOC elements of the current process might be:

- Supplier — plant controllers
- Input — individual general ledgers
- Process — manual consolidation of financial statements
- Output — consolidated financial statement
- Customer — Chief Financial Officer (CFO)

The proposed SIPOC could be similar to the one shown as Exhibit 17.3.

Document the Current Process

Although most traditional SDLCs focus on the "to be" state, describing the system that will be constructed rather than the one that's currently running, Six Sigma companies with their insistence on fact-based decisions know that they must understand the current process prior to making any changes to it. Documentation of the current process is normally done through the use of a process map. Because the team is still working at the macro level at this stage in the project, teams typically create a top-level process map (see Exhibit 5.11) rather than a detailed or functional map. Later phases will identify more details and warrant the use of detailed or functional maps.

Exhibit 17.3 SIPOC for General Ledger Consolidation

Supplier	Input	Process	Output	Customer
Plant and Headquarters Staff	Daily Transactions		Consolidated Reporting (Balance Sheets, P&L, Income and Expense)	CFO
Plant Controllers	Monthly Closing Data	Consolidated General Ledger System	Individual Plant Reporting (Balance Sheets, P&L, Income and Expense)	Plant Controllers
Executive Committee	Cost Reduction Targets		Departmental Reporting (Balance Sheets, P&L, Income and Expense)	Department Managers
CFO	Chart of Accounts			
	Financial Calendar			
			Reduced Costs	Executive Committee

Define High-Level Requirements

It is only after the previous tasks are complete that the team is ready for the traditional SDLC's third step. Although detailed requirements will be specified in the system analysis phase, it is important to establish high-level requirements to determine the scope of the project. While there are a number of ways of determining requirements, as shown on Exhibit 5.8, one-on-one interviews and focus groups are the techniques most commonly used at this stage of the project. In both cases, it is helpful to conduct structured interviews. The elements of structured interviews include:

- Participation by two team members: one to facilitate and the other to record answers to questions.
- Preestablished list of questions, which are normally sent to participants in advance of the meeting. A sample questionnaire that can be used to obtain high-level requirements is included as Exhibit 17.4.

Step 4: Validate the Requirements

Following requirements definition interviews, team members need to ensure that they understood their customers' needs. Issuing minutes of the interviews and asking customers to sign an acceptance form frequently does this. While such an approach is one method of validating the requirements, a Six Sigma project would also include a meeting with the customers who had been interviewed. The meeting would have three objectives:

1. *Ensure that the team has a clear understanding of requirements by "echoing" them to the customers.* It is possible for misunderstandings to occur, even when the project team issues minutes. Face-to-face meetings help reduce that likelihood.
2. *Apply the SMART criteria to all requirements.* Once requirements are defined, the team can help customers add the specificity that is needed to make them meaningful.
3. *Have customers prioritize the requirements and quantify the degree to which they are currently met.* This step is important for ensuring that the project team focuses on the right things. Exhibit 5.15 shows a completed customer requirements matrix.

In addition to clarifying requirements and helping to ensure that the project is properly focused, holding a second meeting helps to keep customers involved in the project. The importance of this cannot be

Exhibit 17.4   Customer Requirements Questionnaire

Organizational Structure and Objectives
1. What is your role or responsibility?
2. How is your department organized?
3. What are your department's primary goals?
4. How do you know when you have met them?
5. What problems have you had in meeting your goals over the past year?
6. What new obstacles do you foresee that might prevent you from meeting your goals?
7. How is the department's performance measured?
8. What other measurements do you make and report?

Critical Success Factors
1. What are the most important decisions you are expected to make?
2. If mistakes were to occur, which would hurt your department and the company the worst?
3. If you could have only three pieces of information with which to judge your department's performance each day, what would they be?
4. What is most critical to your department's success?

Current Process
1. Please describe the current flow of work throughout your department.
2. Where are the delays?
3. Do you measure cost per transaction?
   If so, what is it?

Current System
1. On a scale of 1 to 10, how critical is the current system to your department's success?
2. What would be the impact on your department/the company if the system did not run?
3. On a scale of 1 to 10, how well does the current system meet your department's needs?
4. What is the most useful information you receive now?
5. What is the least useful?
6. What information do you need that is not currently provided by the system?
7. On a scale of 1 to 10, how would you rate the information you receive in each of the following categories:
   (a) Timeliness
   (b) Accuracy
   (c) Completeness
   (d) Ease of use/access
   (e) Cost
8. If you could change three things about your current system, what would they be?

overestimated. Although the team must ensure that all meetings provide value to the participants (as well as all participants providing value to the meeting), it is essential to have frequent communication with customers.

With the information gathered in the validation step, the team is ready to begin developing a QFD. An initial QFD such as the one shown as Exhibit 11.13 helps to identify the customers' CTQs and the gaps between their current satisfaction and the company's targets.

Step 5: Develop a Feasibility Study

Whether it is called a business case or a feasibility study, the document outlined in Exhibit 17.1 is normally the means by which a team gains approval for its project. The elements and the Six Sigma tools that can be used to develop them are discussed below.

- *Problem Statement.* Although it is likely that the team will want to expand on it, the problem statement that was developed for the project charter serves as the basis for the feasibility study's problem statement. It is also helpful to include an "as-is" process map in this section.
- *Scope of Project.* The objective of this section is to identify what is — and what is not — included in the project. Inclusion of a preliminary SIPOC similar to Exhibit 17.3 provides a simple pictorial representation of the project, while a top-level map of the "to-be" process is an effective way of communicating the differences between the current and proposed processes. New system functions and manual intervention should be clearly outlined on the "to-be" map.
- *Objectives.* The goal statements that were developed for the project charter can be used to complete this section.
- *Critical Success Factors.* Critical success factors (CSFs) are those elements that must go right for the organization to meet its objectives and the project to be a success. Many of them are identified during the customer requirements interviews; others may be related to technology and are identified as the project team outlines alternative approaches. A technology-related CSF might be, "The system must be available 24/7 with no more than a two-hour outage for maintenance on Sunday mornings."

  Although all CSFs are important, some are more critical than others, just as some customer requirements are more important than others.

Using a ranking process similar to the customer requirements ranking described in Chapter 5, the result of which is shown as Exhibit 5.15, and then listing CSFs in descending order provides a clear understanding of which have the greatest impact on the business or the project.

■ *Assumptions.* Assumptions are frequently related to CSFs and define states that must exist if the CSF is to be achieved. An example of an assumption related to the system availability CSF is, "No new database releases will be installed during the development cycle." As for CSFs, assumptions should be ranked and a chart similar to the customer requirements ranking created. The ranking for assumptions is not their importance to the customer but rather the likelihood that the assumptions are correct. It is helpful to list assumptions in ascending probability order to place the highest risk items first.

When there are a large number of CSFs and related assumptions, it is useful to develop a CSF/Assumption matrix and include it in the feasibility study. A CSF/Assumption matrix is a variation on the Six Sigma tool, the Failure Modes, and Effects Analysis described in Appendix D.

A sample CSF/Assumption matrix is shown as Exhibit 17.5. Like an FMEA, this matrix determines a risk priority rating by multiplying the CSF's importance rating and the likelihood that the assumption will not be true. And, like the FMEA, the resulting RPN clearly identifies the areas of greatest risk.

■ *Recommended Approach.* This section of the feasibility study is designed to answer the question of how the project team proposes to reach its objectives. In Six Sigma terms, this is the place to explain how the process will be transformed from "as is" to "to be." If the project is to develop in multiple phases, or if there are several alternative actions proposed, such as the development of a client/server versus a Web-enabled system, a process improvement ranking spreadsheet can be used to quantify the effects of each proposed step. Appendix C describes the process improvement ranking spreadsheet.

■ *Alternative Approaches and Reasons for Not Selecting Them.* Virtually all project teams are expected to consider alternative approaches to reaching their objectives. In addition to providing explanatory text, the inclusion of either a decision matrix (see Exhibit 8.4) or an impact assessment (see Exhibit 8.1) helps present the alternatives in clearly understandable form. If the impact assessment is used, the totals row should be eliminated, because what is being displayed are alternative solutions, not phases or pieces of the project. A third approach, and the one a DFSS company would use, is the Pugh Concept Selection matrix (see Exhibit 12.2). The advantage of the Pugh is its simplicity.

■ *Risks and Recommended Mitigating Actions.* All projects have risks; successful ones recognize the risks and develop a strategy to mitigate them. A simplified Failure Modes and Effects Analysis (FMEA) can be used to quantify the risks and propose corrective actions. Exhibit 17.6 shows a section of a risk assessment and mitigation plan for an IT project. As with other rankings, it is helpful to use a scale of 0-1-4-7-10 to rank each risk's severity. The Failure Probability column, which uses the same scale, rates the likelihood that the current mitigation efforts will fail.

■ *Resource Requirements.* This section of the feasibility study lists all resources that will be required to complete the project. As was true of the "Support Required" portion of the project charter, this should include computer processing time, training materials, and new software as well as personnel.

■ *High-Level Project Plan.* Traditionally, IT projects are planned using standard project management software. In addition to showing tasks and milestones, the project plan should include key deliverables. For simplicity, the schedule portion of the project charter can be used in lieu of a Gantt chart. It has the advantage of showing costs by phase or deliverable.

■ *Cost/Benefit Analysis.* The standard cost/benefit analysis is a calculation of return on investment (ROI). While this is important, impact on the bottom line is not the only consideration when evaluating a project's merits. In addition to providing a calculation of ROI, a Six Sigma project will include other benefits, including reduction in cost of poor quality and an increase in sigma level and customer satisfaction.

Step 6: Obtain Project Approval

The process of obtaining project approval for a Six Sigma project is similar to conventional system development projects. The primary difference is that departments or functions that might not have been required to approve a traditional project are included under Six Sigma. While most organizations would require the department that is funding the project to approve it and, if the cost is high enough, the Controller or CFO to review and approve the cost/benefit analysis and ROI calculation, because of its focus

Exhibit 17.5   CSF/Assumption Matrix

Critical Success Factor/Assumption Matrix					

Critical Success Factor	I M P	Assumptions		O C C	R P N
What must happen? The system must be available 24/7 with no more than a two-hour outage for maintenance on Sunday mornings	How important is the CSF to the customer?	What assumptions exist?	How likely is the assumption to be false?		How great is the risk?
	7	No new database releases will be installed during the development cycle		4	28
	7	The contract with Big Telecom will be renewed prior to July 1.		1	7
					0
					0
					0
					0
					0
					0
					0
					0
					0

on customers, a Six Sigma company would ask all affected groups to approve the project. For an IT project, as noted previously, this could include the data center and help desk organizations.

The reasons for including all groups in the approval process are to:

■ Improve cooperation among stakeholders.
■ Reduce the likelihood of future surprises.
■ Establish communication channels.

Use of an approval checklist (see Exhibit 8.2) may prove helpful if there are a number of signatures to be obtained.

Once the project has been approved, the team is ready to proceed to the second phase of the SDLC: System Analysis.

Exhibit 17.6 Risk Assessment and Mitigation Plan

Project Name:	Date Prepared:	Revision Number:
Prepared By:	Revised By:	Revision Date:

Risk Assessment and Mitigation Plan

	What is the Risk and its Severity?		How Well Do We Mitigate It?			Action Plan				Results of Actions		
Risk Category	Risk	S E V	Current Mitigation Plan	F A I L / R I S K	R P N	Actions Recommended	Resp.	Target Date	Actions Taken	S E V	E F F	R P N
Commitment	The champion lacks enthusiasm or influence.	0			0							0
	The project is outside the champion's direct span of control.	4	Steering committee has been formed with all key executives; bi-weekly meetings will be scheduled to review the project and make critical decisions	4	16							0
	The customer community is skeptical or resistant to the project.	7	Weekly rumor control meetings.	7	49	Hire Change-is-Us to run "coping with change" seminars.	Smith	1/115/02				0
	Project funding is inadequate.				0							0
	Benefits of the project are not well quantified.				0							0
Team Composition	The team does not include members from all key departments/functions.				0							0
	Team members are unable to commit to the time required for the project.				0							0
	The team lead is assigned to the project less than full time.				0							0
	The team has never worked together.				0							0
	Team members are located at sites in different time zones.				0							0
Project Definition	Team members have little or no knowledge of the functional area.				0							0
	The project scope is not well defined.				0							0
	The project requirements are not well defined.				0							0
	Project deliverables are not well defined.				0							0
Effect on Customers	The project will require changes to the customer department's organizational structure.				0							0
	The project will result in reductions in staff.				0							0
	The project will require policy changes.				0							0
	The project will require procedural changes.				0							0
	The project will require the development of new training programs.				0							0

Exhibit 17.6 Risk Assessment and Mitigation Plan (continued)

Risk Assessment and Mitigation Plan

Project Name:		Date Prepared:	Revision Number:
Prepared By:		Revised By:	Revision Date:

What is the Risk and its Severity?		How Well Do We Mitigate It?			Action Plan				Results of Actions		
Risk Category	Risk	SEV	Current Mitigation Plan	FRAIISLK	RPN	Actions Recommended	Resp.	Target Date	Actions Taken	SEV	EFV	RPN
Complexity	The scope of the project affects more than one department/functional area.				0							0
	This project is dependent on the completion of one or more other projects for its success.				0							0
	One or more projects depend on the completion of this project for their success.				0							0
	The project is estimated to last more than twelve months.				0							0
	The team size is greater than twelve.				0							0
	The team will use new development tools and/or techniques.				0							0
	The project requires use of a new programming language.				0							0
	The project requires use of a new DBMS.				0							0
	The system requires 24/7 availability.				0							0
	Response time must not exceed one second.				0							0
	The data that will be converted to the new system is of poor quality.				0							0
Commitment	The system will require interfaces to more than four existing systems.				0							0
Resource Availability	The project requires acquisition of new computer hardware.				0							0
	The project requires acquisition of new system software.				0							0

Chapter 18

System Analysis

The second phase of a traditional waterfall SDLC appears deceptively simple. It has one primary objective: completing the requirements definition that was begun in Project Initiation. It is in System Analysis that the high-level requirements identified in the first phase are transformed into a detailed specification.

Although System Analysis may be viewed as nothing more than an expansion of the feasibility study with the objectives of confirming requirements and creating a conceptual design of the system, the work involved is anything but simple. If the project is to be successful, the requirements specification that is produced in this phase must include everything that is needed to solve the business problem that was the reason the project was initiated.

It is no exaggeration to state that the accurate and complete definition of requirements is the single most important task in the entire system development process. The reason that this is true is that those requirements are the input to all future phases. As the GWC Order Entry team learned in Chapter 6, variations in inputs are a major cause of variations in output; that is, defects.

IT professionals have long used the acronym GIGO (garbage in, garbage out). Although the term is typically used in conjunction with data — to indicate that if erroneous data is entered into a system, the output will be equally bad — the concept of GIGO applies equally to the system development process. If the inputs (requirements) are garbage, the outputs (the system) will also be garbage.

Chapter 6 explains this concept in Six Sigma terms by stating, $y = f(x)$. That is, the output (y) of the process is a result of the input (x) and the process itself (f). Because in system development, requirements are the input to the process, the $y = f(x)$ equation translates to:

> The system (y) is a result of the design and construction (f) that were based on the requirements (x).

That is, if inaccurate requirements are input to the development process, the result will be an inaccurate system (GIGO). A corollary to GIGO is NINO (nothing in, nothing out). If requirements are incomplete, the result will be an incomplete system.

While code generators, reusable code, and testing tools have helped streamline later phases of the SDLC, they are only as good as their input, a fact that not every tool vendor emphasizes. An advertisement for a system development tool guarantees error-free software. What IT manager could resist that lure? However, reading the fine print reveals that the guarantee applies only if the requirements are complete. Although the vendor does not state it in those terms, NINO and GIGO apply to the guarantee.

It is essential to have complete and accurate requirements if the resulting system is to meet customer needs and be defect-free. Unfortunately, obtaining those complete and accurate requirements is far from simple. As noted previously, one of the major disadvantages of the waterfall approach to system development is that customers are frequently unable to define their total requirements this early in the project. That failure can have two potential consequences:

1. If requirements are left incomplete or inaccurate throughout the entire life cycle, the result will be a system that does not meet the customers' needs.
2. If requirements continue to evolve throughout the later phases, the result can be the "scope creep" that IT departments dread, which leads to delays in the project schedule and increased costs.

In either case, IT will not accomplish its goal of delivering a system that satisfies its customers.

Although there are no guarantees, using Six Sigma processes and tools can help improve both the completeness and the accuracy of the requirements and thus increase the probability of developing the system that the customer really wanted.

To develop the best possible requirements specification, the following steps are recommended:

1. Understand the current process.
2. Identify the requirements.
3. Prioritize the requirements.
4. Identify potential process improvements.
5. Determine which improvements will have the greatest impact on the highest priority requirements.
6. Create a detailed "to-be" process map.
7. Assess the impact and risks of the proposed process improvements.
8. Complete the development of the conceptual design.
9. Complete the requirements specification document.
10. Obtain approvals.

While many of these steps were performed during Project Initiation, it is important to repeat them in the System Analysis phase because the level of detail is greater. Project Initiation provides generalities. System Analysis demands specifics.

Step 1: Understand the Current Process

Prior to developing requirements, it is essential to understand the current process completely. While that may sound intuitive, many projects begin with only a basic understanding of the current system, whether automated or manual, in the belief that what is important is the new functionality. With its focus on fact-based decisions, a Six Sigma company would argue that it is essential to understand exactly what is happening currently before making any changes. No project team would consciously automate a defective process, yet unless that process is understood, it is possible to do exactly that.

The objectives of this first step are to develop a baseline from which to make improvements and to understand which of the proposed improvements will have the greatest impact. To do that, it is necessary to understand all facets of the current process, including its defects and their causes. Not only does a thorough understanding of the process help avoid the perpetuation of defects, but it also helps ensure that no potential requirements are missed.

While it is possible to document a process in pure text, a simpler way of promoting common understanding is to use a detailed process map or, if a number of different departments are involved, a functional process map. Although a top-level process map may have been developed during project initiation, it, by definition, included only the major steps in the process. At this point, it is important to expand the preliminary process map to include all steps. It is particularly important to include exception and rework processing because these provide opportunities for improvement. Even if the project team does not plan to conduct a complete process reengineering study, there are benefits to be derived from eliminating rework loops. Similarly, the team should identify delays in the process. Whether or not the company has embraced all aspects of lean manufacturing, the new system will benefit from the elimination of as many forms of waste (see Exhibit 6.3) as possible.

A Six Sigma company knows the importance and the value of keeping customers involved in the project. Development of the process map is one task where customer involvement is of particular importance. While the top-level process map may have been developed by the customer department manager or a senior member of the staff, all levels of the customer organization should be included in the development and validation of the detailed process map. Not only is it a Six Sigma principle to involve the people closest to the process, but it is also common sense. Those who actively participate in the process are the ones who understand it best.

It is possible that a "hidden factory" exists and that the manager is not aware that errors are being caught and corrected outside the officially defined channels. If requirements are based solely on the manager's definition of what ought to be happening rather than what actually does, the resulting system may prove inadequate. Because the rework and checking that the hidden factory performs were not identified, the new system will not resolve the underlying problems. The hidden factory will still be needed, and the project is unlikely to achieve its projected benefits. Having the right people involved in the definition of the current process helps prevent this problem from occurring.

Once the map is developed, the project team should schedule a follow-up session with the customers. The purpose of this meeting is to review the map and validate it, confirming that team members understood what they had been told.

The detailed process map becomes a key input not only to the definition of requirements, but also to the revision of policies and procedures and the development of training programs. Like all inputs, it is important that it be accurate.

Once the process is mapped, the team should define and measure its defects using the techniques outlined in Chapter 6. As noted above, "defects" should encompass delays and wait states in the process, as well as the production of erroneous results. The purpose of defect identification and measurement is to further clarify the problem statement and to continue the identification of the areas where changes can have the greatest impact. The goal is, as always, to help the team make fact-based decisions. It is only by quantifying the problem (the defects) in the current process that the team can state with assurance the benefits the proposed solutions will bring.

As shown in Exhibit 16.3, the phases of the traditional waterfall SDLC do not map cleanly to Six Sigma's DMAIC. Although the previous steps in System Analysis are part of the Definition and Measurement phases of DMAIC, it is important to move into Analysis and perform a root cause analysis once the defects have been identified. Not only will this help understand how improvements can be made, but it may also identify areas where procedural rather than system changes can prevent defects. Like moving the fax machine in GWC's Order Entry department, these are often "low hanging fruit" and can be implemented quickly with lower cost than system modifications.

Step 2: Identify the Requirements

Once team members have completed mapping and analysis of the current process, they are ready to develop detailed requirements. Like the development of the detailed process map, representatives from all levels of the customer organization should perform this step. Although Exhibit 5.8 shows a number of methods for obtaining requirements, at this stage of the system development process, focus groups and interviews are the most commonly used techniques. The reason for choosing them rather than surveys is the need for personal involvement and the dialogue that results from open-ended questions.

In preparation for the requirements definition interviews, the team will normally use three documents:

1. The preliminary requirements identified during Project Initiation
2. The detailed process map
3. The list of defects and their root causes

Just as the previous step transformed a high-level process map into a detailed one, in this step the team should take the general requirements that were identified in Project Initiation and work with customers to make them specific. For example, a general requirement might have been to "Allow online entry and validation of employee name and address." To determine the specifics of that requirement, the project team might ask:

1. Will employee name be entered in first name, last name order?
2. Do you want to include middle names or only middle initials?
3. How many suffixes can an employee's name have?
4. How many lines of supplemental address do you need to store?

5. Do you want to provide for a mailing address separate from the primary residence?
6. Do you have employees who live outside the United States? If yes, in which countries?

The objective of asking these questions is twofold: (1) to determine details about the requirement and (2) to stimulate discussions that might reveal other requirements.

In addition to reviewing the high-level requirements and expanding them into detailed ones, the team should consider the detailed process map as a source of requirements. It is helpful to ask the following questions as each step of the detailed process map is reviewed:

1. What must happen to make this step succeed?
2. How can this step be made better, faster, cheaper, and easier?

These open-ended questions can identify requirements that might otherwise not be mentioned until later in the life cycle.

While the team is conducting customer interviews, they should remain mindful of the Kano model (see Exhibit 11.8) and the fact that many important requirements are unspoken. Customers may not list system uptime or transaction response time as requirements because those could be their basic expectations. They may also not ask for online notification when they are close to exceeding their budget for a specific item because the capability was not available in the existing batch process. Real-time updates and the possibility of early warning could become the excitement factors that change the system from "acceptable" to "excellent."

When working with the list of defects, the team should ask, "How can we prevent this?" The response can be transformed into a requirement, which can be decomposed into one or more detailed requirements.

At the same time that the requirements are documented, the team should also establish acceptance test criteria. This step has two benefits:

1. It provides essential input to the development of an acceptance test plan.
2. It helps ensure that the requirement is valid.

Developing test criteria is an extension of applying the SMART criteria. If the preliminary requirement were "Address must be validated," making it SMART might change the requirement to "State must be an abbreviation from the Postal Service list of U.S. states and zip code must be five numerics." Since this is in fact two requirements, the statement should be separated into the two components and test criteria should be established

Exhibit 18.1   Requirements and Acceptance Criteria

Requirement	Acceptance Criteria
State code must be an abbreviation from the Postal Service list of U.S. states	Valid U.S. state codes are accepted
	System will not allow entry of more than two characters
	Invalid states (alpha) are rejected
	Numeric state codes are rejected
	Blank state codes are rejected
Zip code must be five numerics	Valid zip codes are accepted
	System will not allow entry of more than five characters
	System will not allow entry of alphabetic characters
	Zip code 00000 is rejected
	Entries of less than five numerics are rejected

for each. Exhibit 18.1 provides an example of acceptance test criteria for these requirements.

Although the primary focus at this point in the system development life cycle is typically on process functionality, as noted above, it is also important to define the customers' expectations for basic needs such as response time and system availability. Similarly, if a help desk operation will be involved, the expectation of its service levels should be defined along with the timeframes within which any batch processing must occur.

Establishing complete requirements is not a simple task; however, using brainstorming techniques and structured interviews can increase the success rate.

Step 3: Prioritize the Requirements

One of the pitfalls that traditional SDLCs encounter is the development of a plethora of requirements, all of which IT attempts to incorporate into the new system. Although this effort can be viewed as good customer service, because it has as its objective the satisfaction of all customer requirements, it can boomerang and result in customer dissatisfaction. This is particularly true when the inclusion of all requirements extends the project schedule.

A Six Sigma project recognizes the importance of asking customers to prioritize their requirements. The prioritization process is similar to developing a Pareto chart because it identifies the changes that will have the greatest impact on customer satisfaction. The objective is to ensure that the system IT develops will solve the correct problem. In DFSS terms, the team needs to identify the customers' CTQs, and then ensure that each step of the system design and development process focuses on satisfying those CTQs.

Prioritization can be accomplished by developing a customer requirements matrix as shown in Exhibit 5.15. Although it is possible to prioritize requirements during the same session in which they are identified, there are several benefits to waiting at least a day. First, the delay gives the project team the opportunity to divide requirements into logical groupings and to produce a draft requirements matrix. The act of transcribing requirements from notes into a more formal document has the added benefit of helping team members ensure that they understood the customers' comments. The transcription process may also trigger more questions.

Just as important is that customers will have had a chance to think about the process map and the questions they answered during the requirements definition interviews. Their mental review may identify new requirements.

When the group reconvenes, they should view the session as an opportunity to do four things:

1. *Validate the requirements they identified during their last meeting.* The validation process involves ensuring that the requirement was correctly understood and transcribed, and that the function it describes is indeed necessary.
2. *Identify new requirements.* These requirements may be the result of the customers' reflection on prior sessions or the team's review of previously identified requirements.
3. *Prioritize all requirements.* Although it possible to use any ranking scale, the 1-4-7-10 scale proposed earlier allows clear distinctions in importance.
4. *Obtain customers' current level of satisfaction.* Again, the 1-4-7-10 scale provides clarity.

Following the prioritization meeting, the team should distribute an updated requirements matrix to all participants and ask customers to confirm its accuracy.

Although it is possible to work with the simple customer requirements matrix, a company trained in DFSS recognizes the value of constructing a QFD. Chapter 11 outlines the advantages of using a QFD. One of those advantages is that the four levels of the QFD provide a single repository of key requirements and the ways in which they will be met. It should be noted that the four levels of the QFD have different names when applied to software development than when used for development of a product:

- QFD1 — Business Requirements
- QFD2 — Functional Specification
- QFD3 — System Design
- QFD4 — Operations Planning

Although the names are different, the underlying structure and the way in which the QFD is used are the same as shown in Chapter 11. In both cases, the QFD allows the team to prioritize requirements and ensure that the most critical requirements are satisfied.

While the waterfall approach appears to dictate sequential thinking, the reality is that a customer CTQ captured as part of the initial interviews may result in the identification of features and functions at levels other than business requirements. Rather than ignore those ideas because it is not the right time in the schedule to address them, Richard Biehl encourages his students to work all levels of the QFD simultaneously. In Exhibit 18.2 Biehl provides an example of how a customer's requirement for privacy translates to each of the four QFDs.[1]

Exhibit 18.2   Use of the Four Levels of QFD in Software Development

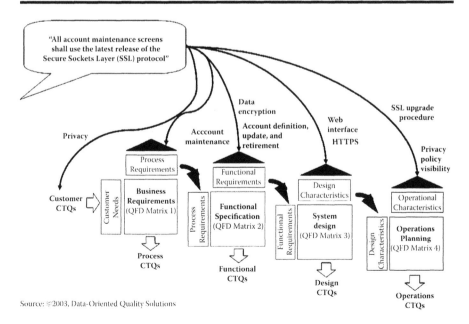

Source: ©2003, Data-Oriented Quality Solutions

The use of a QFD and its embedded calculations simplifies the process of determining which customer requirements are the most important and where the greatest gaps between needs and current satisfaction exist. Appendix F provides an explanation of each field on the QFD, including the formulas.

Step 4: Identify Potential Process Improvements

Once requirements have been identified and prioritized, the team should hold a brainstorming session to identify potential solutions to the requirements. Although at this point in the project it is assumed that a new computer system will be developed, the solutions should not be limited to software. As the GWC OE team discovered, simple procedural changes such as moving the fax machine or eliminating the review of high-volume orders can be equally effective in resolving problems. All possible solutions should be documented.

A cost/time ranking such as the one shown in Exhibit 7.8 may help the team focus its efforts. An alternative, and the one a company trained in DFSS would use, is the QFD. Unlike the cost/time ranking, the QFD relates each potential improvement to a customer CTQ and provides a greater level of focus than is possible with a simple cost/time ranking.

It is possible that the identification of detailed requirements may have invalidated a portion of the system that was envisioned when the feasibility study was developed or that new sub-systems will need to be added to the proposed system. Although a traditional SDLC does not require updates to documents created in previous steps, if the team is using a TMAP, these changes should be noted in it.

Step 5: Determine Which Improvements Will Have the Greatest Impact on the Highest Priority Requirements

As the GWC OE team learned, low-cost quick fixes may not result in increased customer satisfaction. To determine which of the proposed process improvements or system functions should be implemented, the team has two choices:

1. A process improvement ranking spreadsheet as outlined in Appendix C
2. A QFD

Although either one will provide the team with the information to make fact-based decisions about which functions to automate first, the

QFD offers more precision. The "how" portion of the QFD allows the team to measure the impact each potential improvement will have on each requirement. The QFD also clearly identifies which requirements are being addressed and points out any gaps. The process improvement ranking spreadsheet does not provide that level of detail. It may, however, be all that is needed for a small-scale project.

Each tool assists the team in making fact-based decisions and in prioritizing the development of features and functions.

As noted, one of the shortcomings of the traditional SDLC is that project implementation schedules are frequently lengthy and that by the time a system is ready for production, its value to the business is diminished. One way to mitigate that risk is to do what the GWC OE team did and develop the system in phases. Phased implementation can be viewed as a variant of the "pick low hanging fruit first" principle, and the process improvement ranking spreadsheet or QFD can be used to determine which functions should be implemented first.

Although it is important to keep the thought process map updated throughout the project, this is one of the most critical steps to document on the TMAP because major decisions are made in it. The QFD, time/cost, and process improvement rankings provide key inputs to those decisions but the rationale should be explained in the TMAP.

Step 6: Create a Detailed "To-Be" Process Map

Once the team has decided which process improvements should be implemented, they are ready to develop a detailed "to-be" process map. Although this is not part of a traditional SDLC, there are several advantages to creating one:

1. It provides a clear pictorial representation of the proposed system, showing both automated and manual tasks and their interrelationships.
2. Distribution and review of the map improves communication — not only among the team, but also with all affected departments.
3. The map can be used as input to the revision of policies and procedures and the creation of training materials.
4. Development of the map can identify gaps in the process or missing requirements.

The resulting map should be included in the final requirements specification document, and — like all of the SDLC documents — it should be updated during the remaining phases of the development life cycle, if changes are made that would alter the process.

Step 7: Assess the Impact and Risks of the Proposed Process Improvements

Before finalizing the process map and completing the requirements specification, the team should assess the impact and the risks of the system and process improvements being proposed. A risk assessment and mitigation plan (see Exhibit 17.6) or full FMEA (see Appendix D) is useful for describing and quantifying the risks, as well as proposing mitigating actions.

Similarly, an impact assessment (see Exhibit 8.1) can be used to identify all functions that will be affected by the new system. The team may want to replace the "Employee" and "Customer" columns with the names of all departments that will be impacted, so that there is no ambiguity.

Step 8: Complete the Development of the Conceptual Design

The team is now ready to complete its conceptual design of the new system. The first step is to review the recommended approach from the feasibility study to determine whether it should be modified, based on the detailed requirements. Once the approach has been finalized, the conceptual design can be documented. This is typically an expansion of the "Recommended Approach" section of the feasibility study and should include a flowchart showing the major functions and sub-systems of the proposed system.

Exhibit 16.4 indicates that the DFSS phases that correspond to System Analysis are Definition and Development. Although it is not part of the traditional SDLC, the project can benefit from the inclusion of several DFSS techniques at this point:

- *Model the design.* This step (Step 3 in Chapter 13) allows the team to take advantage of the DFSS lever (Exhibit 10.1) by identifying potential problems early enough that they can be corrected easily and at minimal cost. Exhibit 10.2 points out that two major forces affect a design: (1) the customer and (2) the process. The focus of the project thus far has been on the customer. While that is undeniably important, it is also critical to ensure that the proposed system is feasible; that is, that the infrastructure has the process capability needed to run the new system. The team should consider a series of designs of experiment (DOE) to determine at what levels the system will overload the current infrastructure. If new servers or additional bandwidth are needed, this is the time to identify them.

■ *Develop quality measures.* Although development of metrics is often relegated to the final stage of a project, it is preferable to begin identifying them as part of the conceptual design. There are two primary reasons for this:

■ *Increase focus.* Knowing how success will be measured helps the team understand what is most critical.

■ *Identify gaps.* It is possible that as key metrics are developed, the team members will realize that they are not gathering all the data needed to generate those metrics. It is easier and less expensive to add fields at this point in the project than during Implementation, when coding and testing are complete.

As discussed in Step 5 of Chapter 13, the team should develop both a scorecard and a dashboard for the system.

Step 9: Complete the Requirements Specification Document

If the team has followed the preceding steps, development of the requirements specification document involves little more than assembling and packaging the documents they have already developed. Exhibit 18.3 provides a suggested outline for a requirements specification, along with a brief explanation of the contents of each section.

Step 10: Obtain Approvals

The team is now ready to have the requirements specification approved. An approval checklist (see Exhibit 8.2) may be helpful in documenting the steps required and the individuals responsible for each.

Reference

1. Biehl, Richard, *Six Sigma Topic Sampler.* Data-Oriented Quality Solutions, 2003, p. 33. Available at www.doqs.com.

Exhibit 18.3 Contents of Requirements Specification

Section Number	Section Name	Information to Be Included
1	Introduction	The project name and scope (summary).
2	Assumptions	A list of any assumptions that were identified subsequent to the development of the feasibility study.
3	Process Flow	The "to be" process map.
4	Project Risks	The risk assessment and mitigation plan.
5	Requirements and Acceptance Criteria	The requirements and acceptance criteria matrix. If a QFD was constructed, it may be included.
6	Conceptual System Design	A description of the proposed architecture (online vs. batch, client/server vs. web-based, etc.) as well as a flow chart showing proposed subsystems and the functions that they will automate.
7	Impacted Groups	The impact assessment.
8	Approvals	A listing of all approvals that are required for the document.
9	Appendices	A copy of the feasibility study and any other documentation that was developed during System Analysis.

Chapter 19

System Design

Following the definition and prioritization of requirements, the traditional SDLC moves into the System Design phase. Although a conceptual design was identified during System Analysis, it is during Design that this general outline of the system is turned into very specific design documents from which a system can actually be developed. The objective of this phase is to transform the requirements that were developed in the previous phase into a blueprint for a computer system.

System Design consists of three sub-phases: (1) functional design, (2) technical design, and (3) program design. Like the rest of the SDLC, these follow a waterfall approach and are done sequentially, with the output of one phase becoming the input to the subsequent one. DFSS can assist in this process. Companies trained in DFSS techniques will use a QFD to ensure that requirements flow properly from one phase to the next as shown in Exhibit 18.2. They will also seek to identify and then prevent potential failures at each stage using an FMEA (see Appendix D).

Functional Design

It is during the functional design stage that the team describes — in very specific terms — what the system is to do. While previous descriptions were general, it is here in the functional design specification that all the details are provided.

The functional design specification can be viewed as a description of everything that the customer will touch: input screens and output reports, along with any processing that is needed to transform input into output. Because of its potential impact on the customers, it is important that they (the customers) be involved in each step of this design process. Although IT could in theory develop a functional design without further customer participation, simply working from the requirements, a Six Sigma company would not allow that to occur. To ensure that customer requirements are met *completely*, customers must be active participants.

Consider, for example, the order of fields on an input screen. While IT could arrange them to provide the most visually pleasing screen, that order might result in difficult data entry, particularly if data entry is done from existing forms with a differing field order. Similarly, the format of a report might not be conducive to the use the customer plans for it. While IT can — and should — provide suggestions for good design, it should also work closely with the customers to ensure that the system meets expectations.

While screens and reports are being designed, the project team should also evaluate existing policies and procedures to determine whether they need modification.

Although there are no Six Sigma tools developed specifically for the functional design stage, adherence to the principles of remaining focused on the customer and communicating frequently will increase the likelihood of the phase being successful. It is also important to keep the thought process map updated, because the design specification indicates the result of decisions, not the logic that led to them. The TMAP is the single source of overall project history.

As noted, a QFD can help the project team in several ways. It can be used to:

- *Prioritize features.* With its ranking scale, the QFD clearly demonstrates which features and functions will have the greatest impact on requirements. Paying careful attention to the column totals (the Impact section) can help the team avoid scope creep by identifying features that have minimal impact and could be eliminated.
- *Ensure all requirements are addressed.* The Customer Requirement/Product Feature intersections and, in particular, the Importance of All Features totals on each Customer Requirement row highlight requirements that have not been fully satisfied. If the team can identify these shortcomings early in the process, the odds of fully satisfying customers are increased.
- *Provide input to the next phase.* The linkage of one QFD to the next, with the CTQs of the first becoming the requirements of the next, helps the team ensure that nothing is lost between phases. This is particularly critical if different team members are responsible for different documents.

Every project team recognizes the importance of building in quality. Unfortunately, schedules are often so demanding that the team does not take the time to identify and correct defects before they can occur. The predictable result is additional work later in the life cycle. The use of an FMEA at each stage can help identify potential problems and eliminate them before they can occur. Although not part of the traditional SDLC, the use of an FMEA, like the use of a QFD, can improve the quality of the system.

Working with key customer representatives, the project team's goal is to develop a functional design specification that accurately and completely reflects the system to be developed. Exhibit 19.1 shows a sample of one portion of a functional design specification. It is important to note that nothing is left to chance. The actual screen design is shown, along with the length of each field and all validation that is to be performed. For reports, the source of each field, including any calculations that are required, would be shown.

It is also important to note that the underlying technical details, such as the database structure and the division of the system into individual programs, are not defined at this point. That level of specification will occur in the Technical Design stage.

While a traditional SDLC includes approval of all documents as a necessary step, it does not specify any techniques for obtaining that approval. Using the Six Sigma principles outlined previously — customer focus and constant communication — the team should consider conducting design review sessions with customers. These will provide the opportunity for discussion and may identify discrepancies or errors.

Technical Design

If the functional design sub-phase described *what* was to be accomplished, then the technical design sub-phase answers the question of *how* to translate functional requirements into a system. It is during this sub-phase that the overall system architecture, major system components, and interfaces to and from existing systems are finalized and that the database is designed. The output is a technical design specification. Exhibit 19.2 shows the components of a typical technical design specification.

Although it would appear that this portion of the SDLC is strictly technical and need not involve customers, it is important that they be involved in several steps, particularly the design of the database. It is equally important that the involvement be appropriate. The objective is to elicit information from customers, not to frustrate them. Truly customer-focused companies understand the importance of speaking the customer's

Exhibit 19.1   Sample Functional Design Specification

GWC Functional Specification	
System	GWC Integrated Personnel and Payroll system (GIPP)
Sub-system	Employee self-service
Date created	August 13, 2001
Created by	George Greenbelt
Revision number	N/A
Revision date	
Revised by	
Function Description (Repeat for Each Function)	
Function	Entry/update of employee demographics.
Purpose	The employee demographics function allows employees to update their records online. It consists of two screens: one for name and address, the other for dependents.
Frequency	The screens may be updated at any time that GIPP is operational.
Security	Access to the screens is permitted only after the entry of a valid social security number (SSN) and the associated personal identification number (PIN) using the "Employee Entry" screen described below. The initial entry of SSN and a default PIN will be done by the Human Resources specialist at the time of hire. Employees may change their PIN using the "PIN Change" screen described below.
Input	Upon entry of a valid SSN and PIN, the system will display the following screen. All fields currently stored on the database will be retrieved and displayed. **Employee Demographics** **Employee name** *First name* *Middle initial* *Last name* *Suffix* George G Greenbelt Jr. **Employee Address** *Street* 101 Main street *Supplemental address* Apartment 3C *City* Hidden Falls *State* NY *Zip code* 13000 **Update**

Fields	Field Name	Length	Validation
	First name	25	Mandatory field. All characters must be alphabetic.
	Middle initial	1	Optional field. If entered, must be alphabetic.
	Last name	25	Mandatory field. All characters must be alphabetic.

Exhibit 19.1 Sample Functional Design Specification (continued)

	Suffix	3	Optional field. If entered, must be a valid entry from the "Suffix" table.
	Street	25	Mandatory field. No validation will be performed.
	Supplemental address	25	Optional field. No validation will be performed.
	City	25	Mandatory field. No validation will be performed.
	State	2	Mandatory field. Must be a valid entry from the "US States" table.
	Zip code	5	Mandatory field. Must be five numerics.
Processing	When the employee clicks the "update" button, the system will validate the entry. If all fields are correct, the system will display the following message: "Your changes have been applied." If validation errors are detected, the following messages may be produced:		
Error messages	*Field*	*Error message*	
	First name	First name must be entered.	
	Last name	Last name must be entered.	
	Street	Street must be entered.	
	City	City must be entered.	
	State	State must be entered. An incorrect state code was entered.	
	Zip code	Zip code must be entered. An incorrect zip code was entered.	
Output	There are no reports generated as a result of this function.		

language rather than expecting them to learn IT's lingo. Consider the following example.

As part of Information Engineering, one of the structured methodologies that was developed in response to the ad hoc nature of early SDLCs, IT departments began to create Entity Relationship diagrams (ERDs) to define their databases. Exhibit 19.3 shows a simple ERD.

Each of the boxes in the ERD represents an entity. That entity will become a table in the database or, in customer terms, it is a logical

Exhibit 19.2   Contents of Technical Design Specification

Section number	Section name	Information to be included
1	Introduction	Project name, scope of project (summary).
2	Process flow diagram	Graphical illustration and, when required, an explanation of the process to be automated, illustrating the inputs and outputs of each major step, the relationship between steps and any manual efforts.
3	System architecture	Graphical illustration and, when required, an explanation of the hardware and software components of the proposed system, including the relationships between the software components and interfaces to external systems.
4	Database specification	Description of any new databases that will be created. This should include at a minimum the data dictionary. It may also include entity relationship diagrams and CRUD matrices.
5	Reusable components	Listing of all existing software utilities that will be used in the proposed system. "Utilities" include individual programs, software packages and procedures.
6	Hardware requirements	Listing of all computer hardware that will be used for the proposed system. In addition to computers, printers, networks and other components should be included.
7	Support software requirements	Listing of all support/system software that will be used for the proposed system. This should include database management systems as well as any unique operating system software requirements.
8	Test strategy	A high level description of the test procedures that will be developed for the proposed system. This should include the scope of each type of testing: unit, system, integration, acceptance, stress.
9	Approvals	Listing of all approvals that are required for the document.

grouping of related pieces of data. The lines that connect those boxes have verbs or verb phrases that show the relationships between the boxes. There are two verbs on each line because the ERD defines two different relationships, namely how A is related to B and how B is related to A.

Exhibit 19.3   Entity Relationship Diagram

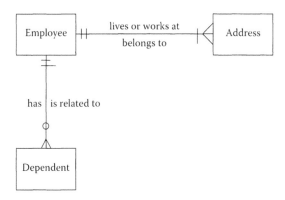

When determining the relationship between two entities, the verb to the right of the line is the relevant one. In the example in Exhibit 19.3, an employee *has* dependents, and a dependent *is related to* an employee.

To further complicate the diagram, there are not simply boxes, lines, and verbs, but also symbols. The symbols at both ends of the lines reflect the optionality and cardinality. Optionality indicates whether or not there must be a relationship between the two entities. In the sample ERD, the "O" near the "dependent" box symbolizes the fact that an employee does not have to have a dependent. This is an optional relationship.

Cardinality indicates the maximum number of occurrences that can exist in a relationship. A straight line means "one," while a crow's foot means "many." The crow's foot next to the "dependent" entity box shows the fact that an employee can have more than one dependent.

The ERD is complicated by the fact that there are two sets of symbols next to each entity box, because, as noted previously, each of the lines is meant to be read in two directions. Reading the symbols on the relationship lines between "employee" and "dependent" results in the following statements:

- An employee can have between zero and many dependents.
- A dependent is related to one and only one employee.

Because they knew that customer involvement was essential, IT departments asked customers to participate in the creation of these diagrams. These efforts were not always successful. Although members of the IT staff may find ERDs easy to understand, customers frequently do not. While the information contained in an ERD is critical to a database design, the notation and the terms used to describe that notation are foreign to many customers.

Exhibit 19.4   CRUD Matrix

	Entity		
Process	Employee	Address	Dependent
New hire	C	C	C
Self-service	RU	RU	CRUD
Termination	RD	RD	RD

With its focus on customers, a Six Sigma company would agree that the customers should not have to learn the notation and that IT would construct ERD diagrams behind the scenes. The team would, however, engage customers in structured interviews to obtain the relationship information that is contained in the diagrams. Leading questions, such as "How many addresses can an employee have?" and "Can more than one employee have the same work address?" will elicit the information needed to create an ERD.

IT may also want to create CRUD matrices. CRUD is an acronym for create, read, update, and delete, the actions that are normally performed on a piece of data or an entire table within the database. A CRUD matrix associates processes or individual screens with database entities and is designed to ensure that all aspects of an entity's life (creation, update, and deletion) are planned. A sample CRUD matrix is shown as Exhibit 19.4. Again, customers should be involved in the discussions that lead to the creation of the matrices. Because CRUD matrices are easier to understand than an ERD, customers may want to participate in their actual development. In either case, they should review the results, even if IT has to translate the documents into English.

Defect Prevention

Before the technical design specification is circulated for approval, the team should schedule a structured walk-through. The purpose is to conduct an impartial review of the document, identifying problems and areas for improvement. In Six Sigma terms, the walk-through is designed to reduce defects. Participants are normally other members of the IT department, including Quality Assurance.

Although the objective of a traditional SDLC walk-through is to reduce defects in the current project, a Six Sigma company knows the importance of improving the entire system development process. As a result, not only should all defects be identified, but their root cause should also be determined. When appropriate, corrective actions can be taken to ensure that the errors are not repeated on this or any future projects. Use of the Six Sigma tool, the Failure Mode and Effects Analysis (FMEA), facilitates

Exhibit 19.5   FMEA after Design Reviews

Failure Modes and Effects Analysis (FMEA)

| Process Name: | GWC Integrated Personnel and Payroll System (GIPP) | | Date Prepared: 8/20/01 | Revision Number: 0 |
| Prepared By: | George Greenbelt | | Revised By: | Revision Date: |

	What Could Happen?			Why and How Often?			How Do We Prevent It?			Action Plan				Results of Actions			
Process Step	**Potential Failure Mode**	**Potential Failure Effects**	S E V	**Potential Causes**	O C C	**Current Controls**	F A I L	P R O B	R P N	**Actions Recommended**	**Resp.**	**Target Date**	**Actions Taken**	S E V	O C C	D E T	R P N
Technical design review	Zip code validation routine was not identified as reusable code	Additional coding (40 hours) would have been required; two modules would have required maintenance	7	Web site listing all reusable modules had not been updated with zip code module	4	None	10		280	Add "reusable code added to repository" line to QA checklist	Quentin Ashton	08/24/2001					0
	Test strategy did not include creation of regression database	Future maintenance efforts would be delayed by the need to create the database	10	Lack of training; associate had been scheduled, but class was canceled	4	None	4		160								0
Program design review	Input screens lack unique identifiers	Support will be more difficult, since Help Desk will have no easy way of identifying the screen in question	10	Lack of standards	10	None	10		1000	Add unique identifier to design standards	Susan Standard	08/24/2001					0
									0								0
									0								0
									0								0
									0								0
									0								0
									0								0
																	0
									0								0

the documentation of errors and their corrective actions. The FMEAs constructed up to this point focused on what *could* go wrong with the system. This one identifies errors that *have actually occurred* and is used to determine the flaws in the system development process that led to those defects. The objective of this FMEA is to mistake-proof IT's process and prevent the recurrence of those errors. Exhibit 19.5 shows a sample FMEA after the technical and program design specification reviews.

Throughout the technical design sub-phase, it is important to keep customers informed of progress and, as always, to keep the thought process map updated. Once the technical design specification is complete and approved, the team is ready for program design.

Program Design

The final step in System Design, program design documents the individual modules that will comprise the system. The output is a program specification that will be used to generate code, either manually or using a code generator. Exhibit 19.6 shows the components of one program design specification.

Unlike other portions of System Design, customer involvement is minimal during program design. The team should, however, conduct structured walk-throughs and document all defects on the FMEA that was begun during technical design so that lessons learned can be shared with other projects.

Exhibit 19.6   Contents of Program Design Specification

Section Number	Section Name	Information to Be Included
1	Description	A high level description of the program's functionality.
2	Inputs	A description of all input used by the program, including its purpose, frequency, and source. For screens, layouts should be included.
3	Processing	Description of all processing to be performed, including calculations, error handling, and security.
4	Outputs	A description of all output generated by the program, including its purpose, frequency, and destination. For reports and screens, layouts should be included.
5	Called programs	A listing of any programs that may be called by this program, including the ownership of the called program.
6	Called packages/ procedures	A listing of any packages or procedures that may be called by this program, including the ownership of the called modules and the functions that will be invoked.
7	Database specification	Information about any databases that are created or modified by this program. Table names and affected fields should be listed.
8	External parameters	A listing of any external parameters, including the purpose.
9	Test plan	The test plan, including all test cases and expected results.
10	Approvals	A listing of all approvals that are required for the document.

Chapter 20

Construction

The fourth phase of the traditional system development life cycle is Construction. Because its objective is the production of executable program code, this phase is sometimes called "Coding" rather than "Construction." No matter what name is applied, it is important to note that the objective should be more than generating executable code. The objective should be to produce defect-free code that meets the customer requirements defined in the previous phases. Although this is an implicit goal of all projects, making it explicit helps to keep the team focused.

In classic Six Sigma terms, Construction is part of the Improve phase. In DFSS, it is a continuation of Development. This is the stage where solutions are implemented and processes are improved. When the solution is a computer system, either programmers write code or a code generator produces it. In either case, Construction is the SDLC phase that has the least scheduled customer involvement. Traditionally, IT develops code without intervention or assistance from other groups.

Structured Walk-Throughs

Because one of IT's goals is to develop defect-free code, many organizations conduct structured walk-throughs of code. Like design walk-throughs, the purpose is to provide an impartial review of the code, identifying problems and areas for improvement. In addition to members of the IT development staff, it is helpful to include at least one person from the proposed support organization in these reviews. That person, recognizing that his or her responsibility will be the ongoing maintenance and enhancement of the system, will provide a different — and valuable — perspective to the code review.

The objectives of the structured walk-through are to:

1. Ensure that there are no logic flaws.
2. Ensure that the code meets IT's coding standards. Such standards could include naming conventions, use of validation tables rather than hard coded logic, and restrictions on nesting levels.
3. Improve the maintainability of the system. As noted above, the participation by someone who will assume responsibility for the system can help in identifying areas where coding changes may make long-term support less costly.

In his book entitled *Software Testing and Continuous Quality Improvement*,[1] Lewis provides a number of checklists that can be used as part of a structured walk-through. These focus on the production of efficient, maintainable code.

A Six Sigma project would expand the role of the structured walk-through to include the following objectives:

1. Ensure that the code satisfies the customer's requirements. It is useful to compare the code's functionality against the customer requirements matrix that was developed during System Analysis or against the QFD, if one was created.
2. Uncover errors in the design or requirements definition processes. It is possible that as the team walks through the code, they will discover incomplete or erroneous requirements or design specifications. These errors should be reviewed with the customer to ensure that the team's understanding is correct.

Defect Prevention

Code walk-throughs are designed to identify and correct errors. Six Sigma companies know they must do more than correct defects; they must seek to prevent them. As a result, their focus is greater than the current project. They want to improve the entire system development process. The first step is to measure defects.

When errors are found or areas that could be improved are identified, they should be documented. It is not uncommon for programmers to discover that requirements are missing or ambiguous when they begin to code a module. A typical reaction is to make the change and continue with the project. If this occurs without documenting the problem, IT has created its own "hidden factory." As discussed in Chapter 1, the hidden factory is the informal detection and correction of defects. While this approach achieves the goal of correcting an individual problem, it obscures the magnitude of the problem and does nothing to prevent its recurrence.

As was true in the Design phase, a Six Sigma team's goal is not simply to ensure that the current system is defect-free, but also to improve the Construction phase for all subsequent projects. To accomplish this goal, the team will do more than document and correct errors. It will also measure them and perform an analysis of both the causes of the defects and the life-cycle phase in which the errors were introduced. This can be viewed as an expansion of the Root Cause Analysis shown as Exhibit 7.6.

Although there are no Six Sigma tools designed specifically for quantifying system development defects, the principles of measurement and analysis can be used to develop tools. An example is the Error Analysis spreadsheet shown in Exhibit 20.1. This spreadsheet allows team members to quantify the types of errors they uncovered, the root causes, and the life-cycle phases in which they were introduced.

When the team has finished all the structured walk-throughs of the Construction phase, it will consolidate the various Error Analyses to determine where the majority of the problems occurred and what caused them. A Pareto chart similar to the one shown in Exhibit 7.7 can be used to analyze the frequency of errors. Items with a high frequency will be subject to further analysis and a corrective action plan, and will be documented on the FMEA begun during the design reviews (Exhibit 19.5).

Like all SDLC phases, Construction involves reviews and approvals. These can be documented on the Approval Checklist (see Exhibit 8.2).

References

1. Lewis, William E., *Software Testing and Continuous Quality Improvement.* Boca Raton, FL: Auerbach, 2000.

Exhibit 20.1   Error Analysis

| System Name | GIPP | Prepared By | George Greenbelt |
| Module | GIPP0001 | Date | 09/14/2001 |

Error	Type of Error			Root Cause					Phase error was Introduced				
	Erroneous logic	Missing logic	Pgm stds violated	Ambiguous reqmts	Carelessness	Design defects	Incomplete reqmts	Lack of training	Coding	Program design	Technical design	Functional design	Requirements definition
Requirement to validate zip code was not incorporated into module		1			1				1				
Requirement to validate state code was hard coded rather than using standard state code table			1					1	1				
Requirement for a country code is missing		1					1						1
Totals	0	2	1	0	1	0	1	1	2	0	0	0	1

Chapter 21

Testing and Quality Assurance

Testing, the fifth phase of the traditional SDLC, is part of the Improve phase in the Six Sigma DMAIC model. Although the Six Sigma step is simply "Implement," inherent in that statement is the need to ensure that the solution being implemented is defect-free. The corresponding DFSS phase is Verification.

In traditional SDLC terms, testing can be viewed as the quality assurance step because it is during this phase that the quality of the software that was developed during Construction is proven. The reality, of course, is that quality assurance should begin when the project is initiated and should be an integral part of each step. This is particularly true of Six Sigma projects, where the goal is to eliminate defects as early as possible in the process and to prevent them from occurring in other similar processes. Similar to all aspects of DMAIC, testing needs to be customer focused and fact-based.

The objectives of the Testing phase are to:

- Demonstrate that the developers have understood and met customers' requirements.
- Show that real people can use the system in the real world.

The differences between the two objectives are more than semantics. It is possible to have met customer requirements for functionality and still have a system that is virtually unusable. If, for example, response time is slow or the system requires so many workstation resources that end users cannot run their normal office applications concurrently with the new system, it does not meet the second objective. This potential problem is the reason why a DFSS project models a solution before implementing it.

There are two primary steps included in the testing phase: (1) develop a test plan and (2) execute it. Although some IT departments perform ad hoc testing, those that follow a formal methodology recognize the importance of developing a comprehensive written test plan and executing it through the use of a rigid test schedule. In Six Sigma terms, a test plan helps reduce variation and ensure that measurements of defects are repeatable and reproducible.

The Test Plan

The first step in creating a test plan is to identify the types of testing that will be performed. Typically there are five distinct tests scheduled as part of a development project: (1) unit, (2) system, (3) integration, (4) stress, and (5) acceptance. Each serves a different purpose. With the exception of stress and acceptance, which are sometimes performed concurrently, the tests are executed sequentially. Exhibit 21.1 outlines the types of testing, when they are performed, and who should participate.

Exhibit 21.1 Types of Testing

Testing Category	What Is the Objective?	What Is Being Tested?	When Is It Performed?	Who Should Participate?
Unit	Verify that an individual program module performs according to its specifications.	Program logic	As soon as the module is complete.	Developers, Quality Assurance
System	Verify that the system as a whole operates according to its specifications.	Interfaces within the system	When all modules have been tested and all bugs resolved.	Developers, Quality Assurance
Integration	Ensure that the interfaces between systems function as planned and that the system meets the required performance levels under normal conditions.	Interfaces to and from external systems; operation in the "real world" environment	At the completion of system testing.	Developers, Quality Assurance
Stress	Test the system's limits and performance under extraordinary circumstances.	System robustness under high volumes of data and/or low resource availability; ability to recover from system failures.	At the completion of integration testing.	Developers, Quality Assurance
Acceptance	Verify that the system meets all customer requirements.	Functionality and ease of use	At the completion of integration testing.	Customers, Quality Assurance

In a traditional SDLC, customers are involved in only the final phase of testing, acceptance. Recognizing the value of having customers involved as early and as often as possible, a Six Sigma system development project would include customers in all phases. While their involvement may not be as extensive as the developers' or Quality Assurance's involvement in the early stages, customers provide an important perspective and may be able to identify usability problems that are not apparent to the other testers.

Customers should also be involved in the creation of the test plan. Just as they participated in the development of acceptance criteria for each of the requirements (see Exhibit 18.1), they can provide valuable input to the test schedule, acceptance criteria, and critical success factors. Exhibit 21.2 shows the contents of a typical test plan.

When developing a test plan, the team can benefit from several of the techniques it used in previous phases of the SDLC. The first of these is the structured walk-through. As each section of the test plan is completed, the project leader should convene a walk-through, including members of the Quality Assurance team as well as members of the team who will be responsible for the ongoing support of the system. Although many organizations do not include the maintenance organization at this point, there are several advantages to having them participate.

- As was true during the Construction phase, the support organization provides a different perspective from that of the development team.
- Because they will be responsible for the ongoing maintenance and enhancement of the system, members of the support organization have a vested interest in ensuring that the tests that are performed exercise all possible combinations of data and logic.

Similar to other walk-throughs, this one should be viewed as an opportunity to improve the entire system development process, and errors should be documented on the FMEA that was started in prior phases (see Exhibit 19.5), then analyzed using tools such as the Pareto chart.

Test Cases

Although Testing is part of the Improve step in the DMAIC model, many of the steps can be viewed as measurements. As such, it is important that they are repeatable and reproducible. This is one of the reasons why a formal test plan with predefined test cases and expected results is important. Without them, testing can be haphazard, and recreating error conditions is difficult.

Exhibit 21.2   Contents of Test Plan

Section Number	Section Name	Information to be Included
1	Introduction	List of types of testing to be performed.
2.0	Unit test plan	
2.1	Test strategy	Scope of testing to be performed; objective of testing.
2.2	Roles and responsibilities	List of all individuals who will participate in the test; this includes reviewers as well as actual testers.
2.3	Test environment	Environment in which test will be performed; any special requirements (testing software, special security, etc.).
2.4	Test schedule	High level schedule of when tests are to be performed.
2.5	Test cases and expected results	A list of all test cases to be entered along with the expected results.
2.6	Other acceptance criteria	A list of acceptance criteria that may not be linked to an individual test case; e.g., response time.
2.7	Critical success factors	A list of all assumptions that may affect the completion of the test. May include assumptions about the maximum time required to review and approve test results as well as accuracy of data conversions, etc.
3.0	System test plan	*Will include all the subsections shown for the Unit Test Plan.*
4.0	Integration test plan	*Will include all the subsections shown for the Unit Test Plan.*
5.0	Stress test plan	*Will include all the subsections shown for the Unit Test Plan.*
6.0	Acceptance test plan	*Will include all the subsections shown for the Unit Test Plan.*
7.0	Approvals	A listing of all approvals that are required for the document.

Actual creation of test cases should be done by a combination of the developers and customers in conjunction with Quality Assurance. The importance of having independent professional testers involved in the process cannot be overemphasized. Both developers and customers test with the objective of proving that the system works. This is their natural bias. Professional testers, on the other hand, have as their objective proving that the system *does not* work. They are the ones who will stress the limits, who will ignore normal boundaries and enter what should be impossible combinations of data. They will refuse to enter mandatory fields; they will attempt to enter the same record twice or to retrieve a record that they have deleted. They are the ones who have the tenacity to test every field on every screen. Because they have no pride of authorship in the system, they are willing to uncover every possible flaw. They are, in short, essential to the development of a defect-free system.

The Unit Test

Although all testing is designed to prove the functionality of the system, nowhere is this more important than in unit testing. This is the first chance that the team has to validate its coding. Although it can be viewed as a tedious task, it is essential to test every branch of program logic, because this is the only way to identify and eliminate defects. Initially, unit testing is performed with valid test data to prove that the program works as designed. This is analogous to the first part of prototyping, where the team seeks to ensure that the product meets customer requirements.

Once team members are convinced that the program functions properly when given correct input, they should test erroneous conditions, trying to break the system as the Just Right Widget team did in their Accelerated Stress Testing during prototyping. Again, the goal is to identify and eliminate defects. Test cases should include the highest and lowest acceptable values for each field, invalid values, null fields, and various combinations of fields. For an example of field combinations, when testing state and zip code, one test case should include a valid state code with a zip code that is valid only in another state, such as "NY" and "07960" (the latter is a New Jersey zip code).

Actual test results should be recorded on the test case log; and when bugs are uncovered, they should be documented. Although a traditional SDLC does not mandate it, a Six Sigma project will analyze this data to determine whether there are common root causes. Exhibit 21.3 shows a sample test case log.

Exhibit 21.3   Test Case Log

System	GIPP				Tested By	Quentin Assurance				
Module	GIPP0001				Date	November 14, 2001				
Case Number	Data Entered	Expected Results	Actual Results	Date Retested	Retested By	Retest Results	Comments	Date Closed	Closed By
30002	State code "AA"	Error message: "An incorrect state code was entered"	System accepted invalid code	11/21/01	QA	Correct error message was produced		11/21/01	QA
30003	No zip code	Error message: "Zip code must be entered"	Error message: "Zip code must be entered"	11/15/01	QA	Correct error message was produced		11/15/01	QA
30004	Zip code 10021	Value accepted	Value accepted					11/14/01	QA
30005	Zip code Ab123	Error message: "An incorrect zip code was entered"	System produced correct error message					11/14/01	QA

The System Test

Once all of the individual modules have been tested and all bugs resolved, the team is ready to perform system testing. The objective of system testing is to uncover errors in the interaction between modules. As with all testing, the team should exercise all interfaces and test invalid combinations as well as the expected ones. For example, if one program is expected to pass a parameter to another, a test case with no parameter and others with invalid ones should be included. Results of this and all tests should be documented on the test case log.

The Integration Test

Integration testing has two major objectives. The first is to validate the interaction between the new system and all existing systems that interface with it. Like system testing, it is important to determine the system's behavior under ideal and erroneous conditions. If a step in the new system depends on files being produced by an external system, test cases should include no input file, a null file, duplicate files, and files with totally erroneous data and file formats.

The second objective of integration testing is to determine the system's performance under normal operating conditions. While the first stage of integration testing is typically done with limited numbers of test cases, because the objective is to test specific conditions, the second stage will use what are expected to be normal volumes of data, as the team must ensure that the system meets the customers' performance requirements. Previous tests may have been done in a lab environment with dedicated workstations and no other applications running. This portion of integration testing should be done in a "real-world" environment with all applications that would be expected to be running on a normal day being exercised at the same time.

If data from existing systems is to be converted and loaded into the new system, a preliminary conversion should be run so that the integration test can use live data.

The Stress Test

Once team members have completed integration testing and are convinced that the system functions as desired under normal conditions, they should perform stress testing. The objective of stress testing is to determine the system's behavior under extraordinary conditions. There are three primary "stressors" to be tested:

1. Security
2. High transaction volumes
3. Disasters

When testing security, the team should validate both logical and physical access controls. That is, how well do log-on IDs work and how secure is the data? The tests to be conducted should include not only attempts to hack the system, but also tests of database checkpointing and rollback procedures.

High volume testing, although frequently overlooked, is an important part of stress testing. The team should know how a system will perform under transaction volumes that are double, triple, and quadruple the expected volumes. Not only is it possible that transaction volumes may increase with time, but it is also possible that customers have underestimated the normal volume. Similar to the stress test that the Just Right

Widget team performed, these tests are designed to determine how robust and reliable the system will be.

Failure to perform high-volume testing can have career-limiting effects. Consider the case of a large corporation that replaced printed pay stubs with online access to pay information. Although this was viewed as nothing more than an extension of its highly successful employee self-service program, the team failed to consider the impact of tens of thousands of employees attempting to access the Web site at the same time and were forced to revert to printed stubs until the servers could be upgraded. While this failure to do high volume testing was embarrassing, had the application been online trading, the effects could have been far more costly to the corporation.

Although most system development projects include the creation of a disaster recovery plan, not all teams actually test the plan prior to putting the system into production. They should. It is important to simulate system failure at key times, such as month-end processing for financial systems, as well as during normal operations, and to demonstrate that the recovery procedures function as designed and are adequate to meet the customers' needs. The last phrase, although sometimes overlooked, is important. While daily backups may appear adequate, in high transaction situations where the customers have no paper trail of their input, having to recreate an entire day's work may be difficult. In these circumstances, more frequent backups may be warranted.

When developing the test scenarios for stress testing, the team should apply the RAVE criteria to the measurements. The tests that are performed should be:

- Relevant
- Able to detect process changes
- Valid and consistent from time to time
- Easy to execute

Relevance is rarely a problem; however, the ability to detect changes might be. Varying transaction volumes by a only small number can result in an inability to detect process changes. Similarly, increasing volumes too dramatically can result in overcompensating for the problem.

Consistency is critical during testing because it helps reduce variation. Although the system might ultimately run on two different servers, when resolving problems, it is important to ensure consistency by performing all testing on the same server. Then, once the system is stable on that machine, testing can (and should) be performed on the second server to ensure that it produces the same results as the first one.

As always, tests should be as easy to execute as possible.

The Acceptance Test

Acceptance testing is the final step before the system is released to production. At this point, the team should be convinced that the system will run properly under both normal and extraordinary circumstances. Acceptance is the "put it all together" test, the objective of which is to verify that the system meets all customer requirements. Customers, it is important to note, include groups such as the Data Center and Network Operations, as well as the department that initiated the project.

Acceptance testing tests everything, not just the system's functionality. It is during this phase of testing that customers validate the system documentation as well as the system itself. The ultimate customers should ensure that the user guides and procedures they have developed match the system, while the operational departments should validate all runbooks and procedures they have been given. Even training materials should be checked against the system itself. Acceptance testing is similar to the first stage of a DFSS Verification pilot. It is a small-scale running against what the team hopes will be the production system.

Six Sigma Tools for Testing

As was true in the previous phases of the SDLC, throughout the various testing stages, it is important not only to document and correct defects, but also to analyze them. The objective is twofold: (1) to ensure that the system under development is defect-free and (2) to improve the system development process itself. That is, defect prevention as well as correction.

An Error Analysis similar to the one shown as Exhibit 20.1 will help the team quantify and categorize the errors that are uncovered during testing. By conducting a root cause analysis and generating a Pareto chart, the team can identify the most frequent errors. To help prevent their recurrence, these should be reported on the project's overall FMEA (see Exhibit 19.5), and corrective actions should be developed.

Chapter 22

Implementation

The final phase of the traditional SDLC is Implementation. This is the point where the system is complete and is turned over to production. There are four major steps involved in implementation:

1. Customer training
2. Customer documentation
3. Data conversion
4. Project evaluation

The first three steps are part of the Improve phase of DMAIC; the last step is the first step of Control. All can be considered part of DFSS's Verification phase.

Customer Training

Although it is sometimes addressed as an afterthought, the development and delivery of customer training is an essential part of system development. Because it is so closely tied to the customer, Six Sigma companies know how important it is to train and train properly.

One of the most effective ways to approach customer training is to view it as a sub-project and to employ the same Six Sigma tools that were used during the initial phases of the overall project. Because the project already has a champion, the first steps should be to establish a project charter and form a team. As shown in Appendix A, the charter documents the team's objectives and responsibilities along with a high-level schedule and critical success factors. Because it is likely that the training team will include people such as professional trainers and course designers who have not been involved in previous phases, a formal project charter is helpful in ensuring that all participants have a common understanding of the goals and the expected level of commitment.

The next step should be to identify customer requirements for training. It is important to note that what customers need and want may differ from IT's understanding of requirements. A system developer will create a training course designed to teach people how to use the system, while customers want training that shows them how to use the system *to do their jobs*. The difference is fundamental. Customers view the system as a tool, whereas IT sees it as a product.

Obtaining customer requirements need not be a lengthy process. The team leader can convene a focus group with representatives from the customer department and use that session to define expectations and requirements. It is important, however, to document requirements and to obtain customer sign-off, ideally during a second face-to-face meeting. Prioritization of requirements using a requirements matrix (see Exhibit 5.15) is also useful because it helps the training team focus on the right things. Although it is possible to use a QFD for the prioritization, this is one case where the rigor of a QFD may be overkill or, in terms a lean expert would prefer, overprocessing (see Exhibit 6.3). As was true in previous phases, the steps of documenting and reviewing requirements help to ensure that everyone involved in the process has a common understanding of what is to be done.

Once requirements have been defined, the team can determine the appropriate training medium. While classroom training was once the only option, teams can now develop Web-based or other computer-based training (CBT). Because of its self-paced nature, CBT is particularly useful for refresher training. If there is disagreement about the type of training to be developed, a cost/time ranking similar to Exhibit 7.10 or, if needed, an impact assessment (see Exhibit 8.1) can help the team make fact-based decisions. A Pugh concept selection matrix (see Exhibit 12.2) can also be used.

Because it is important to clarify the role that the new system will play in the customers' daily work, the training materials should include one or more process maps. These provide a pictorial representation of the various steps involved in the overall process and help establish the context for the system. When there are different functions or roles involved, such as clerks, reviewers, and approvers, a functional process map helps delineate individual responsibilities. Similar process maps are helpful in training other customers, including the data center.

Once training has been conducted, the team should assess its efficacy. Although many of the techniques used to gather customer requirements see (Exhibit 5.8) can be used, the most common method is to ask for customer feedback via a formal survey at the end of the training session. A sample training survey is included as Exhibit 22.1.

While some companies calculate only average ratings to determine the success of their training programs, as the GWC OE team learned, averages can be misleading. It is helpful to create a histogram see (Exhibit 6.12) to see the distribution of ratings. If there is wide variation, the team should analyze the data to determine where improvements can be made.

While an initial survey is helpful in determining the quality of the training materials and the instructors' skills, it does not address the issue of how much knowledge students retained. A follow-up survey 30, 60, and 90 days after the initial training, focusing on how easy the students found the system to use and what aspects of training they wished had been given greater or lesser emphasis, is of equal importance. This is the "real-world" effect of the training. Lessons learned at this point should be documented on the TMAP and, if serious problems were uncovered, on the project's FMEA (see Exhibit 19.5).

Training is often a time when customers identify new requirements for the system. Although it is unlikely that full implementation will be delayed until the enhancements are made, the requests should be documented. The use of a requirements matrix (see Exhibit 5.15) allows the customers to assign a priority ranking to each requirement.

Customer Documentation

In the ideal world, all documentation is completed prior to acceptance testing so that it can be used and validated during the testing process. In the real world, documentation is often the final step, and impending deadlines result in the effort being short-changed.

As was true of training, it is important to gather customer requirements before developing documentation. The stereotype of massive volumes of paper that serve little purpose other than gathering dust on a shelf is all too often true. Had they been surveyed, customers might have told the development team that they needed brief online help rather than a pound of paper. By convening a focus group, the team can learn what types of documentation will be most valuable to the customers. Again, it should be noted that the Operations staff and other groups that will touch the system should be included in the survey of appropriate documentation. The tools that were used to evaluate training methods can also be used for documentation.

Exhibit 22.1 Training Survey

Training Assessment

Location: _____   Date: _____

Instructor: _____

Participant's Name (optional): _____

Please rate the following aspects of the training using a scale of 1 to 5 where 1 is awful and 5 is excellent. You'll note that we've asked you to rate each of the lessons as well as the course as a whole.

System Navigation

Content of lesson	1 2 3 4 5
Pacing of lesson	1 2 3 4 5
Usefulness of examples to your job	1 2 3 4 5
Ability to use function after the lesson is over	1 2 3 4 5

Getting Started

Content of lesson	1 2 3 4 5
Pacing of lesson	1 2 3 4 5
Usefulness of examples to your job	1 2 3 4 5
Ability to use function after the lesson is over	1 2 3 4 5

General Ratings

Usefulness of training materials	1 2 3 4 5
Instructor's knowledge of topic	1 2 3 4 5
Instructor's training skills	1 2 3 4 5
Overall course rating	1 2 3 4 5

Comments

Although documentation may have been drafted in prior phases, it is likely that it will need to be refined following acceptance testing and training. If substantial revisions are required, the team should document the types of modifications that are needed to determine whether there are common causes that could have been prevented. If so, the TMAP and FMEA may need to be updated.

Data Conversion

Although the programs needed for data conversion should have been designed, coded, and tested in prior phases, it is during Implementation that they are executed in a production mode. Because this is live data, it is possible that errors will be uncovered as the data is converted. These should be tracked in the Error Analysis (see Exhibit 20.1), with frequent errors and the planned corrective actions documented in the FMEA (see Exhibit 19.5). As was true throughout the SDLC, the objective is to improve not just this project, but also the overall system development process.

Project Evaluation

A typical SDLC ends with a formal project evaluation or, as it is sometimes called, a post mortem. The objectives of this step are to determine how well the system met customer requirements and what problems were identified during the life cycle. Customer satisfaction is typically obtained through surveys, while the assessment of the life cycle is more likely made through brainstorming sessions. In Six Sigma system development, these evaluations are a continuation of the data collection and analysis that occurred throughout the project.

While a post mortem is important to identify defects and potential improvements, it should not be the final step in the life cycle. A Six Sigma project will go beyond project evaluation and establish a control plan as shown on Exhibit 9.2. The purpose of the control plan is to ensure that the benefits that were expected are achieved and sustained. If, for example, one of the projected benefits was a reduction in the cost per transaction, the control plan should identify the expected cost, the method for calculating it, and a reaction plan should the cost reduction target not be met.

If it did not do this as part of System Analysis, the project team should identify metrics that provide a clear measurement of the project's benefits and provide for regular reporting of those metrics. Scorecards and dashboards (see Exhibits 13.5 and 13.7) are useful tools for displaying metrics.

Finally, although it is a step that is all too often neglected, the team should celebrate its success.

Although it has shortcomings, a waterfall SDLC can be an effective method of developing software. Using Six Sigma tools will increase the likelihood of success and help identify ways to improve not only one project, but also the entire system development process.

V

SIX SIGMA AND LEGACY SYSTEMS

The traditional SDLC ends when the system is installed, ignoring the fact that systems are living things that must change to adapt to new business environments and that the longest — and most costly — stage in a system's life is its post-implementation support. As a result, maintenance should be approached in a structured manner similar to the rest of the SDLC. Use of Six Sigma tools can simplify the process and increase the likelihood of success.

Chapter 23 provides an introduction to legacy systems and presents the case for formal change management, while Chapter 24 outlines the system change process and makes a case for release-based maintenance.

Chapter 25 categorizes maintenance and shows how the DMAIC model can be applied to it. It also introduces steering committees and service level agreements, showing how both can be used to improve communication, increase customer focus, and ensure that decisions are fact based.

Chapter 23

Introduction to Legacy Systems

For many IT professionals, the term "legacy system" evokes images of a 20-year-old program that is about to be superseded by a new piece of software, typically an integrated system that was designed to replace a hodgepodge of ancient programs. While this is a valid definition, it can also be argued that all systems become legacy the moment they are placed in production. Whether 20 days or 20 years old, the systems face similar challenges. They must continue to run properly, even when the infrastructure changes; they must adapt to a changing business environment; and they must be flexible enough to accommodate new functionality. In short, they must be maintained.

The Challenge

As shown in Section IV of this book, the traditional SDLC ends with the implementation of the system and appears to assume that the system will remain static. That is, of course, an invalid assumption. The reality is that systems are constantly evolving. There are three primary reasons for this:

1. *Incomplete or inaccurate requirements.* No matter how carefully the team worked with customers to define requirements, something is almost always missed. Additionally, as customers begin to experiment with the system during the various testing phases, they

frequently discover new uses for the system, some of which will require modifications to the software. As a result, it is not unusual to have an extensive list of proposed enhancements and modifications even before the system is first put into production, and that list normally grows throughout the system's life.

2. *Incomplete testing.* Although developers and the Quality Assurance team attempt to test every possible condition, some combinations of conditions may be missed. As a result, the system might break or function incorrectly. These bugs must be fixed.

3. *Business changes.* It is virtually an axiom that the underlying business requirements that triggered the initial development of the system will alter in some way during the life of that system, necessitating modifications to the software. Similarly, regulatory requirements and changing infrastructure (new hardware, new versions of operating software or databases) may require the system to be modified.

Not only are systems constantly evolving, but they are also evolving over extended periods of time. It is a generally accepted principle that the life of a system exceeds the length of time required to develop it. If not, there would be little incentive to develop it in the first place. A second principle is that systems live longer than anticipated. Although at one time, system developers expected COBOL mainframe systems to have a life span of five years, reality is that it is not uncommon to find 20-year-old COBOL programs still in existence. What this means is that support of systems — what is commonly called "maintenance" — becomes the longest phase of the SDLC.

It is also the one where errors are the most costly. Although no one wants to have late delivery of a new system, the impact of schedule slippage is normally less than the discovery of errors in a production system. Once a system has been placed into production, customers begin to depend on it and to replace whatever manual systems preceded the new system. Soon the dependency is complete. At that point, system outages and erroneous output can place the business at risk.

Need for Change Management

The cover of Martin and McClure's classic book entitled *Software Maintenance*[1] represents a system's life as an iceberg, with development being only the tip. The largest part of the iceberg is the one that is hidden beneath the water: support. Continuing the iceberg analogy, ships (or, in this case, IT departments) ignore the bulk at their peril. They know that change is ongoing and that, to be successful, it must be managed.

For all of the above reasons, maintenance should be approached in a structured manner similar to the rest of the SDLC. The first step in developing that structure is to establish formal change management. In this as in maintenance itself, the use of Six Sigma tools and techniques can simplify the process and increase the likelihood of success.

When DFSS Can Help

While it might seem that DFSS techniques would have no applicability to legacy systems because, as Exhibit 10.3 illustrates, DFSS is best suited to the development of new systems rather than improvement of existing ones, there are times when following the DFSS process is appropriate, particularly when new functions are being added and when new sub-systems are proposed. Those projects, because of their similarity to new development, can benefit from the use of DFSS techniques.

Reference

1. Martin, James and McClure, Carma, *Software Maintenance*. Englewood Cliffs: Prentice Hall, 1983.

Chapter 24

Change Management in the IT Department

Just as IT departments recognized the need for formal processes for developing software and implemented traditional SDLCs to meet this need, they also recognized the need for a structured way to manage change to those systems. The corollary to this statement is that, just as not all IT departments have adopted development methodologies, not all have embraced formal change management. For those departments that lack these processes and for those that have change management but want to review its effectiveness, Six Sigma tools can be helpful.

It should be noted that although the following discussion of change management is slanted toward application maintenance, the concepts can be applied to all types of change, including the changes to requirements and design that occur during system development. In all cases, the goals are to reduce variation by having a standard process and to ensure that the results of that process meet customer requirements.

There are four primary tasks included in the establishment of a change management system:

1. Understand and document the process.
2. Define success.
3. Identify and mitigate risks.
4. Ensure that the process is followed.

In Six Sigma terms, the steps translate to define, measure, analyze, improve, and control. That is, successful change management follows the classic DMAIC model.

Step 1: Understand and Document the Process

The first step in developing effective change management is to understand what is currently being done, to streamline and improve the process, and to document the improved process. The Six Sigma tool of choice for this documentation is the process map, specifically the functional process map. Because multiple departments and multiple functions within IT are involved in change management, the use of a functional process map clearly delineates individual responsibilities and where hand-offs occur. Exhibit 24.1 provides an example of a functional process map for software maintenance.

As noted on the functional process map, other tools can be used in the actual change process. These include the Request for Services (see Exhibit 17.2) and the Approval Checklist (see Exhibit 8.2). Depending on the size and complexity of the requested modification, the team can also use an Impact Assessment (see Exhibit 8.1) and an FMEA (see Appendix D).

Once the preliminary "as-is" process map is created, the team should review it with all affected groups to ensure that the map accurately reflects the flow of responsibility. A review of the map shown as Exhibit 24.1 reveals that several process steps have been omitted. Although it is possible that a change to the system may require customer training, there is no reference to either training materials or the actual training sessions. Before the team members begin to improve the process, they need to ensure that it is completely understood and documented.

When the "as-is" map is complete, the team's next task is to determine how the process can be improved. Whether or not the company has adopted all aspects of lean manufacturing or what Womack and Jones call "lean thinking,"[1] the team's objective should be to identify and eliminate as many forms of waste (see Exhibit 6.3) as possible. In explaining the title of his book, Michael George states, "Lean Six Sigma for service is about getting results rapidly."[2] That should be IT's goal for the change management process.

As the first step in eliminating waste, the team should identify non-value-added steps and unnecessary wait states, then try to devise ways to eliminate, or at least reduce, them. To improve customer satisfaction, it is often important to reduce the time between submission of an RFS and receipt of the time and cost estimate, because during that stage of the process, the customer may have the impression that the request has

Exhibit 24.1 Change Management Functional Process Map

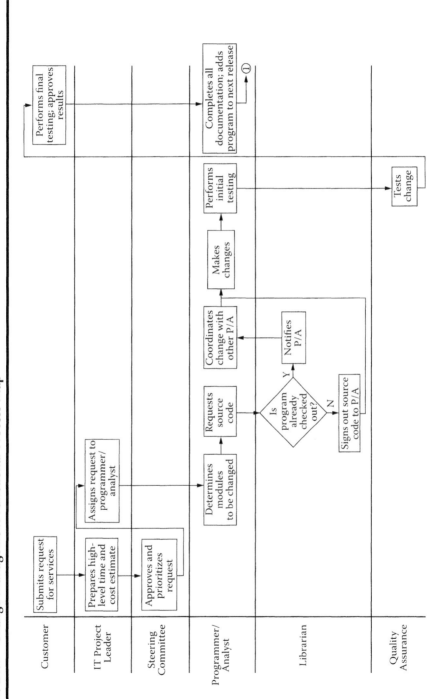

Exhibit 24.1   Change Management Functional Process Map (continued)

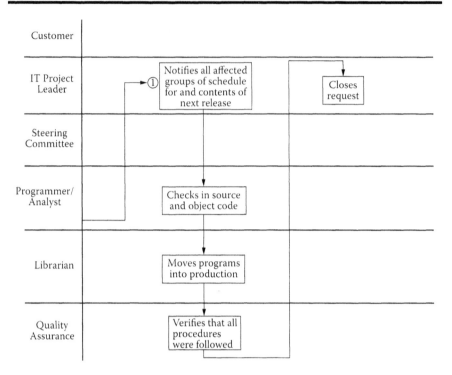

fallen into a black hole. The team may find that adding a step, confirmation of receipt, improves the overall process because it eliminates customer calls and the time required to research the status of a request. Note that those steps (customer calls and related research) were part of a hidden process and did not appear on the original process map.

As is true of most steps, identifying and eliminating waste may be an iterative process. When the team believes it has created the final "to-be" map, it is time to schedule another round of reviews.

Step 2: Define Success

After defining the process, the team needs to determine what constitutes success. Because this is a Six Sigma project, the assessment must be based on facts rather than opinions. Simply put, the team must establish a series of metrics to measure the process.

If beauty is in the eye of the beholder, so too is success. While IT may measure success by a reduction in the request backlog, customers may be unhappy because one critical request was not completed on schedule. IT should work with its customers to establish these metrics because they may have different perspectives of success. As any Six Sigma company knows, what is important is the customers' perceptions. However, it is also important to ensure that customer expectations are realistic and that there is a common understanding of those expectations and how they will be measured.

When defining the metrics, the team should ensure that they include the SMART and RAVE characteristics. For example, although a customer might define successful system maintenance as "everything works right the first time," the team would be correct in pointing out that "works right" is not specific enough to ensure that the measurement is objective. Furthermore, "everything," although a desirable goal, is not attainable. A more appropriate quality metric would be "99.8 percent of all changes placed in production within the calendar month required no rework and resulted in no lost productivity within the customer department."

Once success is defined, the team should develop both scorecards and dashboards. The scorecards will be used to communicate with the customer on a monthly basis, while the dashboards provide daily status to the IT staff, helping to keep them on track for meeting the customers' expectations.

Step 3: Identify and Mitigate Risks

Change involves risk. Every time a production system is modified, there is a risk that the change will introduce an error that is not caught by testing. This unexpected side effect of correcting the original problem can wreak havoc with production systems and is the reason most IT departments insist on complete regression testing. However, when a critical system crashes in the middle of the night, regression testing is often impractical.

Because it is not feasible to maintain systems in their original state with no modifications, the team's objective is to identify possible risks and ways to mitigate them. Brainstorming is one method of identifying potential problems. Documentation of actual defects is another. In either case, the FMEA (see Appendix D) and Risk Assessment and Mitigation Plan (see Exhibit 17.6) are effective tools for documenting the team's findings and recommendations. Exhibit 24.2 illustrates an FMEA that one change management team developed. As with all FMEAs, this one should be a "living" document, updated whenever new errors are uncovered or when risk mitigation plans are modified.

Release-Based Maintenance

Six Sigma companies know the value that reducing variation has in preventing defects. One of the most common and effective methods of

Exhibit 24.2 FMEA for Change Management

| Process Name: | GWC Change Management | | Date Prepared: 11/14/01 | | Revision Number: N/A |
| Prepared By: | George Greenbelt | | Revised By: | | Revision Date: |

Failure Modes and Effects Analysis (FMEA)

	What Could Happen?			Why and How Often?		How Do We Prevent It?			Action Plan				Results of Actions			
Process Step	Potential Failure Mode	Potential Failure Effects	SEV	Potential Causes	OCC	Current Controls	FAIL PROB	RPN	Actions Recommended	Resp.	Target Date	Actions Taken	SEV	OCC	DET	RPN
Emergency Bug Fix	Erroneous code is placed in production	Problem is exacerbated; system crashes	10	Incomplete testing	1	All changes are tested; QA certifies results; previous version of source and object code is retained	4	40								0
Routine Change Implementation	Not all modules are transferred to the correct libraries	Program does not work as expected	7	Carelessness	7	None	7	343	Implement release-based maintenance; require formal QA sign-off	GG	11/30/2001					0
Routine Change Implementation	More than one person is modifying the same module	Subsequent release does not include all modifications	10	No control of source code	4	None	4	160	Implement source code control using automated tool; add review of check out and check in procedures to QA audit procedure	QA	12/14/2001					0
								0								0
								0								0
								0								0
								0								0
								0								0
								0								0
								0								0
								0								0

reducing the risk associated with application maintenance is to implement release-based maintenance. The precept of release-based maintenance is that, except for emergency bug fixes, modifications to a system are applied in batches on a predetermined schedule rather than being implemented on an ad hoc basis whenever an individual change is complete. The advantages of this approach include:

- The frequency of system modifications is reduced, thus reducing the number of opportunities for failure.
- Releases are planned and scheduled like any project. Risks are reduced because a standard process is followed with an implementation schedule that includes all needed tasks. Once again, variation is reduced.
- Releases can be scheduled for the least critical times for the customers. If an error should occur, its impact would be less than if it were introduced during a key cycle. Furthermore, releases can be scheduled at a time when IT staff and customers are available to review the results.
- Costs are reduced because standard tasks such as quality assurance testing are performed less frequently.
- Defects should be reduced by the use of standard processes, including complete testing and sign-offs.

Although initially customers might be skeptical about the approach because some enhancements will be delayed, the improved quality and reduced risk normally convince them that the policy is a valuable one.

Step 4: Ensure that the Process Is Followed

The final step in change management as in any Six Sigma project is to establish a procedure that ensures that the process is followed and that the improvements continue to be achieved. That is, a control strategy must be developed. This includes the establishment of metrics that will accurately reflect the quality of the process and the development of steps to invoke if the process is "out of spec." The Six Sigma tool designed to document this process is the Control Plan (see Exhibit 9.2).

Chapter 9 outlines the steps that are typically included in this phase of a project. As discussed in Chapter 9, it is important to do more than draft a Control Plan. A process must be established to ensure that the measurements are taken and that any variations are addressed. Equally important, responsibility for the execution of the process must be clearly defined.

Change, whether it is to an existing system or to other aspects of the system development process, must be managed if it is to be successful. By treating change like any other process and employing Six Sigma tools, variation can be reduced and quality improved.

References

1. Womack, James P. and Jones, Daniel T., *Lean Thinking*. New York: Free Press, 2003.
2. George, Michael, *Lean Six Sigma for Service*. New York: McGraw-Hill, 2003, p. 17.

Chapter 25

System Maintenance and Support

Maintenance — the term evokes images of hordes of programmers making routine, single-line changes to code. Reality is far different. In many IT departments, all post-implementation support of a system is termed "maintenance." Under that definition, both responding to customers' questions about functionality and implementing large enhancements would be considered maintenance, along with fixing bugs and making the dreaded one-line coding changes. This apparent expansion of scope is the reason some IT shops have renamed their maintenance organizations "application support." By changing the name, they have made official what maintenance programmers have known for decades: that the work is multifaceted. And, as Chapter 23 points out, maintenance is the bulk of the iceberg that constitutes a system's life.

Before explaining how Six Sigma can benefit system maintenance, it is helpful to understand what it involves.

Categorizing Maintenance

Purists divide post-implementation work into three categories:

1. Maintenance
2. Enhancements
3. Support

Although, as noted below, there is some dispute over the difference between maintenance and enhancements, there is little discussion about support. The distinction that is made between support and the other two categories is that support involves no change to program code, while the others do. This might lead to the conclusion that support is a "functional" rather than a "technical" role and should be part of the customer department rather than IT. This conclusion is invalid. While the support function requires excellent customer interfacing skills, it is also a technical position because substantial investigation of the code may be required to resolve customer questions.

Maintenance, the first category, is subdivided into three groupings:

1. Corrective: fixes to bugs and other program errors. Corrective changes are designed to restore the system to its originally designed functionality.
2. Adaptive: work required by regulatory changes or changes in the business. These changes may add functionality but are nondiscretionary.
3. Perfective: modifications that add functionality but are not mandated.

Because enhancements also add functionality, the line between perfective maintenance and enhancements is a gray one. Many IT shops make the distinction based on the size of the modification, measured either in function points or hours of effort required.

Six Sigma and System Support

No matter how the work is classified, it is all related to change. In the case of program bugs, the customer discovers that something has changed when it should not have changed. Modifications reflect the fact that the business has changed, and the system must keep pace with it. Even questions about functionality deal with a dimension of change, because something is different. A new customer or a potentially new use for the system triggers these changes.

Maintenance is the process of changing a system, and as such it should be managed like any other project. And, like any Six Sigma project, what is important is ensuring that the process focuses on the customer so that the right changes are made at the right time in the right way.

The DMAIC model is helpful in establishing an effective support organization. The steps outlined in Chapter 24 provide a guideline to the process:

■ *Define* the work that is currently performed. Because the processes employed involve more than one department, a functional process map similar to the one shown as Exhibit 24.1 is an effective tool for documenting and understanding the maintenance function. The basic change management function shown in this exhibit can be expanded to include steps that are unique to maintenance and enhancements, with another process map developed to show the steps involved in resolving customer questions. As is true of all Six Sigma projects, the definition phase should include the identification of customers. Customers of system maintenance frequently include the Computer Operations department and the Help Desk, as well as those shown on Exhibit 24.1.

■ *Measure* the current effectiveness of the process. How satisfied are customers? How long does a typical modification take? What is the longest or shortest time required to implement a change? How many defects does the process have? Because it is typically a goal of IT to provide quality service as quickly as possible, measurement should include the time required to complete each step in the change process, including all wait states. This information will be used in the next step.

■ *Analyze* the variations and defects in the process to determine the root causes. Are delays the result of other departments not knowing the proposed schedule and not having needed staff available? Are there ways to eliminate the delays and make the process lean? What other forms of waste can be removed? Are defects caused by incomplete testing? Are customers unhappy because they are not involved in the work prioritization process?

■ *Improve* the process by removing the opportunities for variation and ensuring that the changes to be made are those that will have the maximum impact on customer requirements. In short, make fact-based, customer-focused decisions.

■ *Control* the resulting process by implementing metrics that identify shifts in performance and provide the mechanism for correcting them. Because they are updated frequently, dashboards are effective methods of identifying problems early enough in the process that they can be corrected before they have a serious negative effect on performance.

Customer Focus

Although it is important to develop a process to eliminate variation, it is equally important to ensure that the process focuses on and truly understands customers' needs and that the support organization has the skills to identify those requirements. While the work involved in maintenance is multifaceted, coding is only a small portion of it. Understanding customer requirements and analyzing the system to determine exactly where the modification should be made are typically the major efforts involved in any maintenance project.

The key element in all support, as was true in the development of the system, is the clear definition of customer requirements. Because, as was noted previously, incorrect changes to a production system can have a negative impact on the overall business, it is important that requirements be completely defined and that the effect of any system modification be fully understood. This is the reason a typical request for services (see Exhibit 17.2) includes at least one level of approval beyond the original requester.

Unfortunately, simply understanding what the customer would like done and how to implement that change does not ensure that IT will satisfy its customers. As Chapter 5 points out, it is important that customers prioritize their requirements and that all customers, not simply the ones who requested it, understand the impact of the change that is being proposed and agree with it.

Although there are a number of ways to prioritize requests, a Six Sigma IT department, recognizing the importance of customer involvement in all aspects of the support process, may go beyond prioritization and institute customer steering committees for the systems it supports.

The Steering Committee

One of the hallmarks of a Six Sigma company is the emphasis it places on teamwork. The steering committee is a specialized team, a group of customers with a vested interest in a specific system or group of systems. Its role is not only to review and prioritize individual requests for changes to the system, but also to prioritize the use of resources (human and machine) and to ensure that the system is operating at the desired level. A steering committee is truly the "voice of the customer." As such, it is important to have the right customers as members of the team.

The steering committee is typically convened by the Chief Information Officer (CIO) or a program manager within Information Technology, and that individual may serve as the facilitator or leader. Although the leader normally issues invitations to customer department heads, in large organizations it is common for department heads to delegate their responsibility and for lower ranking staff to be members of the steering committee. This is not a problem as long as the individuals chosen have the authority to speak for their departments.

As with all teams, it is important that the members of the steering committee have the right attributes. The characteristics shown in Exhibit 5.2 are as important for the steering committee as they are for Six Sigma process improvement projects. It is also important that the team members be knowledgeable about the system's functionality and its use within their departments.

One or More Committees?

One of the decisions that must be made before a steering committee is convened is whether it will oversee only one system or a number of them. Recognizing that customers are busy and that they will not want to attend meetings that appear to have little or no relevance to them, some IT departments may believe that it is wisest to have individual meetings for each application, while others will want to have only one steering committee for all systems.

Although there are a number of ways to make this determination, the decision between having a separate steering committee for each application and combining multiple systems can be based on the following criteria:

- Are the systems interrelated? If so, they should be grouped together, because changes to one system may affect another. In this case, it is important that all customers be aware of proposed modifications and be able to evaluate their impact on their departments.
- If the applications are not interrelated, do they use the same technology (programming language, database, and hardware platform)? If they do and if it would be feasible to transfer staff from support of one system to another based on business priorities, the systems should be grouped. In this case, the steering committee would be asked to weigh the value of a proposed modification on the business as a whole and to determine whether work on another system should be deferred while a high-priority request is completed for the first system.

It is also possible to have two levels of customer meetings: one to prioritize routine requests, the other to serve as a true steering committee, evaluating overall performance and high-level resource shifts. In this case, the lower-level meeting would typically address only a single system.

Under some circumstances, a steering committee may not be needed. These circumstances include:

- The system is stable and has few requests for enhancements.
- There is only a single customer department that uses the system, and all requests are approved by a single person within that department.

The majority of systems, however, can benefit from being managed by a steering committee.

Charters and Agendas

When the steering committee is first convened, it is helpful to develop a team charter. Although this need not be as extensive as the typical project charter (see Appendix A), a written document that outlines the team's commitments is an effective tool for ensuring a common understanding. Exhibit 25.1 shows the format of a steering committee charter.

Exhibit 25.1   Steering Committee Charter

Summary			
Process Impacted	General ledger, accounts payable and accounts receivable systems		
Team Leader	George Greenbelt	Champion	Oscar Early
Start Date	September 17, 2001	Target completion date	On-going
Project Description	Review system support, prioritize outstanding requests for service, review and revise service leaves as needed.		
Team Membership				
---	---	---	---	---
Name	Role	Department	% Time	GB Trained?
George Greenbelt	Team leader	IT	4 hours per month	Yes
Giselle Ledger	Team member	Finance	2 hours per month	Yes
Alan Payer	Team member	Finance	2 hours per month	No
Adele Received	Team member	Finance	2 hours per month	Yes
Schedule				
---	---	---	---	---
Milestone/ Deliverable	Target Date	Owner	Estimated Cost	Comments
Initial Meeting	9/24/01	George Greenbelt		
Initial SLA Review	1/02/02	GG		
Revision History			
Revision Number	Authors		Date

Exhibit 25.2   Steering Committee Meeting Agenda

GWC Finance Systems Steering Committee Agenda
Monday, October 22, 2001
Conference Room 1

Time		Responsibility
10:00 – 10:10	GRACE	Greenbelt
10:10 – 10:30	Review of monthly metrics	Greenbelt
10:30 – 10:50	Review of project from customer perspective	Ledger
10:50 – 11:25	Review and prioritization of open requests	Greenbelt
11:25 – 11:30	Other business	Greenbelt

Minutes will be issued by close of business Tuesday, October 23.

It is also helpful to have a standard agenda for the steering committee's meeting. Exhibit 25.2 outlines a typical agenda. As noted, one of the steering committee's responsibilities is the prioritization of requests. Development of a cost/time/impact ranking similar to Exhibit 7.10 is helpful in this process. The other key responsibility is the assessment of how well the system is functioning. This is typically accomplished by reviewing actual performance against service level agreements.

Service Level Agreements

As Six Sigma companies know, it is important to make decisions based on facts. When evaluating the IT department's support of a system, it is normal to have a series of metrics that report the level of support provided. Although this is an essential part of the evaluation process, unless there are clearly identified expectations for support, the metrics are of little value. If, for example, IT reports that system availability for the month was 95 percent but there is no context, who can say whether this is a good or bad level of support? Was system availability 98 percent for the preceding six months? What level does the customer require? To avoid this problem and set the context, IT and the customer should establish service level agreements.

A service level agreement (or SLA as it is normally called) is a formal contract that specifies the level of support to be provided. There are three principles that should be employed when developing an SLA:

1. *Apply the SMART criteria.* As was true when customer requirements were developed, SLAs should be SMART. Although all of the characteristics are important, it is essential that the SLA be relevant. For example, an SLA related to customer calls might measure response time as follows: "99 percent of all severity one problems will be responded to within five minutes of their being entered into the call tracking system. Coverage will be provided 24/7 365 days a year." This service level is specific, measurable, attainable, and timebound. It may not, however, be relevant. What is meaningful to customers is normally how quickly a problem is *resolved*, not how quickly the analyst responded to a call. Similarly, an SLA for enhancements might be, "1000 function points will be placed into production, defect-free, each month." The problem with this service level is that customers rarely understand function point counting, making the SLA if not irrelevant, then at least confusing to them.

2. *Keep it simple.* Although it is possible to develop long, intricate SLAs that cover every possible situation, the best are those that are simple and easy to understand. Wherever possible, legalese should be avoided in favor of simple declarative sentences. "We will resolve or find a work-around for all severity one problems within eight hours of the problem being logged into the call tracking system. We will provide 24/7 coverage to meet this commitment." This SLA is simple and easy to understand. Additionally, the use of the first-person plural pronoun sets a tone of commitment and partnership with the customer.

3. *Focus on the key few.* While it is tempting to establish dozens of SLAs, the reality is that only a few will be of critical importance to the customers. These are the ones that should be carefully developed, monitored, and reported each month. Typically, key SLAs number no more than five and might include:
   a. *System availability.* Was the system running when needed? This SLA may have several parts, depending on the time of day or month. The Finance department, for example, is normally more concerned about system availability during the closing cycle than at other times during the month.
   b. *Speed of bug fixes.* How quickly were problems resolved? Again, there may be several parts to this SLA, depending on the severity of the problem. Severity three or nuisance problems do not require immediate 24/7 resolution.

c. *Schedule fidelity.* How well did IT meet its target dates, particularly for enhancements?

d. *Cost of poor quality.* If defects were introduced when changes were made or if the system was not available when needed, what effect did this have on the customers? It is possible to quantify COPQ in terms of hours of work lost as well as lost sales or increased costs.

e. *Customer satisfaction.* How happy are the customers with the service being provided? Customer satisfaction is normally assessed through the use of a survey, as discussed below.

Exhibit 25.3 shows a portion of an SLA.

Exhibit 25.3   Sample SLA

Service	*Service Level*
Respond to and resolve functional and operational problems with the system.	We will resolve or implement a work around for 99 percent of all problems, based on their severity, within the following timeframes:
	Severity *Resolution Time*
	1 1 hour
	2 8 working hours
	3 3 working days
	We will resolve or implement a work around for the remaining 1 percent in no more than double the time shown.
	We will provide coverage 24/7, 365 days a year except for a two-hour system maintenance period between 2 and 4 p.m. Eastern time each Sunday.
Ensure that system is available when required.	System will be available and fully operational 99 percent of the time between 8 a.m. and 6 p.m. Eastern time, Monday through Friday, excluding company holidays. "Fully operational" means that all system functions will be present and that 100 concurrent users will experience response time delays of no more than one second.

Once SLAs have been established, they should be treated like formal contracts. This means that they should be written and signed by both parties. There should be penalty clauses for failure to meet the agreed-upon SLAs and — although this is less common — there should be rewards for consistent overachievement of the service levels.

As with all aspects of change, communication is important. SLAs should be explained to both the IT staff and the customer departments. This helps to improve communication between the groups and to ensure that there is a common understanding of expectations and responsibility. IT needs to know how it will be measured, and customers need to agree that these measurements reflect their requirements.

Similarly, performance against the SLAs must be tracked and should be reported not only to the steering committee, but also to the IT staff and the customer department. A scorecard similar to the one shown as Exhibit 9.4, which displays historical performance as well as goals, is an effective way to report metrics. Again, the objective is to focus on what is important to the customer and to provide facts about how well the customers' requirements are being met in as simple a format as possible.

Customer Satisfaction Surveys

Six Sigma companies recognize that it is possible to meet all objective criteria of success and still have dissatisfied customers. This is why they issue customer satisfaction surveys: they want to ensure that they have delighted their customers.

Surveys are, however, a two-edged sword. It is possible to decrease customer satisfaction by sending out a survey. If customers feel that responding to a survey is a nuisance or that their responses are ignored, they will — understandably — not be pleased, and the results of the survey will reflect that displeasure.

A few steps can help to make surveys meaningful:

1. *Keep them short.* While some surveys are several pages in length and ask dozens of questions, the most effective are the ones that take less than a minute of the customer's time to answer. This is a corollary to the "focus on the key few" principle of SLAs. When compiling the questionnaire, it is helpful to ask, "What action will I take based on this?" and "If I could only gather five pieces of information, would this be one?" One survey asked customers whether the IT staff was professionally dressed, leading a cynical customer to ask if the dress code was more important than delivering quality services.

2. *Keep them focused.* If IT is surveying customers for multiple reasons, it may be desirable to create surveys tailored to each type of service provided. Exhibit 25.4 shows the difference between surveys circulated to customers who reported a production problem and those who requested a system enhancement. The production support survey is shorter, reflecting the fact that the elapsed time was less than for an enhancement, and that the customer would have had less contact with the person performing the work.

Exhibit 25.4   Customer Satisfaction Survey

Customer Satisfaction Survey Production Support

Problem Number:

System:

We value your opinion.

We recently responded to a problem or question ticket that you opened. Please let us know how well we met your needs.

Category	Ranking					
	Excellent	Very Good	Satisfactory	Fair	Poor	N/A
QUALITY OF WORK Did our work meet your requirements?						
ON-TIME DELIVERY Did we resolve the problem/question when we promised we would?						
DEFECTS Was our work defect free?						
OVER ALL SATISFACTION How would you rate the quality of service we provided?						
COMMENTS						

Would you like a follow-up call to discuss your ratings? _____ (Yes) _____ (No)

If yes, please complete the following:

Name	
Phone	
Preferred time to be called	

Exhibit 25.4   Customer Satisfaction Survey (continued)

Customer Satisfaction Survey Enhancement

Project Number:

System:

We value your opinion.

We recently completed a system enhancement for you. Please let us know how well we met your needs.

Category	Ranking					
	Excellent	Very Good	Satisfactory	Fair	Poor	N/A
QUALITY OF WORK How well did our work meet your requirements?						
ON-TIME DELIVERY Did we complete the work when we promised we would?						
DEFECTS Was our work defect free?						
PERFORMANCE TO BUDGET Was our work completed within budget?						
ISSUE RESOLUTION If problems occurred, how well did we resolve them?						
PERSONNEL ASSIGNED How would you rate the staff assigned to your project?						
COMMUNICATION Did we keep you adequately informed about our progress?						
OVERALL SATISFACTION How would you rate the quality of service we provided?						
COMMENTS						

Would you like a follow-up call to discuss your ratings? ____ (Yes) _____ (No)

If yes, please complete the following:

Name	
Phone	
Preferred time to be called	

3. *Keep them simple.* Use the simplest English possible and ensure that each question asks for only one piece of information. Compare "Were you apprised of the projected timeframe for the project? Did we communicate our progress pursuant to our agreement? Was the project completed to your satisfaction within an appropriate time?" with "Did we complete the project when we said we would?" In the first case, the customer had to make subjective decisions (What is an "appropriate" time?) and faced a dilemma if the IT staff member had completed only part of the question. What if she had told him of the projected timeframe but had not communicated progress? Which rating would be appropriate? In the second example, there was no confusion.

4. *Send them at the appropriate time.* There is no single answer to the question of what is the appropriate time. Although some IT departments choose to survey all customers on a quarterly basis, they run the risk of customers who submitted only one request during that period having forgotten what services were provided by the time they receive the survey. To avoid that problem, IT may choose to survey customers at the completion of a piece of work. While this is appropriate for the customer who has occasional requests, receiving a survey for each request could be annoying to a customer who submits multiple requests in a month. Just as it may be necessary to create more than one survey, IT should consider being flexible about the timing with which it distributes surveys.

5. *Provide individual feedback, if requested.* All surveys should include a question asking if the respondent would like to be contacted about his or her ratings and comments. Even if survey results are compiled and reported quarterly, if the response requests follow-up, IT should ensure that it is done almost immediately. A dissatisfied customer's dissatisfaction will only grow if complaints are ignored. Conversely, even if they have not requested follow-up, if customers praise a specific member of the IT staff, it is appropriate to respond with a simple "thank you."

6. *Publish the results.* No one likes being part of the black hole syndrome, where surveys are collected but there are no visible results. If customer satisfaction surveys are to provide value, the results should be summarized and published on a regular basis — typically quarterly. In addition to the individual quarter's results, it is helpful to display both the goal, as defined in the SLA, and previous periods' results. This will allow people to see trends. Additionally, if the results do not meet the goal, the survey should be accompanied by an explanation of actions planned to improve performance. Exhibit 25.5 provides a sample report of customer satisfaction results.

Exhibit 25.5   Customer Satisfaction Report

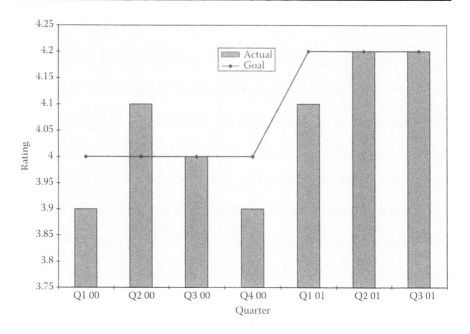

Ensuring Successful Maintenance

Whether it is called maintenance or support, the work that is done after a system is first implemented represents up to 75 percent of the system's total cost. It is critical to the business and to IT's continued credibility that this work be performed efficiently and effectively. The key to this success is to treat maintenance like any other project. That means:

- Create a well-defined process.
- Ensure that customers are involved in every step of the process.
- Define and communicate expected results.
- Establish clear accountability for achieving those results.
- Measure performance and implement procedural changes when needed.

In short, focus on customers and quality.

VI

INCORPORATING SIX SIGMA INTO OTHER DEVELOPMENT METHODOLOGIES

In response to the shortcomings of the traditional waterfall SDLC, the IT industry developed a number of different methods for developing systems, notably Rapid Application Development (RAD), prototyping, and spiral or iterative development.

Chapter 26 explores the advantages of RAD, distinguishing between joint requirements planning (JRP) and joint application development (JAD) sessions, and explaining the roles that facilitators play in both types of meetings.

Chapter 27 discusses prototyping and its extension, spiral development, along with the Six Sigma tools that will enhance them.

The final chapter of Section VI outlines the technical challenges that accompany client/server and Web-based development projects and shows how the tools used in the Measurement and Analysis phases of Six Sigma can help identify and reduce the variation inherent in these technologies.

Chapter 26

Rapid Application Development

Although the traditional waterfall SDLC is a proven method for developing systems and provides a high level of structure to the process, as noted in Section IV, there are distinct disadvantages to it, most notably the elapsed time between definition of requirements and the delivery of a system, and the lack of customer involvement throughout the process. The concept of rapid application development or RAD was one of the IT industry's answers to these problems.

Unlike the waterfall SDLC, with its dependence on manually generated specification documents and program code, its long timeframes, and its low level of customer involvement, RAD is characterized by short timeframes, extensive customer involvement, and the use of computer-aided software engineering (CASE) tools, which automate portions of the development cycle.

A Six Sigma company would applaud RAD because it reduces variation, shortens cycle times, and increases customer focus. Although these are advantages, they can be enhanced. It is possible to increase the effectiveness of a RAD project through the use of standard Six Sigma concepts and tools. Furthermore, because RAD projects are, by definition, new development, they can benefit from the application of DFSS tools and techniques.

JRP and JAD

RAD projects begin with JRP (joint requirements planning) and JAD (joint application development) sessions. The primary difference between the two is that JRP is used to develop the high-level requirements for a system, while JAD sessions develop the detailed specifications. As is suggested by the names, in both cases, the work is done as a joint effort between customers and the IT department. These steps correspond to the Project Initiation and System Analysis phases of a traditional SDLC or Definition in the DMAIC model. RAD corresponds to the Identification and Definition phases of DFSS's IDDOV.

The success of JRP and JAD, like the success of Six Sigma projects, depends on a number of items, including selecting the right participants, facilitator, and location. It is also essential that the problem to be solved and the goals of the project be clearly defined and understood before the JRP and JAD sessions begin. Without this common vision, normally established and articulated by the champion, the project may not achieve the desired results. The project charter (see Appendix A) is the tool of choice for defining and communicating the project's goals.

The Role of DFSS

Although RAD was developed long before DFSS became part of the business vocabulary, the RAD methodology can benefit from the inclusion of DFSS tools and techniques. Because customer involvement is critical, the project team needs to ensure that all customers are identified. The value chain map (see Exhibit 11.3) can help with that identification. The use of a SIPOC (see Exhibit 11.5) enables the team to clearly visualize the boundaries of the project, while the QFD (see Appendix F) with its multiple levels ensures that requirements are captured, prioritized, and addressed at the appropriate stage of the life cycle. Other tools and their applicability are noted below.

Selecting the Participants

As is true of all projects, it is essential to have the correct people participating. While the overall project will have a core team, some of whom will join the JRP and JAD sessions, it is important to ensure that the right customers participate in the these meetings. JRP will normally involve higher-ranking members of the customer departments because this is where the overall strategy is set, while JAD will focus on the staff members who perform or supervise the work. In both cases, however, the project leader should consider the characteristics of effective team members (see Exhibit 5.2) when inviting people to participate in the sessions. In addition to the characteristics shown in the exhibit, it is equally important that the customer team members have an in-depth understanding of their function, their strengths, shortcomings, and opportunities for improvement.

While a formal project charter may not be created specifically for a JRP or JAD session, an abbreviated version similar to the Steering Committee Charter (see Exhibit 25.1) is useful in ensuring that all team members understand the schedule, time commitment, and overall purpose. This is in addition to the project charter, which addresses the entire project. It is helpful to send a copy of the JRP or JAD charter minus the participants' names to department heads and other staff members who are deciding who will attend, because the charter specifies both time commitments and the proposed schedule and will help the decision makers select the appropriate participants.

The Role of the Facilitator

Because of the intense nature of the sessions, many companies utilize a trained facilitator for JAD and JRP. The facilitator may or may not be familiar with the function that is being automated, but he or she should possess the following skills:

- *Facilitation.* Facilitation, the dictionary explains, is the act of making easier. The fundamental reason for having a facilitator is to simplify the process of JRP and JAD by providing a structured forum, leading the group, and encouraging active participation. One of the first things a facilitator may do is to conduct ice-breaking exercises designed to help transform the participants from a group of individuals into a team.
- *Communication.* The facilitator's responsibilities include asking the right questions to elicit the needed information. Facilitators are normally trained to ask open-ended questions and to devise exercises that will encourage all team members to be active participants. One such exercise might be brainstorming the future state of the function to develop a framework for a new system.
- *Listening.* Just as important as asking the right questions is the ability to hear what is not said. A participant may answer that her view of the future includes all customer orders being placed online. In response, the facilitator may ask whether the profile of the customer of the future requires access to a computer or whether

there will still be a need — albeit reduced — for telephone and faxed orders. Use of the Kano model (see Exhibit 11.8) and an explanation that important requirements are frequently unspoken can help the team identify the full spectrum of customer needs.

▪ *Negotiation.* One of the facilitator's key skills should be the ability to build consensus. It is important that the team emerge from the JRP or JAD sessions with a common, agreed-upon understanding of what is required for the new system and how it will work.

In summary, the facilitator's role, like that of a Green Belt or a Black Belt on Six Sigma projects, is to guide the team through the process, ensuring that the correct tools are used and that the desired results are achieved.

Optimizing the Meeting Location

When appraising a house, realtors claim that three things are important: (1) location, (2) location, and (3) location. While this might be an exaggeration for JAD and JRP sessions, there is no doubt that the correct location can improve the chances for success. Ideal locations have three characteristics:

▪ *Off-site.* Because JRP and JAD sessions are often multi-day meetings, they benefit from being held off-site. Not only does this provide a break from the participants' routine and emphasize the importance of the sessions, but physically distancing participants from their offices and the concomitant disruptions also contributes to the meeting's success.

▪ *Well-equipped.* Facilitators recognize the importance of having the correct tools at their disposal. These include, at a minimum, flipcharts or electronic whiteboards with markers in a variety of colors. Some facilitators find that using different colors to represent different types of information is helpful to participants. Problems can be scribed in red, while solutions are green, and open items are blue. Because it is desirable to refer to the results of brainstorming and other exercises throughout the session, the ideal room will have walls that permit the hanging of flipchart pages and sufficient space for multiple flipchart easels to be in use simultaneously.

▪ *Adequately sized.* All-day and multi-day sessions are, by their very nature, stressful for participants. Having rooms that are over-sized for the number of participants will increase participants' comfort and improve the probability of success. Some facilitators find a

U-shaped table conducive to team formation, particularly if the room provides areas for the group to break into smaller teams for individual exercises.

Effective Sessions

Like all meetings, JRP and JAD sessions can benefit from a protocol similar to GRACE. Although the team leader may have distributed the team charter to all participants in advance, it is important to reiterate the purpose of the meeting, to understand participants' expectations (and to recalibrate them, if needed), to explain the process that will be followed, and to establish a code of conduct (see Exhibit 5.4) and meeting roles (see Exhibit 5.3).

While a standard company code of conduct might be adequate for most meetings, during RAD one additional principle is needed. Participants should agree that everyone will own the output of the sessions. No matter what disagreements might occur during the development of requirements or a system design, it is important that the group be committed to reach consensus.

The CASE tools that are used during the JRP and JAD sessions will dictate the format and, to some extent, the content of the products that are generated during the sessions. They should, however, be supplemented with Six Sigma tools. As noted previously, a clear understanding of the problem to be resolved and a common vision of the future are essential. Similarly, although CASE does not dictate it, the project should begin with the creation of a process map, because it is essential to understand the current process before trying to change it. A draft process map may have been drawn in advance and presented to the team for review and correction as part of one of the initial exercises. Refining the process map can be viewed as one of the first steps to building consensus among the group.

Once requirements are identified, they should be prioritized using a customer requirements matrix similar to the one shown as Exhibit 5.15. This helps ensure that the project is properly focused. Using a QFD (see Appendix F) in lieu of the customer requirements matrix (see Exhibit 18.2) allows the team to document requirements at the correct level.

In addition to ranking requirements, customers can further divide requirements into those that must be implemented in the first version of the system and those that, while still important, are less urgent and can be delayed until a subsequent release. This segmentation is useful in developing an implementation plan. It is also helpful in developing a "to-be" process map. Like the "as-is" map, this is not part of standard RAD but helps improve communication and ensure that decisions are fact-based.

At the same time that they are identifying and prioritizing requirements, the team is frequently brainstorming alternative solutions. A Pugh concept selection matrix (see Exhibit 12.2) is an effective way of evaluating potential solutions and designing one that incorporates the best aspects of the others.

Communication

As is true of all projects, open, frequent communication is essential to the success of RAD. It is likely that questions will arise during the JRP and JAD sessions that cannot be resolved at that time. To ensure that they are not overlooked, the facilitator should keep a separate "open issues" list on one of the flipcharts. Prior to the end of the session, the list should be reviewed and responsibilities and target completion dates assigned. A designated member of the team should have responsibility for publishing the list of open issues and providing periodic updates to all team members. Exhibit 26.1 shows a sample open item log. Because the log can be used throughout the project, with completed items removed and new ones added, some teams refer to this as a RAIL (or rolling action item log).

Exhibit 26.1   Rolling Action Item Log (RAIL)

Item Number	Date Opened	Description	Assigned To	Target Completion Date	Status Date	Status	Actual Completion Date
1	9/25/01	Determine number of transactions currently processed each day and when peak periods are	G. Greenbelt	10/31/01; revised to 11/05/01; revised to 12/05/01	10/15/01	Quarter-end volume may not be representative; will extend measurement through October month end	12/05/01
					10/29/01	Customer has requested two months' data; completion has been extended	
2	9/25/01	Ask Fred Finance whether project can be charged against reserve	S.Service	10/01/01		Reserve has been exhausted; project cannot be charged against it	10/01/01

Although CASE tools automate some of the process of system development once requirements have been defined, the basic steps are similar to those employed during a traditional SDLC, and the concepts and Six Sigma tools used during a waterfall development project can be applied to RAD. Chapters 19 through 22 describe the post-requirements definition phases of the traditional SDLC.

The value of RAD, as its name implies, is that it can shorten the system life cycle. Although code generators reduce the time required to actually create a program module, the primary advantage is that by having customers as active participants in the requirements definition and design phases, the chance of missing or misunderstood requirements, both of which cause rework and delays, decreases.

Done properly, RAD means that defects decrease and customer satisfaction increases, bringing system development one step closer to the Six Sigma goal of near-perfection.

Chapter 27

Prototyping and Spiral Development

As noted previously, techniques for system development continue to evolve, with each iteration bringing IT closer to its goals of providing customers with defect-free systems in the timeframe that they need them. Although RAD helps reduce the time required for system development and encourages more active customer participation in the life cycle, developing the system is still a linear process, and as such it has some of the shortcomings of the traditional waterfall methodology. The most important of these is the need for customers to fully define and communicate their requirements at the beginning of the process.

JRP and JAD sessions increase the likelihood of complete and accurate definition and, because CASE tools reduce the time to deliver a system, there is a lower probability that business requirements will change dramatically between the time a project is initiated and when the system is finally delivered. It is, however, unrealistic to expect customers to be able to define their requirements completely, particularly when new technologies are involved. And new technologies are the lifeblood of IT.

When executive information systems (EIS) were first introduced, it was difficult to explain their value to those who had not actually seen them and did not understand the concept of drill-down. Similarly, during the early stages of Web technology, customers who had not experienced shopping or searching for information online had difficulty defining the navigational patterns for their own systems.

Prototyping

One of IT's first answers to these dilemmas was prototyping. The primary purpose of prototyping is to assist customers in the definition of requirements. As such, it is particularly useful when requirements are unclear or when customers are unfamiliar with the technology that IT is proposing to use.

At its simplest, prototyping is the development of a model of the system. Unlike the prototype discussed in Chapter 15, this model typically has minimal functionality but serves to demonstrate screen designs and system navigation. As such, it should be viewed as part of the definition phase in the either the DMAIC or the IDDOV model. It is a tool to assist in the development of requirements. In RAD, prototyping follows JRP and JAD sessions. IT takes basic requirements that were developed during those sessions, creates a prototype of the system, and then presents that prototype to the customers for validation.

The advantages of this approach are:

- *Increased customer participation.* Although they were involved in previous steps, prototyping extends the period that customers remain active participants in the system development. This has the positive effect of increasing the customer's sense of ownership of the finished product.
- *Improved communication.* The prototype provides a new form of communication between customers and IT. If a picture is worth a thousand words, a prototype is worth ten times that. While requirements documents and mockups of screen design such as those included in a traditional functional design specification (see Exhibit 19.1) are helpful in understanding the proposed system, a working model is a far more powerful communication tool and one that is particularly useful in managing customer expectations.
- *Reduced ambiguity.* This is a corollary to improved communication. Not only do prototypes increase the level of communication, but they also enhance it by ensuring that the communication is effective. Just as programmers frequently discover that apparently complete requirements documents have missing pieces once they begin to code from the specifications, so also do customers learn that their understanding of what IT was proposing differs from IT's own vision. Working together to review the prototype, the two groups can develop a common vision. The prototype can also help the team identify the unspoken basic and excitement needs outlined on the Kano model (see Exhibit 11.8).
- *Increased speed.* Because it is a shell rather than a fully functional system and lacks the underlying code that provides editing, exception

handling, and calculations, the development of a prototype is faster and cheaper than developing a complete system. While prototyping may be seen as an additional step that would increase the length of the overall project schedule, the opposite is true. By helping customers validate their requirements and IT's design, prototyping may actually shorten the development life cycle. And, by ensuring that requirements are more closely met in the initial implementation, a prototype will reduce the overall cost of the system by reducing future enhancements.

Although the advantages outweigh the disadvantages, there are pitfalls to the prototyping process:

■ *Customers may want to use the prototype and will be disappointed by the lack of full functionality.* This problem can be mitigated by carefully explaining that what is being presented is only a shell. It should be compared to the small-scale model that architects create as part of their proposal for major buildings. It can resemble the finished product, but the lighting and plumbing are missing. It is not a prototype in the DFSS Verification definition of the term.

■ *Customers may expect a finished product in an unrealistic time-frame.* Because it is relatively quick and easy to develop a prototype, customers may believe that the entire system can be delivered in a matter of days or weeks, rather than months. Again, careful communication will help reduce this risk. The architectural example may prove helpful. Large buildings are not completed overnight.

Because it encourages close cooperation between IT and customers, and because it helps both groups make decisions based on facts, prototyping brings system development one step closer to Six Sigma. The value of prototyping is highest when it is viewed as an extension of the requirements definition and when the results are used as input to the development of design specifications. As with all Six Sigma projects, decisions and the reasons behind them should be documented on a TMAP, errors should be tracked on an error analysis spreadsheet (see Exhibit 20.1) with high frequency problems analyzed and corrective actions developed and documented on an FMEA (see Exhibit 19.5).

Spiral or Iterative Development

The adaptability of IT as a profession is shown by the introduction of spiral development. Recognizing that prototyping had distinct advantages

Exhibit 27.1   Spiral Development

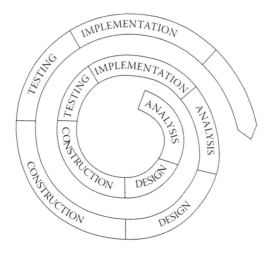

but was also burdened by some shortcomings, the industry attempted to mitigate those disadvantages through spiral or iterative development. The underlying concepts of this methodology are that system development is an evolutionary process, that customers will be able to define only a small portion of their requirements at the beginning of a project, and that there are substantial benefits to be derived from delivering functionality — even limited functionality — quickly.

Rather than force customers to attempt to specify all their needs at one time, in spiral development customers define only the basic outline of a system during the initial requirements definition phase. That limited set of requirements is converted into a system, which is then placed into production. Unlike a prototype, this system, although it is a subset of the final system, has full functionality. It is a complete implementation of the requirements that were defined. The customers use the system and, based on that use, expand their requirements.

As shown in Exhibit 27.1, the cycle is repeated, and each time the system has greater functionality. If this chart looks similar to Exhibit 4.2, there is a good reason. Both spiral development and Six Sigma have as one of their fundamental beliefs that improvement is continuous. Once a cycle is complete, whether it is DMAIC or analysis, design, construction, testing, and implementation, it begins again.

There are a number of advantages to spiral development:

■ *Shortened cycle time.* Because the functionality of each iteration is limited, IT can deliver the system quickly. And, unlike a prototype, this is a fully functional system that customers can use.

- *Increased customer involvement.* Unlike prototyping, where customers were relegated to the background once the prototype was reviewed and IT began to develop the final system, spiral development keeps the customers involved almost constantly. As soon as a version is implemented, customers begin the process of defining requirements for the next version.
- *Increased system flexibility.* It is almost an axiom that business requirements will have changed during a traditional system development life cycle, rendering the system at least partially obsolete before it is implemented. With iterative development, the system's functionality can be altered as business requirements evolve rather than waiting until the full system is completed.

While a traditional IT department might find disadvantages to spiral development, a Six Sigma company would have a different perspective and would consider them advantages rather than shortcomings:

- *Spiral development requires a greater commitment from the customer.* Without virtually constant customer involvement, the system will not be developed, because IT is relying on customers to use the system and then, based on their experiences with it, to define the next set of functionality to be added. A Six Sigma company would consider this need for commitment an advantage, noting that nothing should be undertaken without customer commitment and involvement.
- *It is more difficult to define the end state of a spiral development project than a traditionally developed system.* As customers become accustomed to defining additional functionality, it is possible to have runaway systems that are never declared finished but are constantly tweaked. Again, a Six Sigma company with its belief in continuous improvement would find the iterative aspects of system development an advantage. The same company would, however, ensure that the changes that are requested and implemented are not frivolous and that the system is never considered runaway. Using tools such as the customer requirements matrix (see Exhibit 5.15) and the impact analysis (see Exhibit 8.1), the project team can evaluate the value of requested changes, ensuring that they meet customer requirements. For companies trained in DFSS, the QFD is the tool of choice. Before new features are implemented, the team can analyze the impact each will — or will not — have on customer requirements. The decision to defer or never implement a specific function can be made based on the facts shown on the QFD.

To ensure success, the team should remember that there are two forces affecting their design: (1) customer requirements and (2) process capability (Exhibit 10.2). Before each iteration begins, it is critical to ensure that the infrastructure will have the needed capacity.

Phased Delivery

A hybrid of traditional SDLC and iterative development is phased delivery. In it, although all requirements are defined at the beginning of the project, the actual implementation is broken into phases. This is the approach that the GWC Order Entry team took for its self-service order entry system. Core functionality is delivered as part of the first release, with additional modules implemented later. Unlike iterative development, where the functionality of subsequent releases is determined once the preceding version of the software is delivered, in phased delivery, the content of each phase is clearly defined and the scope of the project is finite.

Phased delivery has many of the advantages of both prototyping and iterative development (shorter cycle times, reduced ambiguity, improved communication, and customer involvement) without the disadvantages. Although the overall project schedule is established at the beginning of the project, if business requirements change as the system is being implemented, it is possible to modify the system at that point rather than wait until it is fully developed. The primary disadvantage is the challenge imposed by attempting to define all requirements at the beginning of the project.

As discussed in Chapter 18, although there are no foolproof methods for ensuring that all requirements are identified, an understanding and application of the Kano model and the use of a QFD can help.

RAD, prototyping, iterative development, and phased delivery all seek to mitigate the disadvantages of the traditional SDLC, and each succeeds to some extent. The decision to use one of these life-cycle models rather than a waterfall methodology is normally based on the complexity of the system to be developed, the degree of customer involvement possible, and the experience of the IT staff. As noted in Chapter 16, the waterfall methodology is well suited for less-experienced staff and does not demand the extensive customer involvement that the newer methodologies do.

All forms of system development, however, can benefit from the rigorous application of the basic Six Sigma concepts:

- Understand the customer's requirements.
- Ensure that the system meets those requirements.
- Keep the customer involved.

Chapter 28

Client/Server and Web-Based Systems

The previous chapters dealt with various methodologies for developing systems and showed how the use of Six Sigma and DFSS tools could enhance them. When discussing client/server and Web-based systems, the primary issue is not methodology, but technology. As a result, a different set of tools comes into play, with DFSS techniques being of particular importance.

The Challenge

Client/server and Web-based systems can be developed using any methodology. What sets them apart from their character- and mainframe-based predecessors is their technical complexity and the variation that results from it. Even the simplest client/server system has inherent complexity because processing is distributed. Instead of having all processing done on the mainframe, some logic is performed on the client workstation and some on the server (which may be anything from a PC to a mainframe). To further complicate the system, a separate database server can provide a portion of the processing. Add to that the fact that different operating systems (or versions thereof) can exist on each of the workstations and that multiple servers, each from a different hardware manufacturer and each running a different operating system, can be used, and the complexity becomes exponential. In Six Sigma terms, the opportunities for variation are high. In DFSS terms, the process capability (see Exhibit 10.2) may not be sufficient to meet customer requirements and create an ideal design.

Although modeling of the design, as discussed in Chapter 13, is important for any new system development project, it is particularly critical on client/server and Web-based systems because of their complexity.

Exhibit 28.1 shows some of the items that IT typically inventories for a workstation. A similar list of components exists for servers. To further increase the complexity, workstations and servers are connected by local area and wide area networks, each with a variety of hardware and software components.

Although this complexity can — and should — be invisible to the customer, it is of vital importance to IT. Before any coding begins, the

Exhibit 28.1   Workstation Inventory

Manufacturer

Model

Serial Number

Operating System

O/S Version

Amount of Memory

Disk Size

Browser

- Vendor

- Version

Word Processing Software

- Vendor

- Version

Spread Sheet

- Vendor

- Version

Email

- Vendor

- Version

Presentation Graphics

- Vendor

- Version

Other Software

- Vendor

- Version

project team should follow the steps for Development of Concept outlined in Chapter 13. Identifying potential failure modes and devising methods to prevent them are as critical as modeling the design. The objective of both is to ensure that the system will be able to meet customer requirements. If the process capability is not available or the system appears to be prone to failure, the design should be reworked until customer requirements and process capability are in balance.

Reducing Variation through Testing

Once the system is designed and coded, additional rigor is required during testing. In addition to proving that the system they have developed delivers the functionality the customer has requested, IT must ensure that response time meets customer expectations and that the software can operate successfully while other workstation-based applications are being used. Perfect functionality is of no value if the system fails the usability test. Unfortunately, that usability can depend on things other than the application IT developed.

To determine the causes of variation and ways to eliminate them, the project team can benefit from the techniques used in the Measurement and Analysis phases of DMAIC (see Chapters 22 and 23). Although it is possible that variations in performance will be identified during the normal testing process, the team should not assume that the absence of a problem means that none will occur. As part of stress testing, the team should attempt to create performance problems by varying as many inputs as possible, then creating a full design of experiments (DOE).

Although the team might hypothesize that the differences they observed in response time are related to time of the day or to a specific workstation operating system, it is important to make changes based on facts rather than suppositions. The team should measure response time, being careful to include as many different workstation, network, and server combinations as possible and to test at various times of the day, with varying numbers of other applications running on the workstations and servers. At this point, because of the sheer volume of data being collected, a statistical software package is helpful in analyzing the data. It can also be used to create additional simulations as the Just Right Widget team did during the Optimization phase of DFSS (see Chapter 14) and again when stress testing the prototype (see Chapter 15).

Producing a control chart (see Exhibit 7.2) will show the upper and lower control limits for the process and will help distinguish between special and common causes of variation. The team may also want to calculate the process capability (see Exhibit 6.20) to obtain the "voice of the process" and compare that to the customers' specifications, the "voice of the customer."

Both the control and process capability charts are likely to confirm what the team already knows, namely that the process does not meet the requirements. The reason for producing the charts is that they quantify the difference between the process and the requirements.

After completing measurements of the variation, the team needs to analyze them to find the causes. To determine whether a specific operating system or workstation model caused the variation, the team might generate a box plot by operating system or workstation model (see Exhibit 7.4). Variations based on time of day can be viewed using a time series similar to the one shown as Exhibit 6.13. The team will also want to determine whether variations have common or special causes (see Exhibit 7.1). If needed, the team can perform a root cause analysis (see Exhibit 7.6) and create a Pareto chart (see Exhibit 7.7) to determine which causes to address first.

The objective of the measurements and the subsequent analyses is to clearly identify and understand the cause of the variation prior to attempting to reduce it. In Six Sigma terms, the team is making fact-based decisions.

It is possible that the analysis will show that the new system cannot meet customer response time requirements when run on a specific hardware and software configuration. While the answer may not be a welcome one if that is a commonly used configuration, knowing the cause makes it possible to correct the problem. Careful measurement and analysis will prevent unnecessary system tweaking and will help the team reduce variation and meet their customers' requirements. Using the DFSS technique of modeling performance prior to developing the system will help reduce the likelihood of serious problems being discovered late in the SDLC. That is, after all, the fundamental reason DFSS was developed — to design in quality and capacity so that process improvement projects are not needed.

VII

SIX SIGMA AND PACKAGED SOFTWARE IMPLEMENTATION

Better, cheaper, faster. For many companies, implementing packaged software is the answer to all three goals. While there is little doubt that under the right circumstances, a packaged software solution can deliver a system better, cheaper, and faster than custom system development, as some companies have learned, the wrong packaged software can be an expensive, time-consuming mistake. This section shows how Six Sigma tools can be used to increase the probability of selecting the right package and of having a successful implementation.

Chapter 29 outlines the steps involved in making a fact-based selection of a software package, while Chapter 30 contrasts the steps involved in implementing packaged software with those of the traditional system life cycle.

Chapter 29

Selecting Packaged Software

In the continuing attempt to reduce the cycle time of delivering a software solution, packaged software or, as it is sometimes called COTS (commercial off-the-shelf) software, can be one of the modern IT department's most effective methods. As its name implies, the software is developed and "packaged" by a software vendor with the goal that it will be used by many different companies.

Advantages of Packaged Software

For the IT department, there are three primary reasons for installing commercial software:

1. *Faster implementation*, because large portions of the "design" and "construction" phases are eliminated. As noted above, reduced cycle time is often a major impetus for selecting packaged software.
2. *Lower cost* than custom development, particularly when the costs of ongoing maintenance are included in the calculation. Note that the cost of actually developing the software is normally greater than a single custom development project; however, because the vendor expects to sell (or, to be technical, to license the right to use) the software to many companies, it need recoup only a portion of its development costs from any one customer. Similarly, the

costs of support and upgrades, commonly classified as "maintenance," are spread among many customers.

3. *Lower risk,* because the software has been (presumably) installed
at other sites and is a proven commodity. The risks of schedule
overruns, budget overruns, and delivery of incomplete or inaccurate functionality are all reduced by the selection and implementation of the correct COTS solution.

Although there are undeniable advantages to commercial software, there
are also pitfalls to avoid. Disaster stories abound of companies that have
spent millions of dollars on software without achieving the projected cost
savings, of runaway schedules that result in the project's being canceled,
and of customer dissatisfaction when the system is finally installed.

Guidelines for Success

While there are no guarantees, there are several keys to the success of a
COTS installation. A Six Sigma company would summarize them as:

■ Understand the customer's requirements.
■ Base all decisions on facts.

A company trained in DFSS would add:

■ Be certain that you have adequate process capability.

The four, more specific, guidelines are:

1. *Be sure the application is suited to packaged software.* Many manufacturing companies speak of "buy versus build" when deciding
how to acquire components. If the component is a commodity,
such as a standard nut or bolt, they will buy it, whereas something
that is unique to their manufacturing process may be built inter-
nally. IT departments should use similar analogies to decide
whether to buy packaged software or develop their own. If the
application is a commodity such as payroll or general ledger,
packaged software is worth considering. If, on the other hand,
the company is trying to develop a unique Web portal, it would
be better served by using a robust set of Web development tools
and creating its own system rather than expending time and effort
attempting to find a packaged solution.

2. *Choose the right package.* While that may seem obvious, it is essential to understand customer requirements prior to selecting software and to ensure that the application meets those requirements. And, as discussed below, it is important to identify all customers and their requirements. For software implementation, customers can include computer operations, network operations and the desktop support group, as well as the end customer. A value chain map (see Exhibit 11.3) can be helpful in identifying customers, as can creation of a SIPOC (see Exhibit 11.5). In either case, it is critical to consider all groups that will be impacted by the system.

   As Exhibit 10.2 shows, choosing the right solution involves more than customer requirements. It also involves the process and its capability. In the case of packaged software, the process to be considered is the infrastructure. Will the proposed system run effectively and efficiently on the company's existing hardware and network? If major upgrades are required, this may not be the right package.

3. *Make minimal modifications to the software.* To achieve the goals of lower cost and faster implementation, which were the impetuses for the COTS solution, it is important that the software be kept as "vanilla" as possible. In addition to streamlining the initial installation, having "vanilla" software will simplify the application of future releases, and minimizing the ongoing maintenance costs.

   Although the idea of making no changes is anathema to many customers, it is possible to minimize changes to the program code if the package is designed for customization by the end user. Many software vendors acknowledge that customers will need to make some changes and provide user exits or customizable fields in their application. If the package does not have that capability and extensive modifications are needed, the second critical success factor has not been met. This is not the right package.

4. *Establish realistic expectations.* Many customers believe that because the company has selected COTS software, implementation will be virtually instantaneous. This is, quite simply, false. While portions of the project life cycle will be shortened, other phases will be as long as if custom software were being developed. Exhibit 29.1 shows how the phases of the traditional waterfall SDLC relate to packaged software implementation. As is true of all projects, customers should be part of the project team, and all affected groups should have a clear understanding of the project schedule and deliverables. Communication is as important in packaged software implementation as in custom system development.

Exhibit 29.1   Changes to SDLC Phases for a COTS Implementation

Waterfall SDLC Phase	COTS Implementation
Project Initiation	Very few changes; issuing an RFI may occur during this stage.
System Analysis	Very few changes; detailed requirements are still needed.
System Design	Streamlined, since design documents will be needed only for interfaces and data conversion modules.
Construction	Streamlined, since only interfaces and data conversion modules will be constructed.
Testing and Quality Assurance	Streamlined, since unit and system testing can be eliminated. Integration, stress and acceptance testing is still required.
Implementation	Slightly streamlined, since vendor may provide basic training materials and customer documentation.

Using Six Sigma to Increase the Probability of Success

Six Sigma tools and precepts can guide IT through the selection and implementation of packaged software and help increase the probability of success. As noted above, a COTS implementation needs to ensure, as is true in any Six Sigma project, that decisions are based on facts and that the customers' requirements remain at the forefront.

To ensure that decisions are fact-based, it is important that the "Define" phase of the Six Sigma DMAIC model not be short-changed. Although it is always important to understand the current process and the problem to be solved, it can be argued that the importance is greater when selecting packaged software because there is less flexibility in a COTS solution than in custom-developed software. The primary advantages of packaged software disappear if it is necessary to make substantial modifications or if the resulting product does not fully meet the customers' needs.

A project charter (see Appendix A), while always valuable, is of particular use in the selection of packaged software because it clearly defines the problem and the anticipated benefits. It is also helpful in calibrating team members' expectations of their responsibilities. While a COTS implementation may have a shorter cycle time than traditional waterfall development, the team still has many of the same tasks to perform.

After forming the team and developing the charter, the team members should ensure that they have a thorough understanding of the current process. Because it is important to understand all the steps, a detailed (see Exhibit 5.13) or functional (see Exhibit 5.14) process map is more appropriate at this stage than a top-level map (Exhibit 5.11). The "as-is" process map becomes one of the facts used in the decision-making process.

At the same time that they are documenting the current process, team members should be listening for unspoken requirements, the basic and excitement needs on the Kano model (see Exhibit 11.8), and identifying opportunities for improvement in the current process. The objective, after all, is to select a package that will resolve as many problems as possible. In DFSS terms, the team wants to ensure that quality is built into the solution so that post-implementation correction of defects is minimized — if not completely eliminated.

Frequent, regular communications with customers should be the hallmark of any system development project. In the case of packaged software, as noted above, it is important to ensure that customer expectations are aligned with the project. Customer understanding of the steps involved in COTS selection and implementation and their buy-in to the concept of possibly modifying processes rather than software are critical to the success of the project.

The Selection Process

A variety of methods can be used to select packaged software. Some companies base their decisions on research services' recommendations. Others choose systems from a vendor that has already provided other packages to them. Still others see demos at conferences or expos or make their decisions based on marketing brochures. A Six Sigma company would take a different approach, working methodically to ensure that it chooses the right package. The following ten steps illustrate one path to making a fact-based decision:

1. Identify the requirements.
2. Prioritize the requirements.
3. Develop a list of potential vendors.
4. Obtain product information.
5. Perform a preliminary evaluation.
6. Conduct initial product demos.
7. Perform a detailed evaluation of "short list" vendors.
8. Identify gaps between products and requirements.
9. Select the final vendor.
10. Negotiate the contract.

Step 1: Identify the Requirements

While it may seem self-evident that a requirements definition should be complete prior to selecting a package, some companies fall into the trap of buying "a solution looking for a problem." Marketing hype, skilled demos, even another company's choice of a particular package may lead either customers or IT to believe that the software is the correct solution for them. That may be true; however, unless the project team has fully defined requirements and ensured that the package meets them, it is also possible that the company will spend time and money implementing a COTS solution, only to discover that it does not accomplish the desired goals.

Requirements for packaged software fall into three categories: (1) functional, (2) technical, and (3) vendor-related. Functional requirements are those that end-user customers develop, and they answer the question, "What must the system do?" These requirements can be obtained by any of the techniques outlined on Exhibit 5.8 or by conducting a JRP session. When complete, it is helpful to document acceptance criteria along with the requirements, as shown on Exhibit 18.1. This will assist in the development of a test plan. Key requirements and the associated acceptance criteria can also be used during the customer demos described in Step 7 below.

Technical requirements are developed by the IT department and relate to the operating environment. They answer the question, "How does the system run?" As noted above, this is a portion of the "voice of the customer." Prior to purchasing a COTS solution, it is important to understand what hardware, operating software, and network resources will be required. If, for example, the software uses a database manager that the company does not currently support, the cost of implementing the package will be increased by the cost of licensing the database and by hiring a DBA (database administrator). Similarly, if the software requires more powerful workstations than are currently installed in the customer department, the total cost of the solution will be greater than originally expected. When the project team recognizes that operations and other parts of IT are customers of the process, technical requirements become just another form of customer requirements.

Vendor-related requirements are normally developed by IT and answer the question, "Who is this vendor?" If one goal of the project is to minimize ongoing support costs by relying on the vendor to update the software, adding new functionality, and ensuring that regulatory changes are addressed, then selecting the right vendor can be equally as important as ensuring that the package has all the functionality the customer needs. Exhibit 29.2 provides a list of questions that can help assess vendors.

Exhibit 29.2   COTS Vendor Assessment Questionnaire

Question	Reason for Asking
How long have you been in business?	Younger companies may not have a proven track record.
How long have you been in the software development business?	This may be a new business, even though the company itself is established. In that case, the track record of the software division is unproven.
What version of the software are you currently selling?	Version 1.0, although theoretically a production version, may be close to beta and, therefore, riskier.
When was the initial version of this package first implemented? ("Implemented" means installed in production mode, not beta.)	Although no guarantee of quality, an older product may be more stable.
When was the current version of this package first implemented?	If the current version involved major changes or additions to functionality, it may be desirable to wait until it has been in production for several months.
How many developers are working on this package?	A small staff means a higher dependence on individuals and greater risk if key staff should leave.
How many customers have this package installed and in full production?	A small installed base may be an indication that the product is either new or somehow inadequate. It is important to distinguish between the number of companies and the total number of installed "seats." One large company may distort the statistics.
How often do you release new versions of the software?	Frequent releases will require more support; no regular schedule of releases could mean that the company has no future plans for the package.
What is the warranty period for the software?	A financial system that has separate quarter- and year-end processing should be warranted through the first time that logic is exercised in production.
What support is included in the purchase price?	Although there is no right answer to this question, it is important to understand what services the vendor supplies.
What other services do you provide?	Vendor-supplied training or conversion services may shorten the project schedule.
What hours/days is help desk support available?	If the system is used 24/7, a fully staffed help desk may be important.

Step 2: Prioritize the Requirements

Once the requirements are identified, they should be prioritized. For packaged software, this is similar to the process normally followed for requirements and would result in the creation of a customer requirements matrix (Exhibit 5.15). Requirements can also be documented on a QFD. Using a format similar to Exhibit 12.1 allows the team to display the result of their evaluation of competitive products along with the requirements. Regardless of the form chosen for recording the requirements, there is a preliminary step. The team should divide the requirements into three categories: (1) mandatory, (2) important, and (3) nice-to-have. The distinctions among the categories are:

1. *Mandatory.* As the word suggests, when all potential solutions are evaluated, if a vendor or package does not satisfy one of these requirements, it is eliminated from further consideration. These are the "show stoppers." Mandatory requirements should be phrased in such a way that responses are binary. Either a requirement is met, or it is not. No subjectivity should be involved in the evaluation of this category of requirements.
2. *Important.* These requirements are important, and the vendor or package will be judged on how closely its solution meets them.
3. *Nice-to-haves.* These are discretionary requirements. How well the solution meets them will be considered the tie-breaker. Customers should clearly understand that, while in custom software development these requirements might be implemented in a second release of the system, it is possible that a packaged solution will never have this functionality. By definition, these requirements are not critical to quality (CTQs).

Once requirements are categorized, the team should prioritize each of them in the important and nice-to-have groups, using a 1-4-7-10 ranking scheme. The ranking will be used as selection criteria in Step 5.

Step 3: Develop a List of Potential Vendors

Other than the additional time required to evaluate them, there are no disadvantages to having an extensive list of potential vendors. The advantage to considering a wide variety of solutions is that the probability of meeting requirements increases. Sources of vendor names include research services, Internet searches, networking, industry group publications and contacts, advertisements in IT journals, and software conferences and expos.

Step 4: Obtain Product Information

Once the list of potential vendors has been compiled, the next step is to obtain information about the product and the vendor. Although this can be done by requesting marketing brochures from the vendor, for larger projects it is common to issue a Request for Information (RFI). An RFI explains the background of the project, its goals and projected timeframe, the number of potential users, and other environmental information. It may also include the requirements that were developed in Step 1. It should *never* include the categorization or ranking of those requirements.

In issuing an RFI, a project team normally indicates a deadline for responses. Although there are exceptions, vendors who fail to meet the deadline and request extensions are typically eliminated from further consideration, because granting one vendor more time than the others can be viewed as unfair treatment of the other vendors. Failure to deliver on time may also be an indication of the vendor's attitude toward deadlines and could presage future problems.

Step 5: Perform a Preliminary Evaluation

Once the responses to the RFI or the product literature are received, the team will begin the evaluation process, comparing the information received to the requirements established in Step 1 and rating how well each of the products satisfies each of the requirements. It is at this point that proposals that fail to meet the mandatory requirements are eliminated.

To avoid having to read entire proposals from vendors that do not meet the basic requirements, the team can designate one person to perform the preliminary screening, reading only those portions of the responses that relate to mandatory requirements. Only those proposals that satisfy all mandatory criteria are passed to the next step, the more detailed evaluation.

Several procedures help to ensure consistent, fair evaluation of the proposals:

- *At least two people should evaluate the proposals.* It is likely that the entire project team will not be able to evaluate the proposals; however, it is important that more than one person is involved in the evaluation to minimize personal bias in the selection process. Because mandatory requirements involve no subjectivity, they can be — and frequently are — evaluated by only one person. All others will be ranked and should be reviewed by multiple team members.
- *Evaluations should be done independently.* Because it is possible for strong-willed individuals to sway a group, this is a corollary to the preceding point. Again, the objective is to ensure as fair an evaluation as possible.

■ *All evaluators should evaluate all proposals.* Although this may appear to place an unfair burden on the evaluators, it reduces one cause of variation and increases consistency.

When the independent evaluations are complete, the team can report its results in a vendor ranking spreadsheet similar to the one shown as Exhibit 29.3. Once a vendor fails to meet one of the mandatory requirements, no further evaluation of that vendor is necessary. As noted, only those responses that satisfy all mandatory requirements are evaluated for important and nice-to-have requirements. Although any ranking scale can be used, a 1-4-7-10 scale (with 0 reserved for responses that are either missing or totally wrong) helps differentiate among responses. The spreadsheet calculates the "Degree of Satisfaction" columns as the product of the importance ranking and the score each evaluator awarded. The spreadsheet also totals columns.

When scoring is complete, the team leader normally collects the individual members' scores and creates a matrix of the totals for important and nice-to-have requirements prior to scheduling a debriefing session with the entire team. If there are a large number of packages under

Exhibit 29.3 Vendor Ranking

Vendor Ranking

Mandatory Requirements		Vendor #1		Vendor #2		Vendor #3	
Must have been in business for more than five years.		Yes		Yes		No	Eliminated
Software must be in production at least one year.		Yes		Yes			
Important Requirements	Importance Ranking	Score	Degree of Satisfaction	Score	Degree of Satisfaction	Score	Degree of Satisfaction
More than 10 Fortune 100 companies have software installed.	7	10	70	7	49		
Help desk available 24/7.	10	7	70	7	70		
Total for Important			140		119		
Nice-to-Have Requirements	Importance Ranking	Score	Degree of Satisfaction	Score	Degree of Satisfaction	Score	Degree of Satisfaction
Warranty period > 1 year.	7	0	0	0	0		
Training services available.	7	4	28	7	49		
Total for Nice-to-Have			28		49		

consideration, the rankings can be used to eliminate low-scoring vendors from future consideration. Otherwise, all vendors who satisfied all mandatory requirements continue to the next step.

Step 6: Conduct Initial Product Demos

In this step, all previously qualified vendors are invited to demonstrate their products to the project team. At this stage, the demos are typically the vendors' standard marketing presentations, rather than being customized for the company. Vendors will normally present an overview of their corporate history, sales growth, and list of key customers in addition to demonstrating the product itself. From the project team's view, the objective of these presentations is to evaluate the products' ease of use and to confirm that the functionality the vendors claimed was present is indeed included in their software.

Because it likely that a number of demos will be scheduled, it is important that the team have a debriefing session after each demo to discuss what was presented and to rank the vendors. As was true in the previous step, it is important that at least some members of the team participate in all demos to provide consistency, and ranking should be done individually prior to having a group discussion. As is true throughout the process, results of the demos and the team's evaluation should be documented. Whenever possible, the team should develop evaluation criteria prior to the demos and treat them as they did other requirements. That is, the team should rank the vendors' performance against those evaluation criteria.

At the conclusion of this step, the team should be able to reduce the potential vendors to a "short list."

Step 7: Perform Detailed Evaluation of "Short List" Vendors

To select the final vendor, the team should perform an in-depth evaluation of its short list. Normally this consists of three steps:

1. *Reference checks.* It is important to distinguish between marketing hype and reality, and one way is to ask customers who are currently using the software how satisfied they are with both the product and the vendor. Although it is expected that a vendor will supply the names of only satisfied customers, it is still possible to distinguish between vendors by asking open-ended questions of the references. Questions that frequently elicit valuable answers include, "If you could change one thing about your experience

with this vendor, what would it be?" and "What do you like most (or least) about the software?" To ensure consistency, it is important to develop the list of questions prior to conducting the reference checks and to have a single person make all the calls. That team member should provide written copies of the responses to the entire team. When all references are complete, the team can review the results and award ranking scores to each vendor based on its references.

2. *Customized demos.* To ensure that the software will meet the company's requirements, it is important to see how easily the company's data can be entered into the system and whether the resulting output meets customer expectations. The team can use the requirements and acceptance criteria developed in Step 1 to create a test script. Although the vendor may want to enter the data, a team member should have a checklist of all requirements that will be tested and should evaluate how well the software met them. This can then be translated into a numerical ranking.

3. *Site visits.* As a final step in large projects, the team should ask to visit at least one customer who is currently using the software. This can be viewed as an extended reference check, and it should be done without the vendor being present because that may provide more candid answers. Additionally, if the vendor is relatively small or unknown to the project team, a visit to the vendor's offices may be warranted to reassure the team of their stability. Results of the site visits should be documented and evaluated. As was true of each preceding step, the goal is to provide as objective a ranking as possible; that is, to make a fact-based decision.

Step 8: Identify Gaps between Products and Requirements

It is possible that a clear winner will be apparent at the conclusion of Step 7. Even if that is the case, it is important to evaluate any gaps that exist between customer requirements and the proposed software's functionality and to determine how easily those gaps can be bridged. If customization of the software will be required, the team should estimate the cost and time required to make the modifications. A variation of the Cost, Time, and Customer Impact Ranking (see Exhibit 7.10) can be used to quantify the gaps. As shown in Exhibit 29.4, in this case, the Customer Impact column reflects the impact of not bridging the gap. A QFD with competitive product assessment (see Exhibit 12.1) can also be used. If any of the functionality gaps would result in a high-priority customer requirement not being met, key customers should be notified. At this point, although unlikely, it is still possible to determine that none of the

Exhibit 29.4   Cost, Time, and Customer Impact Requirements Gaps

Vendor # 1

Gap	Cost to Bridge	Time to Bridge	Customer Impact if Not Bridged
No provision for Canadian provinces in address line	Low	Low	High
No provision for Canadian postal code in address line	Medium	Low	High
Allows only 10 dependents	High	High	Low

packaged solutions meets customer requirements closely enough to be implemented and that custom software will be needed.

Step 9: Select Final Vendor

Using all of the previous evaluations, the team should now be ready to select the solution that most closely meets the customers' requirements. A ranking matrix similar to the one shown as Exhibit 29.5 is helpful for quantifying the results of all the previous steps. It should be noted that, although cost has not been an explicit part of the evaluation, it is possible that one of the requirements may have been "Per seat cost may not exceed $100." While it would appear that this would be a mandatory requirement and that any vendor who failed to meet it would be automatically disqualified, because price is normally negotiable, some teams prefer to exclude costs from their evaluation and focus on functionality. At this point, if two products are closely ranked, the decision will often be made on the basis of cost.

It is important when selecting the finalist to document the reasons for not choosing the other vendors, as it is not unheard of for a disappointed vendor to approach senior management and request further consideration. Having a clearly documented selection process and verifiable facts as the basis for the decision can prevent rework or having the selection overturned.

Step 10: Negotiate the Contract

The final step, and one that is normally handled by the Procurement/Purchasing and Law departments, is to negotiate the contract. The project team should participate in the process to ensure that any unique requirements are addressed, but actual pricing negotiations are normally done by Procurement, while Law handles the terms and conditions.

Once the contract is signed. the team can begin the process of implementing the packaged software.

Exhibit 29.5   Final Vendor Ranking

Final Vendor Ranking

		Vendor #1			Vendor #2		Vendor #3	
Mandatory Requirements								
Must have been in business for more than five years.		Yes			Yes		No	Eliminated
Software must be in production at least one year.		Yes			Yes			
Important Requirements	Importance Ranking	Score	Degree of Satisfaction	Score	Degree of Satisfaction		Score	Degree of Satisfaction
More than 10 Fortune 100 companies have software installed.	7	10	70	7	49			
Help desk available 24/7.	10	7	70	7	70			
Total for Important			140		119			
Nice-to-Have Requirements	Importance Ranking	Score	Degree of Satisfaction	Score	Degree of Satisfaction		Score	Degree of Satisfaction
Warranty period > 1 year.	7	0	0	0	0			
Training services available.	7	4	28	7	49			
Total for Nice-to-Have			28		49			
Initial Demo	Importance Ranking	Score	Degree of Satisfaction	Score	Degree of Satisfaction		Score	Degree of Satisfaction
Screen navigation was intuitive.	10	7	70	7	70			
Functionality matched product literature.	7	10	70	7	49			
Total for Initial Demo			140		119			

Exhibit 29.5 Final Vendor Ranking (continued)

Final Vendor Ranking

Reference Checks	Importance Ranking	Score	Degree of Satisfaction	Score	Degree of Satisfaction	Score	Degree of Satisfaction
		Vendor #1		**Vendor #2**		**Vendor #3**	
References responded included at least one customer in our industry.	10	0	0	10	100		
References included at least one customer of our size.	7	10	70	0	0		
All references responded "very likely" to "would you use this vendor again?"	7	7	49	7	49		
Total for Reference Checks			119		149		

Customized demo	Importance Ranking	Score	Degree of Satisfaction	Score	Degree of Satisfaction	Score	Degree of Satisfaction
Vendor was able to enter all of our data without customizing screens.	10	7	70	4	40		
Reports included all data that customers ranked "important."	7	7	49	10	70		
Reports were in the format customers preferred.	4	4	16	10	40		
Total for Customized Demo			135		150		

Site Visits	Importance Ranking	Score	Degree of Satisfaction	Score	Degree of Satisfaction	Score	Degree of Satisfaction
Customers rated satisfaction "very good" or higher.	7	7	49	10	70		
Customers demonstrated added value of software.	7	7	49	10	70		
Total for Site Visits			98		140		

Exhibit 29.5   Final Vendor Ranking (continued)

Final Vendor Ranking

Gap Analysis	Importance Ranking	Vendor #1		Vendor #2		Vendor #3	
		Score	Degree of Satisfaction	Score	Degree of Satisfaction	Score	Degree of Satisfaction
There were no "high/ high/high" gaps.	10	10	100	10	100		
There were no more than four "medium/medium/ high" gaps.	7	10	70	10	70		
Total number of gaps did not exceed 10.	4	0	0	4	16		
Total for Gap Analysis			170		186		
Total Degree of Satisfaction			830		912		

Chapter 30

Implementing Packaged Software

Once packaged software has been selected, the process is similar to the implementation of a custom-developed system. Like any other aspect of system development, the implementation of packaged software is most successful if approached as a project with clearly defined tasks and deliverables. Many vendors recognize this and provide project plan templates that can be customized by the customer. If the vendor does not supply one, the project team should develop a formal plan, showing the effort required for each task and the estimated start and end dates. In addition, a functional process map is helpful to delineate responsibilities and show the sequence of major tasks.

For a COTS implementation, the process map might be a high-level one that divides responsibilities into only three categories: (1) customer, (2) project team, and (3) vendor. Alternatively, it might be detailed, breaking the project team into its various IT components: programming, database administration, computer center, network services, quality assurance, etc. While not mandatory, the process map facilitates communication and helps to clarify roles.

If the selection process revealed the need for process changes within the customer department, the project can be viewed as having two major tasks that will occur in parallel:

1. Installing and, if needed, modifying the software *and*
2. Preparing the customer department

The importance of the latter cannot be overemphasized.

Preparing the Customer Department

As Chapter 3 points out, while change may be a fact of life, not everyone welcomes it. IT, as agents of change, must understand the dynamics and the potential problems associated with change and work to make it successful. The often repeated five Ps (prior planning prevents poor performance) apply to all aspects of implementing change. They are particularly important when addressing change that affects people's lives as major shifts in the work environment do.

As noted in Chapter 3, frequent communication is one way of improving the likelihood of success in dealing with change, but it must be appropriate, targeted communication. In short, it should be planned. The following are keys to effective communication of change:

1. *Develop a written communication plan.* The purpose of a formal communication plan is to outline what will be communicated, by whom, and when.
2. *Anticipate the questions that customers will ask.* While this may seem obvious, it is helpful to have a brainstorming session to outline all possible questions that might be raised and to develop answers for them as an FAQ document.
3. *Keep the message simple.* Although there may be more detailed communications later, the initial ones should be basic and presented in easy-to-understand language.
4. *Use graphics.* As a corollary to simplicity, pictures or graphics are effective communication tools, particularly when used to reinforce the verbal messages that are being delivered. When explaining what change is being planned, it is helpful to present before and after process maps, showing how the change impacts the current process. It is also important that the affected groups have access to these maps after the meeting.

While IT is installing the software, the remainder of the project team should focus on managing change within the customer department. This includes developing the new or revised procedures and working with all affected staff to gain acceptance for the changes. Use of the formal and informal communication techniques discussed in Chapter 3 can facilitate this process.

Installing and Implementing the Software

The implementation phase of a COTS project can be viewed as an eight-step process.

1. Communicate the decision and project schedule.
2. Install and test the "vanilla" software.
3. Modify the software and retest.
4. Build the interfaces.
5. Develop data conversion programs.
6. Develop and conduct customer training.
7. Go live.
8. Evaluate the results.

Step 1: Communicate the Decision and Project Schedule

Even if major changes to the customer department will not occur, it is important to notify all affected departments of the vendor selection and the overall schedule for implementation. As is true of all projects, this communication should include the reasons the project was initiated — that is, the benefits that will be derived. And, because it is a COTS solution, it is helpful to explain why the decision was made to use packaged software and why the particular vendor was chosen. Communications should, of course, continue throughout the implementation process. Weekly status updates help keep everyone informed and minimize the apprehension that comes from lack of information and uncontrolled rumors.

Step 2: Install and Test the Software with No Modifications

Although tight project schedules make it tempting to skip this initial testing step, it is absolutely essential that it occur. Testing the base software accomplishes two objectives: (1) it verifies that the "vanilla" software works as the vendor claims it does, and (2) it establishes a baseline for modifications and future releases. Without this step, errors uncovered in testing modified code are far more difficult to debug because they may wrongly be assumed to result from the modifications.

Rather than eliminate the testing step, some companies increase its importance by including successful testing in their contract, tying final payments to the vendor to this demonstrated proof that the system performs as expected.

This testing should not differ from the testing that is done on custom-developed software and should include stress testing to ensure that the system and infrastructure can support the anticipated transaction volumes. A test plan and test case log should be developed. As noted in Chapter 29, if acceptance criteria are established when requirements are identified, they can serve as the foundation for the test plan. Should errors be identified during the testing, they should be reported to the vendor and their correction tracked. Because an additional group, namely the vendor, is involved in the correction process, the standard test case log (see Exhibit 21.3) can be expanded to include dates that the errors were reported to the vendor and other vendor-related information. Exhibit 30.1 shows a COTS test case log.

Step 3: Modify the Base Software and Retest

The gap analysis performed during product selection should have identified the customer requirements that were not met by the package and that required customization. At this point, the team is ready to make those modifications.

One of the key considerations in modifying packaged software is ensuring continued ease of maintainability. Unlike custom software, where IT has total control over the system, with a COTS solution, IT depends on the vendor to provide updates. Each modification that the team makes complicates the process of applying vendor updates. This is why, wherever possible, IT should use vendor-supplied exits for those modifications.

Once the changes are made, it is important to retest the entire system. This testing is analogous to regression testing in system maintenance. Its objectives are to prove that the modifications worked as intended and that they had no unplanned effect on the rest of the system. A standard test case log (see Exhibit 21.3) is helpful for recording the results of testing.

Step 4: Build Interfaces To and From Existing Systems

It is likely that the new system will not exist in a vacuum but will either require data from existing systems or will feed data to them. If the project team has not already done so, they should develop a process map, showing the flow of data among systems. Once the interface programs are coded, they must be tested. In addition, the system that is receiving the file from the interface must be tested to ensure not only that the file is in the correct format, but also that the data is valid. Errors should be tracked and analyzed to determine the root causes. The FMEA shown as Exhibit 19.5 and the Error Analysis (Exhibit 20.1) are helpful in this process.

Exhibit 30.1 COTS Test Case Log

System	Perfect Emp						Tested By	Quentin Assurance				
Module	PE001						Date	November 14, 2001				
Case number	Data entered	Expected results	Actual results	Date reported to vendor	Date fix received	Version number	Date Retested	Retested by	Retest results	Comments	Date Closed	Closed by
150	State code "AA"	Error message: "An incorrect state code was entered"	System accepted invalid code	11/14/01	12/03/01	3.02.4	12/05/01	QA	Correct error message was produced		12/05/01	QA

Step 5: Develop Data Conversion Programs and Procedures

While interfaces transfer data between systems on a periodic, ongoing basis, data conversion programs are designed for a one-time running. Their purpose is to take data from systems that will be discontinued, typically the system that the new COTS is replacing, and prepare it for entry into the new system. Like all functions within system development, data conversion programs need clearly defined specifications and a test plan. The steps to follow are analogous to those used in the waterfall SDLC (see Section IV).

It is possible that not all data that is required for the new system exists in electronic format. It is also possible that existing data is in such a format that it cannot be easily converted. An example of the latter might be free-form addresses that must be converted into separate street, city, and state fields. In both cases, manual procedures may be required for data conversion. To ensure consistency, the procedures should be written, and a quality assurance process should be developed.

Standard project planning techniques outlined in previous sections will help keep the development of the procedures on schedule. Providing written conversion procedures has the added benefit of creating a document that can be used as a template or guideline for future projects, thus reducing variability and cycle time for those projects.

Step 6: Develop and Conduct Customer Training

Customer training requirements for COTS implementation are similar to those for custom development and should follow the guidelines shown in Chapter 22. The primary difference is that a COTS vendor may provide training materials or classes. Although these can be valuable and can reduce (or eliminate) the effort required to develop training programs, it is important to ensure that the training teaches customers how to use the system to accomplish their own jobs. Generic training may or may not accomplish that objective. A comparison of customer requirements to the materials the vendor provides will identify gaps, which can then be documented in a standard gap analysis to ensure that they are not overlooked when amending the training materials.

Step 7: Go Live

The system has been modified; data has been converted; customers are trained. The team is now ready to "go live" with the new system. The "Improve" phase of DMAIC is complete. As the project enters "Control," the team should ensure that all customers and affected departments are aware of the new system's implementation and the benefits that the project has delivered. And then they should take time to celebrate their success.

Step 8: Evaluate the Results

In a Six Sigma company, the project is not complete until the team evaluates the results, ensures that they meet the project goals, and develops metrics and a control plan to ensure that the system continues to deliver the planned improvements. Exhibit 9.2 shows a sample control plan. Although these steps do not differ from a traditional system development project or, indeed, from a classic Six Sigma project, they are important and should not be neglected.

Packaged software can provide IT with faster, cheaper system solutions. By ensuring that customer requirements are fully understood and that an orderly, fact-based process is followed, the benefits can be increased.

VIII

SIX SIGMA AND OUTSOURCING

Although outsourcing can help the IT department reduce costs, shorten delivery cycles, and focus on core competencies, it can also increase the risks to both IT and its customers. In part, this is because IT becomes a customer as well as a supplier. The keys to successful outsourcing are to outsource the right functions to the right supplier.

Chapter 31 outlines the reasons a company might outsource and the associated risks, and provides recommendations of tools and techniques that will help identify and mitigate the risks. Chapter 32 describes typical types of outsourcing and addresses the specific risks associated with each type.

Chapter 31

Introduction to Outsourcing

Outsourcing can be one of the most powerful weapons in the modern IT manager's arsenal, but it is also one of the most misunderstood, and — if not managed properly — one of the riskiest. In part, the risk is incurred because IT becomes a customer as well as a supplier of services and depends on another company to deliver services that IT once provided directly to its customers. Much of the risk can be mitigated by employing Six Sigma tools and concepts; however, it is first necessary to define outsourcing.

Outsourcing versus Staff Augmentation

"We outsource most of our system development," one IT manager declares. "We have contractors from three firms doing the coding. All we do is manage the project." While this is one way of accomplishing system development, it is not outsourcing. Rather, it is staff augmentation. The distinction is an important one.

As shown on Exhibit 31.1, there are fundamental differences between staff augmentation and outsourcing, the most critical of which is day-to-day management of the staff. In staff augmentation, whether they are called contractors or consultants, the people who are hired function as an extension of the IT department. Except for the fact that their salaries and benefits are paid by a different company and their services are

Exhibit 31.1   A Comparison of Outsourcing and Staff Augmentation

Characteristic	Outsourcing	Staff Augmentation
Contract is for	One or more pre-defined services	Individual contributor's work
Reason for contract	Long-term strategic decision not to provide the service in-house	Temporary shortfall in staff or specific skill
Payment terms	Fixed fee, typically stated as a monthly fee	Time and materials; hourly rate or per diem
IT's right to select staff	Limited or none	Full
Day-to-day management of staff	Service provider	IT department
Measurement of success	Service level agreement	Individual tasks
Key to success	Service provider	Individual contributor

temporary, they are virtually identical to permanent staff. IT specifies the skills it wants; it interviews potential candidates; it directs their work. In this case, because it has complete control over the resources used to deliver a service, IT is still a supplier.

Outsourcing is different. In outsourcing, IT becomes a customer because it contracts for a service, not for an individual. In outsourcing, IT transfers responsibility for and control of a specific body of work to another company, holding the supplier responsible for delivery of a predefined service. Although the ultimate customer and the work to be accomplished remain the same, IT is no longer the direct supplier of the service. Exhibit 31.2 uses the value chain map to illustrate the differences that outsourcing would create in the development of the General Ledger consolidation project described in Chapter 17.

In a typical outsourcing engagement, the work to be accomplished is specified in a statement of work (SOW), which may identify multiple services to be provided, each with a different expected level of service. This quantification of the work to be provided is called a service level agreement (SLA). The SLA can be incorporated into an SOW, or it can be a separate document. In either case, it represents the contractual requirements placed on the outsourcer.

Outsourcing can be viewed as being similar to the purchase of packaged software, that is, a "buy-versus-build" decision. While there are similarities, the fundamental difference is that in the case of a COTS solution, IT is acquiring a product, whereas in outsourcing, IT contracts for services. Because these differences are important, this book refers to the providers of packaged software as "vendors" and to outsourcers as "suppliers."

Exhibit 31.2 Value Chain Map With and Without Outsourcing

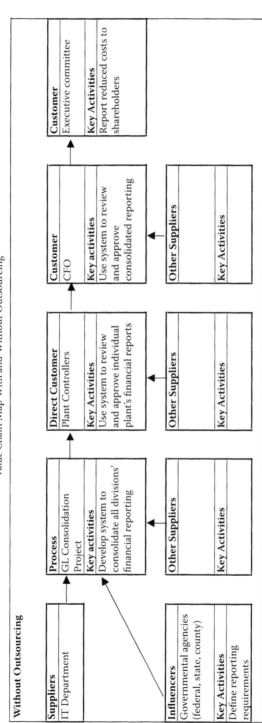

Value Chain Map With and Without Outsourcing

Exhibit 31.2 Value Chain Map With and Without Outsourcing (continued)

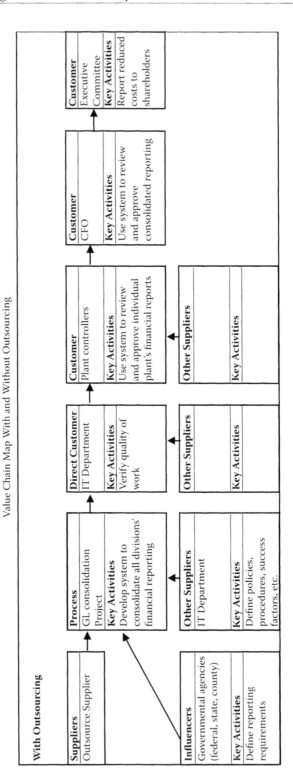

Value Chain Map With and Without Outsourcing

With Outsourcing

Suppliers	Process	Direct Customer	Customer	Customer	Customer
Outsource Supplier	GL consolidation Project	IT Department	Plant controllers	CFO	Executive Committee
Key Activities	**Key Activities**	**Key Activities**	**Key Activities**	**Key Activities**	**Key Activities**
	Develop system to consolidate all divisions' financial reporting	Verify quality of work	Use system to review and approve individual plant's financial reports	Use system to review and approve consolidated reporting	Report reduced costs to shareholders

Influencers	Other Suppliers	Other Suppliers	Other Suppliers
Governmental agencies (federal, state, county)	IT Department		
Key Activities	**Key Activities**	**Key Activities**	**Key Activities**
Define reporting requirements	Define policies, procedures, success factors, etc.		

In understanding the difference between a COTS vendor and an outsourcing supplier, it is important to understand the role each of them plays in the delivery of a system or related services to the ultimate customer. Although the quality of the vendor is a critical part of the purchasing decision for packaged software, reliance on the vendor is only periodic; and if the vendor should go out of business, the COTS solution would continue to run. The major inconvenience would be that the source of periodic upgrades would be gone.

In contrast, because an outsourcer provides services, IT and the customer's reliance on the supplier are constant. If anything, it increases with time as IT transfers additional responsibility to the supplier or loses the in-house resources that previously provided the services that have been outsourced. Under these scenarios, a supplier's failure would have disastrous effects on both IT and the customer. As a result, it is essential that IT consider carefully the decision to outsource and select a supplier who can provided the service for as long as needed. It is also important that customers understand and agree with the decision.

The Outsourcing Decision

Like all decisions in a Six Sigma company, the one to outsource should be based on facts and made only after a thorough assessment of the benefits to be gained and the potential risks that may be incurred. A risk assessment and mitigation plan similar to the one shown as Exhibit 17.6 may be helpful in quantifying the risks.

What to Outsource

Although it is theoretically possible to outsource any IT function, certain ones lend themselves to outsourcing. In general, the function should be repetitive and tactical — not strategic. Using these criteria, system development and maintenance; computer, network, and telephone operations; and the help desk are all candidates for outsourcing. Strategic planning, budgeting, and system design are functions that are traditionally kept in-house.

Personnel-Related Risks

Perhaps more than any other aspect of system development, outsourcing can have a potentially negative impact on the IT department. Although IT is accustomed to being an agent of change, in outsourcing it is IT itself that is being changed. Work that was previously done by IT staff or work that the staff believes should be its responsibility is transferred to an outside company. In many cases, permanent employees are either replaced by the service provider's employees or find themselves transferred to the provider. This is major change, and it should be addressed as such.

While the IT staff is directly impacted by an outsourcing decision, so too are customers. Even if the level of service they receive does not change, the fact that the services will be provided by an outside organization rather than IT may cause discomfort. If permanent IT positions are being eliminated, customers may fear that their own jobs are at risk.

Chapter 3 provides insight into the psychology of change and ways to reduce its negative impact on staff. However, before the decision to outsource is made, it is essential to understand the benefits to be gained and the associated risks.

Reasons for Outsourcing

There are four primary reasons why a company outsources one or more of its functions:

1. *Outsourcing may free staff for other activities.* As it moves to new technologies, a company may want to provide existing staff members with the opportunity to upgrade their skills. For example, when a company is implementing a large integrated system such as an enterprise resources planning (ERP) system, it may choose to transfer responsibility for legacy system support to an outsourcer so that its own staff can focus on the ERP installation.
2. *Outsourcing can provide expertise that is not available in-house.* This is the converse of the first reason. Rather than train its own staff in new technologies or new systems, IT may choose to hire an outsourcer to provide that expertise.
3. *Outsourcing may reduce risk.* If IT has high staff turnover, minimal breadth of coverage of key functions, or is at risk of losing key staff due to early retirement, it may choose to mitigate that risk by transferring responsibility to an outsourcer who will provide continuous coverage and cross-training.
4. *Outsourcing may reduce costs.* Lower costs are one of the key drivers for outsourcing. Although the use of off-shore resources is one way a service provider can lower costs, others reduce costs by employing formal procedures to eliminate waste and non-value-added tasks.

Before initiating an outsourcing strategy, IT should consider what it hopes to accomplish. A formal project charter (see Appendix A) with clearly defined goals will help keep the team focused and will provide objective criteria against which to measure the results of the project.

Potential Disadvantages of Outsourcing

Although there are compelling reasons to outsource certain IT functions, there are potential risks that must be considered, including:

1. *Flexibility is reduced.* Because IT no longer manages the day-to-day activities of the entire staff, it cannot easily transfer people who were supporting one system to another system if business needs shift. Similarly, in the case of a sudden economic downturn, the company cannot lower costs by laying off staff who are now controlled by the service provider. Although contracts typically provide clauses for renegotiating services and fees under these circumstances, the renegotiation process may be longer than IT and the customers would like.

2. *Costs may not be lower.* Some companies have found that outsourcing contracts that were written to reduce their costs do not. The primary reason for this discrepancy is that all needed services may not have been included in those transferred to the supplier. This can occur when the requirements definition phase is curtailed or when the right customers are not included in the project team. In some cases, the negotiated SLAs are lower than those previously provided by in-house staff. This may be the result of an incomplete analysis of requirements, where the team does not fully understand the current service levels, or it may be a deliberate attempt to lower costs by reducing services. Changing from 24/7 coverage of a system to Monday through Friday, 9 to 5, will reduce costs; however, it may not satisfy customers. In these cases, if customers demand resumption of previous service levels, IT may find that it has actually increased its costs. Thorough identification of requirements and definition of desired service levels will help reduce this risk.

3. *Customer satisfaction may suffer.* If negotiated service levels are lower than those previously provided or if the customers' perception is that the supplier provides fewer services, satisfaction may decrease. As noted above, even if service levels do not change, customers may be unhappy with the change from in-house staff to a service provider.

The risks are real; however, outsourcing can succeed if the right strategies are employed. Six Sigma tools and a continued focus on customers will help.

Strategies for Success

There are four factors that, if present, greatly increase the probability of a successful outsourcing engagement:

1. The right supplier
2. A comprehensive, fair contract
3. Clearly defined and attainable SOWs and SLAs
4. A mutual commitment to success

While all of these are important, without the right supplier, outsourcing will fail. Selecting the correct supplier is the single, most important CSF in an outsourcing engagement.

Choosing the Right Supplier

The process for selecting a supplier is similar to that employed for selecting a COTS vendor (see Chapter 29); however, because the role that the outsourcing supplier plays in the ongoing operation of the company is more critical than the COTS vendor's, the selection process focuses more heavily on the company's capabilities and the compatibility between the two corporate cultures. If the outsourcing is to be successful, the two companies must be able to work together and present a single "face" to the customer.

Exhibit 31.3 presents a functional process map for a typical supplier selection process. As is true in all projects, the first step is to define customers and their requirements. It should be noted that while IT is itself a customer, ultimate or end customers must also be included in the process if it is to be successful. While IT is transferring responsibility to a supplier, it is still accountable for customer satisfaction and must ensure that the customers' requirements are considered at each stage of the selection process.

As is true of all projects, requirements should be documented and prioritized. In the case of outsourcing, requirements include not just the services to be provided by the supplier, but also a definition of the nature of the outsourcing the company desires.

Exhibit 31.3   Supplier Selection Process Map

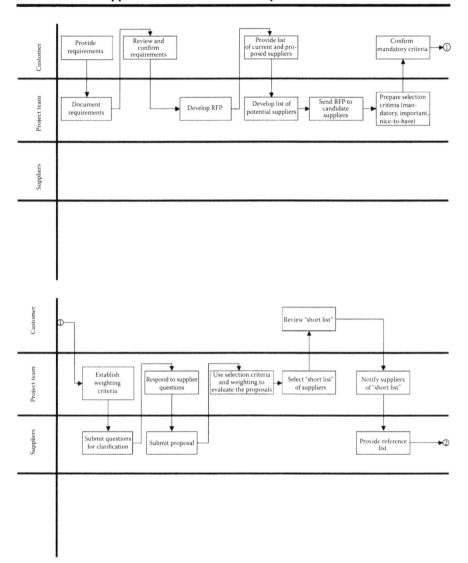

Exhibit 31.3   Supplier Selection Process Map (continued)

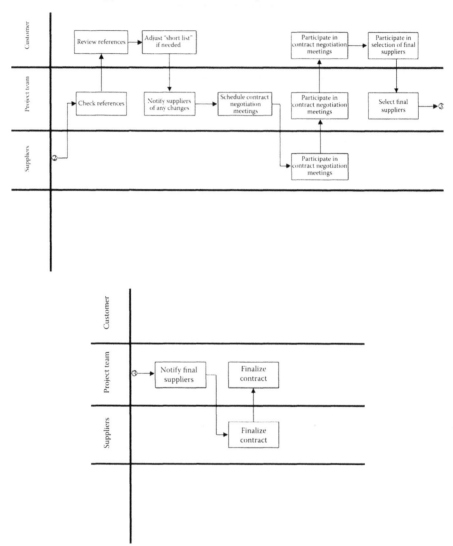

Categorizing the Engagement

The project team should ask (and answer) the following questions:

1. *How long will the outsourcing engagement be?* While the selection of the supplier for a short-term development project is important, a mistake is less costly to the company than an error in the selection

of an outsourcer for ongoing support of all mission-critical systems. The length of the proposed engagement and the criticality of the services the supplier provides will help determine the amount of effort that should be put into the selection process.

2. *How critical to the business is the service to be outsourced?* Successful, timely completion of a development project that will open vital new markets is of greater consequence than the creation of a proof-of-concept system designed to demonstrate the value of a new technology.

3. *Will existing staff be acquired by the outsourcer?* Although some outsourcing is initiated because IT lacks either the number of staff or the specific skills needed for a project, in other cases — most notably when existing "commodity" functions such as help desk operations, legacy system support, and computer operations are being transferred to a supplier — the company may want to transfer some of its own staff along with the responsibility. In this case, cultural compatibility between the two companies is particularly important because employees who were successful in an entrepreneurial company may not be as effective in one with a traditional hierarchical structure, or vice versa.

Staff acquisition can be mandatory or optional, each with its own set of implications:

■ *Mandatory.* The company determines which employees will be transferred to the supplier and typically specifies the compensation and benefits that the supplier will provide. While this ensures that the company's staff has continued employment, albeit with another firm, and shortens the transition time for the supplier, because the outsourcer is gaining expertise, it also lessens the supplier's flexibility. If the supplier had planned to staff the engagement with fewer or lower-cost employees, it may have difficulty meeting its profit targets.

■ *Optional.* In this scenario, the company specifies the employees whose positions will be eliminated by the outsourcing and allows the supplier to hire any of them. This increases the flexibility for the outsourcer without jeopardizing its profit margins and decreases transition time, but it increases stress for the company's employees. Unlike the mandatory option, where displaced staff knew that they would be guaranteed jobs, they are now faced with uncertainty.

4. *Will the outsourcer's staff be located on-site, off-site, or a combination?* The answer to this question impacts three aspects of the engagement: employee morale, communication, and costs:

- *Employee morale.* Although on the surface it involves the least amount of change, having outsourced staff on-site can create morale problems. When outsourcing includes employee displacement, either in the form of layoffs or transfer to the supplier, morale can suffer by having the outsourcer's staff located on-site. Former employees who find themselves doing the same work but for a different employer may have difficulty transferring their loyalty to the outsourcer. Similarly, employees may resent the outsourcer's staff who have taken jobs previously held by their co-workers.
- *Communication.* Having the outsourcer's staff located on-site typically increases communication with customers and remaining IT staff. In a project that requires frequent customer contact or collaborative work, this may be the preferred option.
- *Costs.* Unless the contract is carefully worded, having the outsourcer's staff on-site may increase costs for IT, because it may be required to provide workspace, computers, supplies, etc.

As noted earlier, when evaluating these options, it is helpful to create a risk assessment and mitigation plan (see Exhibit 17.6). Not only does this help quantify the risks, but it is also useful in communicating those risks to the project champion and others who will be part of the decision-making process.

Selecting the Supplier

Once the requirements are defined, the team can begin the formal selection process. This typically includes issuance of a Request for Proposal (RFP) and evaluation of the responses. Unlike an RFI, an RFP typically asks for a formal cost proposal. As was done during COTS selection (see Chapter 29), to ensure a fact-based decision, the team should categorize the customers' requirements as mandatory, important, and nice-to-have, and should establish weighting criteria for them.

In addition to specific technical expertise, as noted previously, the team needs to evaluate the supplier's ability to perform the services now and for the foreseeable future. Particularly in long-term, critical engagements, the team should consider the following criteria and rate them as they did the other requirements:

- *Length of experience.* How long has the supplier been providing these services? A company that has previously provided only staff augmentation services may have difficulty making the transition to true outsourcing. It may not be prepared for long-term, fixed-price work and the need to provide cross-training to mitigate the risk of key staff attrition. Similarly, a large supplier may have outsourcing expertise in one branch but not in the one that will service this account. In this case, length of experience at the corporate level may not be an indicator of probable success for the engagement.

■ *Breadth of expertise.* How many people with the required skill set does the supplier have? If the supplier has to rely on alliances with other firms to provide the number of staff needed for a project, quality may suffer.

■ *Specific experience.* How closely does the supplier's experience match the requirements? If the company is highly decentralized and wants to continue having services provided at a number of sites, has the supplier managed decentralized outsourcing? If the company envisions staff acquisition, has the supplier demonstrated a successful track record of retaining acquired staff?

■ *Corporate culture.* Do the supplier's core values match those of the company? Particularly if the supplier's staff will be located on-site, it is important to ensure that the cultures are compatible. A supplier that encourages an entrepreneurial spirit in its employees may not blend well with a traditional, hierarchical organization that values conformity.

Negotiating the Contract

In addition to reference checking, contract negotiation can be viewed as a continuation of the selection process. Rather than leaving the negotiation to attorneys, it is helpful to have the entire project team involved in the meetings. This allows the team to see how well the supplier's team works together and how well they work with the project team. Because outsourcing is normally a long-term engagement, cultural compatibility is important.

During the various presentations and the negotiations themselves, the team should ask the following questions about the suppliers and rank them:

■ *Did they bring the right people?* While most suppliers will have their attorneys involved in the negotiations, if staff acquisition is involved, they should also bring members of Human Resources. Were decision makers included, or were the supplier's representatives forced to defer decisions to people who were not present?

■ *Do the supplier's representatives function as a team?* If outsourcing is truly a core competency, the team should expect that the supplier's representatives have participated in similar meetings previously and work together as a cohesive team. Failure to do so may signal that the supplier is not as experienced as it claims.

■ *Is the proposed program manager included in the meetings?* It is highly desirable to have the people who will manage the engagement included in the sales cycle, and particularly in contract negotiations. This helps ensure continuity on the engagement and increases the probability of success, because both the company and the supplier have staff who understand why decisions were made.

Use of a vendor ranking chart similar to the one shown in Exhibit 29.5 is helpful for documenting the results of the evaluation process and in removing a level of subjectivity from the final decision.

Selecting the right supplier is the first and most critical step in ensuring successful outsourcing. Using Six Sigma tools and making fact-based decisions, IT can increase the probability of success.

Drafting a Comprehensive Contract

Good contracts make good relationships. While some companies prefer short contracts that outline little more than the services to be provided and the associated costs, most recognize the importance of establishing the terms and conditions (Ts and Cs) of the relationship before an outsourcing engagement begins. A comprehensive contract that includes every possible contingency not only improves communication between the two companies, but also helps to set common expectations. If both groups understand what is to be accomplished and how they will deal with change, they are more likely to have a productive relationship.

Because outsourcing engagements are often long-term, it is important that both parties understand how they will communicate under both normal and extraordinary circumstances and how they will manage change. As a result, many of the clauses of an outsourcing agreement address the following questions:

1. *Communication:*
   a. How will engagement status be reported, how often, and to whom?
   b. What metrics will be collected and reported? How often and to whom?
   c. What is the governance model? Who will be notified and under what circumstances?
   d. How will disputes be handled?

2. Change:
   a. What will happen if the business changes through mergers, acquisitions, or divestitures?
   b. How will short-term business changes such as a sudden downturn or surge in the economy be handled?
   c. How will shifts in priority be addressed?
   d. How will services be added or removed from the statement of work?
   e. How often will service level agreements be reevaluated?
   f. Under what circumstances can the contract be terminated, and how will the termination be handled?

When developing the contract, it is essential that the terms are fair. If either party believes that it will not be treated equitably, the long-term success of the engagement is in doubt. Although outsourcing is not a partnership in the true sense of the word, if each group has a vested interest in the overall success and believes that its own success is possible, the engagement has a higher probability of achieving its goals.

Establishing Effective SOWs and SLAs

Chapter 25 discusses the establishment of service level agreements (SLAs) for system maintenance. SLAs are equally important in outsourcing agreements because they provide the criteria against which to measure the supplier. Whether they are part of the master contract or established as separate legal documents, it is important that the statements of work (SOWs) and SLAs for outsourcing meet the three Cs criteria:

1. *Complete.* As noted above, one of the potential problems with outsourcing is that costs may be understated because not all needed functions are included in the contract. To avoid this, the team should:
   a. Ensure that the right members of the customer department are part of the requirements definition process.
   b. Follow the normal steps for identifying requirements, including prioritizing them.
   c. Work with customers to develop a detailed process map. This will help identify such periodic functions as ad hoc running of jobs, setting up new users' security codes, and performing disaster recovery tests that might otherwise have been overlooked.
2. *Clear.* Once requirements are identified, it is important that they are easily understood. Applying the SMART rules to service levels and statements of work helps ensure clarity. An SLA that requires

the supplier to "perform regular backups of key production files" may create ambiguity. What is the definition of "regular," and which files are "key"? In this case, the SLA should either detail the frequency of backups and name the files to include, or reference another document that contains this information. The latter approach is preferable because modifying a separate document is easier than amending a formal contract such as an SLA.

3. *Customer focused.* No matter how clear and complete the SLA is, if it does not meet the customers' needs, it is of little value. "All severity-one calls will be closed within eight working hours of initiation" is clear. Satisfying it may not, however, result in a high level of customer satisfaction because the agreement does not say "closed and resolved to the customer's satisfaction." To avoid similar problems, customers should be involved in the definition of SLAs and should approve them before they are incorporated into a contract.

While the preceding examples focused on support of existing systems, SOWs for new system development need the same level of the three Cs. It is important that there be no ambiguity over what the supplier is to deliver. If the SOW is for requirements specifications, an outline of the expected document should be included in the SOW. If the supplier is to deliver a completed system, the requirements specification document for that system should be referenced, along with specific clauses defining the level of testing to be performed, documentation to be provided, and training to be conducted. Nothing should be assumed or left to chance.

Although trust is an important part of an outsourcing engagement, a Six Sigma company knows that carefully documenting expectations and ensuring that they are clearly communicated and understood is the way to reduce defects and increase customer satisfaction.

Committing to Success

The final hallmark of a good outsourcing relationship is a mutual commitment to success. While the relationship established between a company and the vendor of packaged software is typically that of buyer and seller, successful outsourcing demands the establishment of something closer to a partnership. The critical success factors for such a relationship include:

- *A clear understanding of each partner's goals.* In Six Sigma terms, this allows each party to make fact-based decisions. If the supplier realizes that the company's highest priority is reducing costs, it will react differently to requests for changes than if it believed the goal is to increase service levels. Similarly, if the company understands that the supplier seeks to increase its market share as well as maintain a specific profit margin, it may be able to provide non-monetary assistance to the supplier in the form of customer references, articles in trade journals, etc.

■ *Shared accountability.* Although the supplier has clear responsibility to deliver specific work, the company needs to understand that if the supplier fails, the company fails to satisfy its customers. As a result, the company should place a high value on making the supplier successful. This does not mean doing the supplier's work but rather setting up procedures that serve as a safety net. Open lines of communication and periodic checkpoints diminish misunderstandings and can prevent major problems. The overall objective is to remain focused on the customer and to recognize that satisfying the customer is both parties' highest priority.

■ *Flexibility.* Reality is that, no matter how good the contract and how complete the SOW and SLA, there will be areas that were not addressed in the legal documents. If both groups are willing to compromise, the relationship will be more than simply a contractual one, and the probability of success increases. Understanding each other's goals and maintaining a customer focus can help the parties recognize where flexibility is most important and how they can achieve a mutually satisfactory compromise.

■ *The WIT factor.* The willingness to do "whatever it takes" (WIT) is one of the key elements that distinguishes successful outsourcing engagements. If both organizations recognize that their objective is to meet the customers' requirements and if neither is willing to accept failure, they will adopt "WIT" as their guiding principle and will function as true partners.

Even if the two companies work as partners, there is one other element required to ensure success: *effective communication.* That communication needs to exist at many levels: between IT and the supplier, between IT and the customer, and between the supplier and the customer. As with any Six Sigma project, it is important that customers are involved at all stages, that their requirements are understood, and that their expectations of what outsourcing will — and will not — provide are clearly defined. Only when all affected groups are working together as a team will outsourcing be successful.

Chapter 32

Effective Outsourcing

The previous chapter presented general guidelines for successful outsourcing engagements. This chapter discusses specific types of outsourcing, the challenges associated with each, and ways to mitigate the risks. In all cases, it is important to realize that, as shown in Exhibit 31.2, IT is a customer, albeit an intermediate one, of the supplier. This means that IT is responsible for clearly identifying its own requirements as well as those of the ultimate customer.

IT is also still the provider of services, although it has contracted with an outside firm to actually deliver those services. As such, IT should identify risks and attempt to mitigate them. Six Sigma and DFSS tools such as the customer requirements matrix (see Exhibit 5.15), the QFD (see Appendix F), and the FMEA (see Appendix D) can help document both requirements and risks.

Where DFSS Can Help

Although outsourcing night appear to have little in common with the development of a new product or system, and therefore be an unlikely candidate for DFSS tools and techniques, some of the concepts are applicable and can increase the likelihood of success. After all, the objective is to build in quality at the beginning of the process — in this case, the outsourcing engagement — rather than correct defects later.

Before initiating any outsourcing engagement, the company should ask the following questions:

1. *Does the outsource supplier have the needed process capability?*
   Exhibit 10.2 illustrates the competing forces that affect a product
   design. Similar forces impact outsourcing, although in the case of
   outsourcing, the *voice of the process* is the supplier's capacity. Does
   the outsourcer have an adequate supply of staff with the required
   skill set? Although the supplier may have already been selected
   using the process outlined in Chapter 31, it is important to ask this
   question when each new SOW begins.
2. *Have all requirements been defined?* In addition to ensuring that
   all customers have been included, it is essential to completely
   identify requirements. Although the rigor of a QFD may not be
   needed, IT should be aware of potential unspoken requirements
   as shown for the Kano model (see Exhibit 11.8) and should ensure
   that basic as well as excitement needs are addressed.
3. *What constitutes success?* In addition to SLAs and milestones, it is
   important to have a clearly articulated definition of success and a
   method of tracking progress toward the achievement of that success.
   Creation of a dashboard (see Exhibit 13.7) with frequent updates
   is one way of measuring and communicating the status of the project
   and preventing minor slippages from becoming critical.
4. *What could go wrong?* The corollary to defining success is the prevention of failure. Rather than wait for problems to occur, IT should
   attempt to identify possible defects and develop ways to prevent their
   occurrence. The FMEA is the tool of choice for this process.

Using DFSS concepts is a formal method of implementing the Five Ps
(Prior Planning Prevents Poor Performance) and can help ensure successful
outsourcing.

Custom System Development

The primary impetus for outsourcing system development projects is a
desire to lower costs. With the emergence of a large pool of relatively
low-cost programmers in locations such as India, the Philippines, and
China, United States-based firms have started to outsource development
to these off-shore companies.

Although there are distinct advantages to using off-shore programming
resources, there are also risks. One of the most critical is the potential for
gaps in communication. A root cause analysis would identify four causes:

1. *Location.* Like all off-site outsourcing, the lack of proximity to customers and IT staff can create communication gaps and misunderstandings.

When U.S. firms are dealing with locations as distant as Asia, the gaps widen because of the logistics of travel.

2. *Time zone.* The difference in time zones between the continental United States and Asia presents similar challenges. Even simple questions that could be readily resolved through a phone call are complicated by the fact that the developers may be separated from their customers by ten time zones.

3. *Language.* Although most Asian developers are fluent in English, they do not speak American English. As a result, misunderstandings can occur because of subtle linguistic differences.

4. *Culture.* Just as important as language are cultural differences. Because some cultures value consensus and harmony, staff may be unwilling to challenge requirements or decisions, to the detriment of the project.

Although these challenges are real, it is possible to resolve them. Developing a risk assessment and working with the supplier to establish a mitigation plan has several benefits. Not only does it quantify the potential problem, but it also helps ensure that IT and the supplier have a common understanding of the risks and that both groups agree with the method designed to reduce them.

Three ways to improve communication are:

1. *Develop regular status reporting.* The supplier should provide weekly written status reports showing, at a minimum, the progress it has made in the past weeks, any problems it encountered, and its plans for the following week. In addition to agreeing on the frequency of status reporting, IT and the supplier should work together to develop a standard format. This will help reduce variation and improve communication by ensuring that all critical areas are addressed. Key metrics from the status reports should be included on the dashboard. To further enhance communication, the governance model should include weekly teleconferences between the United States-based program or project manager and the off-shore staff. As was true of the status reports, a standard agenda facilitates effective communication.

2. *Establish frequent project milestones.* Although phases of the project can extend for multiple months, milestones should be established at intervals no greater than monthly, and the project team should conduct in-depth reviews of the deliverables. This will facilitate mid-course corrections and help ensure that problems are addressed before they become difficult and expensive to correct. It is also important that the format of deliverables is specified and

agreed upon at the beginning of the project. The format and timing of deliverables are part of IT's customer requirements. It is important to display the status of milestones and deliverables on the dashboard.

3. *Insist on an on-site presence from the supplier.* Some off-shore firms have established a hybrid model for their staffing, with the majority of the resources being located in lower-cost locations such as Asia but retaining one or more senior-level staff members at the customer's site. This approach can be an effective way of improving communication. If the outsourcer is not willing to adopt this approach or if visa constraints prohibit it, periodic visits from key members of the off-shore development staff can both foster teamwork and enhance communication.

Packaged Software Implementation

Chapter 30 outlined the steps involved in implementing commercial off-the-shelf (COTS) software. The premise of Chapter 30 was that although IT had decided to buy a software package rather than develop the system in-house, it would be responsible for the actual installation. That is not always the case. Motivated by the desire to complete the implementation of a COTS solution as quickly as possible, some companies hire either the COTS vendor's staff or a firm with expertise in the package to perform the actual installation. In either case, the assumption is that because the outside firms have implemented the software many times, the project schedule will be shorter than it would be if IT were responsible for the implementation. This assumption is normally valid; however, there are two potential problems:

1. *The solution may not fully meet the customers' needs.* There are two possible reasons for this.
   a. While the vendor or other firm may have expertise in the software, it does not have the same business knowledge that someone in the company does. As a result, requirements may not be fully understood and needed customization may not occur.
   b. The vendor may have a single method of installing the software, and that may not fulfill customer expectations. One size does not always fit all.
2. *The company will have no in-house expertise once the system is implemented.* If IT plans to provide ongoing support to customers and to install new releases itself, this can be a serious gap. Although it is possible to rely on the vendor for such support, in most cases that is a costly option.

As was true of other types of outsourcing, it is helpful to develop a risk assessment and to ensure that all decision makers understand the risks and what will be done to reduce them.

One way of mitigating these risks is to insist on having one or two members of the IT staff serve as part of the project implementation team. These people will have as their charter communicating between customers and the rest of the project team, documenting all decisions, and gaining expertise in the package so that they can guide other members of the in-house staff once the system is implemented. If this approach is selected, it is useful to develop both a project charter and a functional process map to clearly identify the roles and responsibilities of the two organizations.

System Maintenance

Companies outsource support of existing systems for a variety of reasons, including lowering costs and risks. The primary challenge associated with outsourced maintenance is meeting customer expectations. Because maintenance engagements are typically long-term, customer requirements and the customers themselves change. The result can be a disagreement over what services are covered by the contract and whether or not the supplier is delivering the desired level of service.

While clear, complete, customer-focused SLAs minimize these problems, one of the most effective ways of meeting the challenge is to establish customer steering committees, as described in Chapter 25. In addition to customers and the IT program manager, the steering committee would include one or more representatives from the outsourcer. By having regularly scheduled meetings to review the status of the engagement and to prioritize requirements, the steering committee helps maintain a customer focus and can identify and resolve problems before they become serious. The tools and techniques described in Chapter 25 also apply to these steering committees.

The Help Desk

Although it is important to have customers involved in the outsourcing of any aspect of IT, it is particularly critical when outsourcing the help desk. By definition, the help desk provides a first line of support for customer problems, making it essential that the service provider is one with a clear understanding of the requirements and a high degree of customer focus. Key customers whose opinion is respected should be part of the selection process so that they can help sell the decision to their departments.

One of the most common reasons for outsourcing help desk operations is the high staff turnover typically associated with it and a desire to mitigate that risk. Outsourcing can help; however, although outside firms may have expertise in running a help desk, they will not have knowledge of the company's unique software applications. Depending on the complexity of the systems being supported, the learning curve may be lengthy, a problem that is exacerbated if the outsourcer also experiences high staff turnover. To help reduce the impact of staff turnover, the company should insist that the outsourcer establish a database to document each problem reported and its resolution. This knowledge base should reduce the training required of new staff and speed problem resolution.

As is true of all outsourcing, it is important that customer requirements are clearly understood and that both customers and the supplier have a common set of expectations. SLAs are of particular importance in help desk outsourcing.

Data Center Operations

Data center operations were among the first functions that were outsourced, primarily because it was possible to lower costs by transferring responsibility to a service provider. Although companies can expect to achieve reduced costs, in addition to the risks that are common to outsourcing, they face the challenge of maintaining control of key decisions, such as when to apply new releases to the operating system and whether or not to replace one vendor's hardware with another's. In both cases, although the change should be invisible to the customer, it may not be. Applying a new release during quarter-end financial closing, for example, could have a negative impact on Finance.

Effective communications can mitigate the risks. Prior to outsourcing, IT should have identified all customers and their areas of responsibility and should have provided that information to the supplier. In addition to establishing a steering committee to review the supplier's performance, the company should institute a review process where all changes are approved before they are implemented. A functional process map is helpful in outlining the supplier and customer's respective responsibilities. And, of course, a carefully drafted SOW with clear SLAs will reduce ambiguity.

The Control Plan

Although companies should enter all outsourcing engagements under the assumption that they will be successful, a Six Sigma company knows that success is not left to chance. That is the reason for the Control phase of the DMAIC model. Prior to actually beginning the outsourcing, IT should work with its customers to establish the key metrics that help measure the success of the project and should develop a formal control plan, clearly outlining the steps to be implemented should the process not remain within the accepted limits. Exhibit 9.2 shows a sample control plan. Exhibit 9.3 is the related reaction plan. When developing metrics, the team may want to ensure that the metrics are valid by creating a metric reliability assessment (see Appendix E).

Used properly, outsourcing can provide a company with increased flexibility and reduced costs. The key to successful outsourcing is to apply Six Sigma's customer focus and reliance on fact-based decisions in choosing the functions to outsource as well as in managing outsourcing engagements.

IX

THE SIX SIGMA IT DEPARTMENT

Although IT itself often suffers from the shoemaker's children syndrome and is too busy improving processes within its customers' departments to analyze and improve its own processes, the DMAIC model can be used to improve the performance of the IT department as a whole. Chapter 33 describes the process of transforming IT into a Six Sigma department.

Chapter 33

Putting It All Together

Previous sections have shown how Six Sigma tools and concepts can be used to improve various aspects of system development, one project at a time. While these improvements are important and will result in reduced variation and increased customer satisfaction, even greater benefits can be obtained by treating IT as if it were a single process and seeking ways to improve that process. The DMAIC model described in Section II and the steps shown in Exhibit 9.5 apply to the process that is Information Technology as much as they did to GWC's order entry process. Although IT is an existing process rather than a new initiative and thus not a typical candidate for DFSS, the use of selected DFSS tools can help in the improvement process, as can application of some lean manufacturing precepts.

Define

The first phase of any project is *definition:* understanding the process, the problems associated with it, the customers and their requirements. Although it is likely that the result of the initial Definition phase will be the establishment of a number of separate projects, each with its own problem statement, if the objective is to transform IT, the process must begin at the highest level, namely understanding the department as a complete entity. Without the "big-picture" perspective, the department runs the risk of developing solutions that are counterproductive or that resolve only a part of the problem, necessitating rework later. To obtain the maximum benefit, the entire department must be involved. This is particularly important if IT wants to implement lean techniques and replace vertical silos of expertise with horizontal workflows where members of different IT functions work together as part of a single team serving one or more customers.

Because recommendations may cross functional lines within the department, it is also important that the project have as its champion either the head of IT or the person to whom that individual reports. Without commitment at that level, the credibility — and therefore the success — of the initiative is questionable.

Step 1: Define the Problem

A potential initial problem statement might be, "IT does not fully understand the relationships among its internal processes." While this statement does not meet the SMART criteria, it provides a starting point and sets the tone of the overall project, which is to understand how each of the functions within IT interacts with the other.

Step 2: Form a Team

Because the objective of the initial project is to understand the department, it is important to include members from all IT functions on the team. The support functions shown in Exhibit 5.1 are of lesser importance at this stage of the project but should be reviewed and potentially included as subsidiary projects are chartered. As is true of all Six Sigma projects, the characteristics of effective team members (see Exhibit 5.2) should be considered when selecting the team.

Step 3: Establish a Project Charter

Although at this point, the team may not be able to quantify benefits, the project charter (see Appendix A) will identify expected team involvement and critical success factors as well as a proposed high-level schedule.

Step 4: Develop a Project Plan

For the initial project, which will consist of only the Definition phase, a separate project plan may not be necessary. Subsequent projects, which will be of longer duration and greater complexity, will benefit from a more detailed project plan than the one included in the project charter.

Step 5: Identify the Customers

When identifying customers, the team should consider not just the traditional customers, namely "end-user" departments, but all groups that use the services of IT. These may include:

- Finance, which receives budget, cost, and other performance data
- Planning, the recipient of the strategic planning document
- Executive offices, which may include IT projects in their briefings to financial analysts
- All IT functions, including Computer Operations, Telecommunications, and System Development, because they rely on each other for data and services

A value chain map (see Exhibit 11.3) is useful for documenting the relationships among the various groups.

Step 6: Identify Key Outputs

In conjunction with the identification of customers, the team should define the outputs that IT provides to each customer. When team members brainstormed to identify customers and outputs, they developed the chart shown as Exhibit 33.1. Further brainstorming resulted in the identification of other customers and outputs, as well as the addition of the Supplier column as shown on Exhibit 33.2. Ultimately, this information will form the foundation for a SIPOC.

Step 7: Identify and Prioritize Customer Requirements

Although team members might believe that they understand their customers' requirements, they should not skip this step. For the initial project, while it is particularly important to identify the internal IT functions' expectations, other customers' needs should not be neglected. The objective is to identify

Exhibit 33.1   Initial Identification of Customers and Outputs

Output	Customer
System requirements	System development team
New system	End user (customer)
Support requirements	System maintenance team
System support	End user (customer)

Exhibit 33.2   Second Identification of Customers and Outputs

Supplier	Output	Customer
End user (customer)	System requirements	System development team
System development team	New system	End user (customer)
End user (customer)	Support requirements	System maintenance team
System maintenance team	System support	End user (customer)
Operations	Running of system	End user (customer)
Telecommunications	Increased bandwidth	End user (customer)
IT finance	Hourly rate calculation	System development/ system maintenance teams
System development/ system maintenance teams	Bills	End user (customer)
IT management	Metrics definition	System development/ system maintenance teams
System development/ system maintenance teams	Monthly metrics	IT management/end user (customer)

what is important to all customers and to determine how satisfied each is with the service or product IT is providing. Creating a customer requirements matrix (see Exhibit 5.15) helps ensure better communication and may identify opportunities for improvement.

The team may prefer to develop an initial QFD (see Exhibit 11.13), because that calculates gaps between current satisfaction levels and the department's goals and factors in the customers' importance rankings when determining development priorities. Regardless of the tool it uses to document requirements, the team should be aware of the Kano model (see Exhibit 11.8) and should seek to identify unspoken requirements.

Step 8: Document the Current Process

The final step in the Definition phase is to understand the current process. To accomplish this, the team should create a detailed process map, showing all steps and their interrelationships. A functional process map (see Exhibit 5.14) can be used and has the benefit of clearly illustrating dependencies among the various IT functions. Alternatively, the team may prefer to develop a traditional detailed process map (see Exhibit 5.13). In either case, it is useful to identify wait states between steps because one of the department's goals should be to reduce all forms of waste (see Exhibit 6.3).

At this point, the initial project is complete. The detailed process map and the high-level definition of customer requirements will have met the project goal of understanding the relationships among departmental functions. IT is now ready to use those documents as the basis for examining its internal processes. By reviewing customer requirements and the degree to which they are satisfied, the project champion can identify areas that should be improved and can charter teams to make those improvements. If a QFD was used, the development priority columns simplify this process and help the champion make fact-based decisions.

It is likely that a number of projects will be initiated as a result of the original process mapping and requirements definition. It should also be expected that, unlike the original project with its generalized problem statement, the second-tier projects will have detailed SMART problem statements. One such problem statement might be "The IT system development budget exceeded plan by 13 percent for each of the past three years, resulting in an unfavorable variance in the G&A (general and administrative) budget. The project's goal is to develop a budgeting process that results in a variance of no more than 8 percent in the next fiscal year and no more than 3 percent in the following year."

Like each of the new projects, this one would follow the full DMAIC model. In the Definition phase, the project team would establish a charter and a full project plan. Although high-level customer and requirements identification was done in the first project, the team would delve more deeply into both areas, focusing on the customers for the system development budgeting process. And, because the problem relates to actual costs as well as the budget, the process map that the team develops would include the determination of actual costs. Because there are a number of inputs to the costing model, the team might develop a SIPOC chart to explain how costs are calculated. Exhibit 33.3 shows an example of a SIPOC chart for the calculation of IT charges to other departments.

Exhibit 33.3   SIPOC Chart for Calculation of System Development Costs

Supplier	Input	Process	Output	Customer
Development staff	Hours worked	Calculation of system development charges	System development charges	Project owner
Computer operations	CPU Minutes			IT Management
Contract staff firms	T&M Charges			Finance department
IT Management	Hourly rate for development staff			
	Bill rate for CPU minutes			

Measure

After fully defining the project, the team moves into the Measurement phase. It is here that the team quantifies the process and determines the magnitude of the problem.

Step 1: Determine What to Measure

Although the SIPOC chart identified the elements of system development costs, the team realized that the most meaningful measurements would be of individual projects because there might be large variations between projects. Furthermore, because budget overruns could occur at any step in the development process, the team decided to measure each phase of the SDLC. As the GWC OE team realized, averages can be deceptive because they do not measure the extent of variation.

At this stage, the team also defined defects. Because the project's overall goal was to ensure budget fidelity, any variance — either over or under budget — was tracked as a defect.

Step 2: Conduct the Measurements

Because the objective was to understand what had caused variation in the past, the team used historical records that included the department's billings and project histories. Depending on their charters, other teams might establish measurements of current processes. A team whose objective was to reduce cycle time would want to measure the current minimum and maximum times for each step of a process and the delays between steps. While historical information might be helpful in determining whether there have been any shifts — either positive or negative — in cycle time, what is most critical for this component is the current "as-is" process.

Step 3: Calculate Current Sigma Level

This is a key step because it provides a baseline against which to measure improvements. It also helps the department focus on its overall goal of performing at the six sigma level. The budget fidelity team measured defects as shown above and counted each phase of the life cycle as an opportunity when calculating DPMO.

Step 4: Determine Process Capability

Calculating current process capability, while not mandatory, is helpful in understanding how closely the process meets customer requirements. It is also helpful to graph the measurements to provide a visual representation of the voice of the process versus the voice of the customer. Exhibit 6.20 shows a process capability analysis.

Step 5: Benchmark Process Leaders

Although some projects may not include this step, if the team is concerned that its goals may not be achievable, benchmarking provides a way of determining how other companies have solved similar problems.

Analyze

In the Analysis phase, teams evaluate the data they collected in the previous phases to determine why variation occurred and how it can be reduced.

Step 1: Determine What Caused the Variation

Working with both the detailed process map and the measurements taken, the team sought to understand why one system development project was completed within its budget while others were not and tried to identify common causes for budget overruns. The questions asked included:

- *Are there non-value-added steps in the process?* The team identified duplicate time reporting as one step that provided no value. As a corollary to this, the team also sought to identify delays in the process so that they, like the non-value-added steps, could be eliminated.
- *Were cost overruns greatest in one phase of the SDLC? If so, why?* Measurements showed that the greatest variances occurred in the testing phase. Further analysis revealed that testing had uncovered incomplete requirements, which resulted in additional coding and testing efforts. A root cause analysis indicated that key customers had not been involved in the requirements definition phase.
- *Were the original cost estimates inaccurate because they did not include all cost components?* The team discovered that in two cases, the projected cost had not included computer and network charges.
- *Were the higher costs incurred because there were schedule overruns? If so, was the cause a poor estimate of time or a change in scope?* The team discovered that some projects suffered from both inaccurate estimates and changes in scope.
- *Were some cost overruns the result of using outside contractors rather than lower-cost in-house staff?* The team discovered that

this was the case but that there had been no in-house staff with the required skills.

Root cause analysis (see Exhibit 7.6) and Pareto charts (see Exhibit 7.7) are helpful in identifying the primary causes of variation and deciding which ones should be addressed first.

Although it is not part of this phase of classic Six Sigma, the team had been trained in DFSS and recognized the value of mistake-proofing their process. To do that, they constructed an FMEA, listing everything that could go wrong with the process and devised ways to prevent those problems from occurring.

Step 2: Brainstorm Ideas for Process Improvements

Using the root cause analysis and Pareto charts, the teams should propose ways to improve the process. As with all brainstorming exercises, it is important to employ the "no bad ideas" rule. While some ideas will be rejected in the next step, every suggestion should be documented during brainstorming. The budget fidelity team's suggestions included:

- Refusing to change the scope of a project without a formal change process that identifies the cost and schedule impacts of the proposed change
- Developing an estimating worksheet that listed all possible cost elements

Step 3: Identify Greatest Impact Improvements

A process improvement ranking (see Appendix C) helps quantify the suggested improvements and their impact on customer requirements, as does the product features portion of the QFD. Teams may also want to develop cost and time rankings (see Exhibit 7.8) to identify "low hanging fruit" that should be addressed first. Although the budget fidelity team's suggestions were low cost, they were not free. In particular, the imposition of a rigid change control process required the development and implementation of a communication plan to ensure that customers understood the reasons for the new procedure.

Step 4: Develop Proposed Process Map

If the process is being changed, as would occur if non-value-added steps were eliminated, the original process map should be revised. In the case of the budget fidelity team, steps were added to incorporate the requirement for change control.

Step 5: Assess the Risks

Teams should also assess the risks of their proposed changes and develop methods of mitigating them using an FMEA (see Appendix D). The primary risk that the budget fidelity team identified was customer resistance to the change control process. The mitigation action was the development and delivery of a communication plan, explaining the benefits of the new procedure. It should be noted that this FMEA has a different focus from the one created in Step 1. The first FMEA addressed the current process and attempted to improve it, while this one analyzes the proposed improvements to determine and correct potential flaws.

Improve

Having developed its proposals, the team is ready to begin the improvement phase.

Step 1: Gain Approval for Proposed Changes

It is important that everyone who will be impacted by the proposed changes review and approve them. If there are a large number of reviewers, an approval checklist (see Exhibit 8.2) helps track the status of approvals.

Step 2: Finalize the Implementation Plan

If changes were made as a result of the review and approval process, the implementation plan should be revised to reflect those changes.

Step 3: Implement the Approved Changes

The team is now ready to implement its proposed changes. Like all Six Sigma projects, actual implementation should include a formal project plan with clearly defined deliverables and milestones, as well as frequent communication of status to all affected groups.

Control

No Six Sigma project is complete without the control phase, which is designed to measure improvements and ensure that they are sustained.

Step 1: Establish Key Metrics

Each project should develop metrics that will be used to track the progress of the improvements. In the case of the budget fidelity project, there was a single metric: a calculation of the percentage variance between actual costs and the budget. Although a summary version was included in monthly reports to senior management, each development project team tracked their actuals versus plan for each stage of the SDLC and included those metrics in their status reports. The metric reliability assessment (see Appendix E) helps determine the validity of proposed metrics.

Because the team wanted to identify variances as early as possible in the process, they also developed a dashboard that was updated weekly and visible to all members of the development staff. The fact that multiple projects' status was shown on the dashboard encouraged friendly rivalry between project teams and helped increase overall quality.

Step 2: Develop the Control Strategy

Recognizing that processes do shift and variation does occur, each project team should also develop a control plan (see Exhibit 9.2) and related reaction plans. For the budget fidelity team, the reaction plan included immediate analysis of any variation that exceeded the annual goal, with quarterly Pareto analysis of root causes.

As is true of all projects, completion of one DMAIC cycle marks the beginning of the next. Exhibit 4.2 shows the iterative nature of Six Sigma projects.

Putting It All Together

IT is a complex function composed of a number of departments, each of which exists to provide services to customers. Although senior management of IT is well aware of that, the various functions within IT sometimes operate as if they were separate, competing departments rather than part of a whole. Projects such as those described above, which seek to understand and communicate the interdependencies among the functions and to promote teamwork among those functions, are an effective method of breaking down the barriers among the groups and ultimately improving customer satisfaction.

Once the department has identified its customers and their requirements and has improved its processes, it should ensure that it continues to meet the requirements and — equally important — that it communicates how well the department as a whole is doing. A departmental scorecard is an effective method of tracking and communicating progress.

As was true of the scorecard that the GWC OE team developed (see Exhibit 9.4), the IT departmental scorecard should consist of only a few metrics and should be designed to provide a high-level status of IT's progress in meeting customer requirements. Typical elements included on the scorecard and the IT functions they measure are:

■ System uptime — computer operations
■ Schedule fidelity — system development
■ Budget fidelity — entire department
■ Customer satisfaction — entire department

Generating the metrics is important. Communicating them is even more critical. And it is not only end users who should receive the communication. The scorecard, which is normally presented as a series of graphs showing goals and monthly or quarterly results, should be made available to all members of IT as well as to customers. Not only are the various functions within IT customers of each others' processes, but they are also the people whose work is being measured. Keeping them involved and informed helps to promote both teamwork and commitment. These are key ingredients in the success of the entire IT department.

Teamwork, customer focus, a commitment to quality, and the determination to make decisions based on facts are the hallmarks of a Six Sigma company. As corporations like Motorola and General Electric can attest, although the journey is not always easy, the results are worth the effort. Fewer defects improve both customer satisfaction and the bottom line.

The Information Technology (IT) department can benefit from incorporating the Six Sigma philosophy and tools into its operation, even if the company as a whole has not embraced Six Sigma, just as IT improved its processes by adopting the SEI CMM maturity path although that did not apply to the rest of the corporation. The structure provided by the DMAIC model helps ensure that IT is working efficiently and effectively, and provides mechanisms for determining which projects will generate the highest level of customer satisfaction. That is, by employing Six Sigma processes, IT will be doing the right thing the right way. The right people will be involved, with their responsibilities clearly defined. Risks will be minimized, and benefits increased.

If that sounds close to perfection, it is important to remember that the goal of Six Sigma is exactly that — nearly defect-free operations. Achieving the goal is not simple. It requires hard work and commitment. It takes time. However, it is possible for organizations that follow the DMAIC model, adopting and adapting Six Sigma tools.

For IT departments willing to make the commitment, the rewards are clear: lower costs and improved customer satisfaction. That is the Six Sigma promise.

X

APPENDICES

Appendix A

The Project Charter

The charter is the single most important document in a project because it is used to establish the project and provides a summary of key information. While other forms are optional, all projects are expected to have a charter. Exhibit A.1 shows a sample charter. The remainder of this appendix outlines the use of the charter and explains how to complete each field.

- *Who creates it?* Although the project's champion may begin to complete some of the basic fields, it is normally the team lead or a designated recorder (scribe) who is responsible for creating the charter.
- *When is it created?* Key fields are completed during the team's first meeting. Others are added at later stages in the project.
- *Who is responsible for updating the form?* The champion or recorder (scribe) has continuing responsibility for the accuracy and completeness of the charter.
- *How often is it updated?* Whenever information shown on the form changes, the charter should be updated.
- *Who can view the data?* At a minimum, the charter should be available to all team members and affected customers (although some companies may insist that financial information be removed before distributing it to external customers). Ideally, the charter should be available to anyone within the organization.

Exhibit A.1 Project Charter

Summary					
Process impacted			Total financial Impact		
Team Leader			Champion		
Start Date			Target Completion Date		
Project Description					
Benefits					
	Units	Current	Goal	Actual achieved	Projected date
Sigma Level	Sigma				
COPQ					
Customer Sat					
Other Customer benefits					
Team Membership					
Name	Role		Department	% Time	GB Trained?
Support Required					
Training required					
Other support required					
Schedule					
Milestone/ Deliverable	Target date	Owner	Estimated cost	Comments	
Critical Success Factors and Risks					
Critical success factors					
Risks					
Approvals					
Role/Title	Name			Date	
Revision History					
Revision number	Authors			Date	

Field	*How to Complete It*
Summary section:	This section serves to document key descriptive information about the project.
Process Impacted	Enter a brief description of the process that is being targeted for improvement. This is one of the key fields that should be entered at the team's first meeting.
Total Financial Impact	Enter the net financial effect of the project; that is, the anticipated cost savings minus any costs incurred during the project. It is unlikely that this information will be available at the early stages of the project, but the impact should be documented as soon as it is estimated.
Team Leader	Enter the name of the person who has been designated the team leader. Like the description of the process, this information should be available and entered at the first team meeting.
Champion	Enter the name of the project champion. Like the description of the process, this information should be available and entered at the first team meeting.
Start Date	Enter the date that the project was initiated. Depending on the company's preference, this can be either the date that the team was chartered or the date of the first team meeting. The start date should be entered at the first team meeting.
Target Completion Date	Enter the date that the "improvement" phase is expected to be completed. Although this field is subject to revision as the project progresses through the various phases, it should be entered as soon as it is projected.
Project Description	Enter a brief description of the project, including a summary of anticipated benefits. Once the formal problem and goal statements are developed, they should be added to this field.
Benefits section:	The purpose of this section is to quantify the projected benefits of the project. Although four potential benefit categories have been listed, it is likely that a project will have other benefits, including cost reduction. These should be described and quantified on separate lines. When "Other Customer Benefits" are quantified, it is important to replace the words "Other Customer Benefits" with the specific benefit to be achieved.

Field	How to Complete It
Benefits — Units	With the exception of Sigma Level, all entries in the benefits section should have the unit of measure specified in this field. An example of COPQ units might be "percentage of sales," while customer satisfaction units might be "scale of 1 to 5."
Benefits — Current	Enter the current or baseline level of this item.
Benefits — Goal	Enter the projected level for this item once the process improvements have been implemented.
Benefits — Actual Achieved	Enter the level that was actually achieved once the process improvements were implemented. This column will not be completed until the Control phase of the project.
Benefits — Projected Date	Enter the date on which the benefits are anticipated to have been realized.
Team Membership section:	This section identifies the people who will serve on the team, their roles, and the percentage of time they are expected to devote to the project.
Name	Enter the team member's name.
Role	Enter his or her role on the team. At a minimum, Team Leader should be identified, with all other participants being listed as Team Members.
Department	Enter the team member's department or, if he or she is an external customer, his or her company affiliation.
Percent Time	Enter the percentage of time the team member is expected to spend on the project. It should be noted that this is an average, and that at certain phases of the project, participation may be at a higher or lower level.
GB Trained?	If a team member has completed Green Belt training, enter "Yes." If the team member is a Black Belt, enter "Black Belt" in this field.
Support Required section:	This section allows the team to clearly identify support requirements other than team members' time and the costs associated with each milestone/ deliverable below.
Training Required	Enter the type of training that will be required. If training must be completed by a specific date, it is helpful to note that, as well as any costs that will be incurred.

Field	*How to Complete It*
Other Support Required	If the project team will need other types of support, such as contiguous workspace or access to specific network drives, enter that information, along with the date that the support is needed.
Schedule section:	This section serves as a high-level project plan, showing — at a minimum — the dates on which each of the DMAIC phases is targeted to be completed. Longer projects may divide phases into smaller milestones and may document the schedule for completion of specific deliverables such as process maps or benchmarking results.
Milestone/Deliverable	Enter the name of the milestone or deliverable.
Target Date	Enter the date on which the milestone or deliverable is expected to be completed.
Owner	Enter the name of the person with overall responsibility for the milestone or deliverable. This may not always be the team leader.
Estimated Cost	If there will be costs in addition to team members' time, enter them here. Costs may include travel expenses. Items listed in the "Support Required" section should not be repeated here.
Comments	This field can be used to indicate the completion of a milestone or to document the reasons for a changed target date.
Critical Success Factor and Risk section:	The purpose of this section is to identify the CSFs and risks that the project faces.
Critical Success Factors	Enter the events that must occur if the project is to be successful.
Risks	Enter the potential reasons that the project may not be successful.
Approval section:	This section serves to document the review and approval of the project charter. Approvals of other project documents are recorded on the individual deliverables.
Role/Title	If the approver is the project champion or sponsor, enter the role; otherwise, enter the individual's title.
Name	Enter the reviewer's name.
Date	Enter the date on which the reviewer approved the project charter.

Field	*How to Complete It*
Revision History section:	The purpose of this section is to document when changes were made to the project charter and by whom.
Revision Number	Enter the revision number. Normally, revisions are given sequential whole numbers.
Authors	Enter the name of the persons who actually revised the document. This may or may not be the person who instigated the change to the document.
Date	Enter the date on which the revision was made.

Appendix B

The Functional Process Map

Process maps are the Six Sigma tools used to provide pictorial represen-tations of the sequence of steps in a process. While other maps depict only the tasks or steps, the functional process map clearly illustrates which department or function is responsible for each step. Exhibit B.1 shows

Exhibit B.1   Functional Process Map

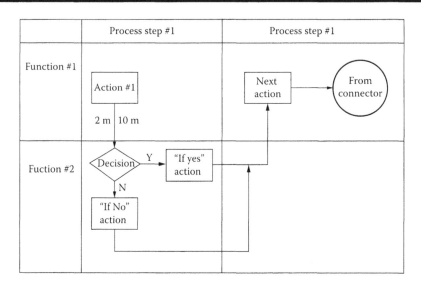

the format of a functional process map. The remainder of this appendix outlines the use of a map and explains how to complete each field.

- *Who creates it?* Anyone on the project team can be responsible for the creation of a functional process map.
- *When is it created?* The initial process map is typically created during the Definition phase of a project. This is often referred to as the "as-is" process. Maps showing the proposed revisions to the process are developed at the end of the Analysis phase.
- *Who is responsible for updating the form?* The individual who created the initial map should assume responsibility for its updates.
- *How often is it updated?* Whenever the team uncovers new steps or dependencies or if the process changes, the map should be updated.
- *Who can view the data?* At a minimum, the map should be available to all team members and affected customers. Ideally, it should be available to anyone within the organization.

Mapping Conventions

1. Rectangles represent actions.
2. Diamonds indicate a decision point. Each diamond will have two lines exiting from it, one representing the action taken if the answer to the question is positive, the other showing the result of a negative response.
3. Circles represent connectors from one page to the next. The corresponding "from" and "to" connectors will have the same number.
4. Lines with arrowheads illustrate the directional flow of tasks and decisions.

Field	How to Complete It
Process Step #1, Process Step #2	Enter along the top of the map the names of the individual process steps being charted. Examples are "Order Entry" and "Packing." If there is only one step, this information can be omitted.
Function #1, Function #2	Enter the names of the departments or the functions within departments that have responsibility for tasks. "Customer" or "Supplier" can be used as function names.
Action #1	Enter the first step in the process, using a verb/object construct (e.g., "Enter customer name and number."). The position of the action box indicates which department or function has primary responsibility for it. In this example, Function #1 initiates Action #1. Draw a line exiting from the action and pointing to the next action or decision. Depending on where the next action box will be placed on the map, the exit line should come from either the right side or the bottom of the action box. In this case, because the next activity is a decision to be made by Function #2, the line exits from the bottom and points to a diamond within Function #2. If the team has identified the minimum and maximum time required for the action, these can be indicated below the box. The minimum time is shown to the left, the maximum to the right. In this case, the range of times for Action #1 is from two to ten minutes.
Decision	Enter the question that requires a decision, using an abbreviated question format (e.g., "Customer in database?"). Draw two exit lines, one from the right side of the diamond, the other from the bottom. Label the line to the right "Yes" or "y," the one from the bottom "No" or "n."

Field	How to Complete It
"If Yes" Action	Following the rules shown for Action #1, enter the action to be performed if the answer to the decision was "Yes." In this example, the responsibility for this action is with Function #1.
"If No" Action	Following the rules shown for Action #1, enter the action to be performed if the answer to the decision was "No." In this example, the responsibility for this action is with Function #1.
Next Action	Following the rules shown for Action #1, enter the next action to be performed. In this example, the responsibility for this action is with Function #2.
Connector	Because the next action will be shown on another page, a connector is needed. Enter a unique number in the circle. The next page will begin with a connector with the same number.

Appendix C

The Process Improvement Ranking Spreadsheet

The process improvement ranking spreadsheet provides a clear, fact-based method of determining which process improvements will have the greatest impact on satisfying customer requirements. Exhibit C.1 shows the format of a process improvement ranking spreadsheet. The remainder of this appendix outlines the use of the spreadsheet and explains how to complete each field.

- *Who creates it?* Anyone on the project team can be responsible for the creation of a process improvement ranking spreadsheet.
- *When is it created?* Ranking occurs at the end of the Analysis phase, once the team has brainstormed possible solutions.
- *Who is responsible for updating the form?* The spreadsheet is rarely revised; however, if updates are needed, the individual who created the initial spreadsheet should assume responsibility for its updates.
- *How often is it updated?* Rarely. Once recommendations have been approved and the Improvement phase begins, there is no need to update the ranking.
- *Who can view the data?* The spreadsheet is often included in the briefing given to the project champion when seeking approval for the proposed improvements. It should be made available to all team members and to interested customers.

Exhibit C.1   Process Improvement Ranking Spreadsheet

Customer requirement	Importance ranking	Effect	Impact on Cust	Effect	Impact on Cust	Effect	Impact on Cust	Total Impact
		3		3		3		
1	2	4	5	4	5	4	5	6
Degree of satisfaction from implementing improvement			7		7		7	

Improvement steps and effects

Field (The numbers in parentheses correspond to the numbers on the Exhibit C.1.)	How to Complete It
Customer Requirement (1)	Enter the requirements from the Customer Requirement Matrix (Exhibit 5.15).
Importance Ranking (2)	Enter the importance ranking that the customer assigned to this requirement (Exhibit 5.15). To provide clear distinctions among requirements, a scale of 1-4-7-10 is recommended.
Proposed Improvement (3)	Enter a brief description of the proposed process improvement.
Effect on Requirement (4)	Rank the proposed improvement's effect on satisfying the requirement, using a scale of 1-4-7-10.
Impact on Customer (5)	This is a calculated field, the result of multiplying the Effect (4) by the Importance (2).
Total Impact on Customer (6)	This is a calculated field, the result of summing each of the Impact fields on this row. It shows the effect that implementing all proposed improvements would have on that specific requirement.
Degree of Satisfaction from Implementing Improvement (7)	This is a calculated field, the sum of all Impacts (5) in this column. It shows the effect implementing this specific improvement would have on all customer requirements.

Appendix D

The Failure Modes and Effects Analysis (FMEA)

The failure modes and effects analysis (FMEA) spreadsheet is used to identify the risks in a process, to quantify the effects that failure would have on customers, and to establish mitigation plans for high-risk items. Exhibit D.1 shows the format of an FMEA. The remainder of this appendix outlines the use of the spreadsheet and explains how to complete each field.

- *Who creates it?* Anyone on the project team can be responsible for creation of an FMEA.
- *When is it created?* Risk assessment often occurs at the beginning of a project when a team seeks to identify areas for improvement. Once a project has been initiated, an FMEA is typically created at the end of the Analysis phase to evaluate the recommended solutions.
- *Who is responsible for updating the form?* Anyone on the team can assume responsibility for the updates.
- *How often is it updated?* The FMEA should be updated when the actions outlined in the Action Plan section are completed. Additionally, because it is a "living" document, the FMEA should be reviewed periodically as part of the Control phase to determine whether there are any new potential failure modes.
- *Who can view the data?* The FMEA is often included in the briefing given to the project champion when seeking approval for the proposed improvements. As a key project document, it should be made available to all team members and to interested customers.

Exhibit D.1 Failure Modes and Effects Analysis

	Failure modes and effects analysis (FMEA)	
Process Name:	Date Prepared:	Revision Number:
Prepared By:	Revised By:	Revision Date:

What Could Happen?			Why and How Often?		How Do We Prevent It?			Action Plan				Results of Actions		
Process Step	Potential Failure Mode	Potential Failure Effects	S E V	Potential Causes	O C C	Current Controls	F A I L (FAIL)	R P N	Actions Recommended	Resp.	Target Date	Date Completed/ Comments	S E V	O C C	F A I L (FAIL) / R P N

Field	How to Complete It
Process Name	Enter the name of the process being evaluated.
Prepared By	Enter the name of the person completing the initial version of the FMEA.
Date Prepared	Enter the date the initial version was created.
Revised By	For all subsequent versions of the FMEA, enter the name of the person who documented this revision. This may or may not be the person who was responsible for the change being documented.
Revision Number	Enter the revision number. Normally, revisions are given sequential whole numbers.
Revision Date	Enter the date on which the revision was made.
Process Step	For each process step being evaluated, enter the name. Depending on the process, individual inputs may be substituted for "Process Step."
"What Could Happen?" section:	This section describes the possible failures and their effect on customer requirements.
Potential Failure Mode	Describe ways in which the process might or does fail. Each potential failure should be listed in a separate row.
Potential Failure Effects	Describe the impact that the failure would have on customer requirements.
Severity	Quantify the impact of a failure on the customer's requirements. To provide clear distinctions among potential failures, a scale of 1-4-7-10 is recommended.
"Why and How Often?" section:	This section quantifies potential causes and the frequency with which the failure occurs.
Potential Causes	List possible causes of the failure. If there are multiple causes for a single failure, each should be shown in a separate row.
Frequency of Occurrence (OCC)	Quantify the frequency with which this possible cause occurs, resulting in failure. Use a scale of 1-4-7-10.

Field	How to Complete It
"How Do We Prevent It?" section:	This section describes the procedures or controls that are currently being used to prevent the failure and the probability that they may not detect/prevent the failure.
Current Controls	Describe the existing procedures that are used to prevent or detect the failure mode. Where formal documents such as an SOP exist, include the number and file name.
Failure Probability	Quantify the probability that the current controls will fail, using a scale of 1-4-7-10.
Risk Priority Number (RPN)	This is a calculated field, the result of multiplying Severity, Occurrence, and Failure Probability. Failure modes with high RPNs should have corresponding corrective action plans developed.
Action Plan section:	This section describes the actions that will be taken to mitigate high-risk items.
Actions Recommended	Describe the action that will be taken to reduce the occurrence or the failure probability.
Responsible Person	Enter the name of the person responsible for completing the action.
Target Date	Enter the date that the corrective action is to be completed.
Date Completed/Comments	Enter the date the action was completed and any explanatory notes.
Results of Actions section:	This section measures the success of the corrective actions by recalculating Severity, Occurrence, Failure Probability and the resulting RPN.
Resulting Severity	Quantify the impact of a failure on the customer's requirements, using a scale of 1-4-7-10. Normally this will not have changed as a result of the corrective action.
Resulting Frequency of Occurrence	Quantify the frequency with which this possible cause results in a failure after the corrective action has been completed. Use a scale of 1-4-7-10.
Resulting Failure Probability	Quantify the probability that the controls will fail after the corrective action has been completed. Use a scale of 1-4-7-10.

Field	*How to Complete It*
Resulting RPN	This is a calculated field, the result of multiplying the Resulting Severity, Occurrence, and Failure Probability fields. If the corrective action has been effective, the Resulting RPN should be lower than the original one.

Appendix E

The Metric Reliability Assessment Spreadsheet

The metric reliability assessment spreadsheet helps a team determine which metrics will have the most validity. Exhibit E.1 shows the format of the metric reliability assessment spreadsheet. The remainder of this appendix outlines the use of the spreadsheet and explains how to complete each field.

- *Who creates it?* Anyone on the project team can be responsible for creation of a metric reliability assessment spreadsheet.
- *When is it created?* Metric assessment typically occurs at the beginning of the Control phase when the team begins to establish its key metrics.
- *Who is responsible for updating the form?* The form is rarely updated; however, anyone on the team can assume responsibility for the updates.
- *How often is it updated?* Rarely. Once metrics have been established, there is no need to revise the spreadsheet.
- *Who can view the data?* All team members and interested customers should have access to the information.

Exhibit E.1 Metric Reliability Assessment Spreadsheet

Process:									
Prepared By:									
Date Prepared:									
Metric	Measurement	Collector	Data reliability	Data repeatability	Collection delays	Collector availability	Total metric reliability	Comments
Averages								

Field	How to Complete It
Process Name	Enter the name of the process for which metrics are being developed.
Prepared By	Enter the name of the person completing the assessment spreadsheet.
Date Prepared	Enter the date the assessment was completed.
Metric	Enter the proposed metric.
Measurement	Enter each of the measurements that form part of a metric in a separate row.
Collector	Enter either the name of the person who will take the measurement or the person's job title/function.
Data Reliability	Quantify the objectivity of the data: 1 = subjective, no historical basis 4 = based on anecdotal historical experience 7 = based on direct observation 10 = obtained directly from an objective source (e.g., computer system, time stamp)

Field	How to Complete It
Data Repeatability	Quantify the degree to which the measurement is repeatable among collectors: 1 = subjective 4 = based on data specific to the collector (e.g., operator's wristwatch) 7 = transcribed from printed source 10 = obtained directly from an objective source (e.g., computer system, time stamp)
Collection Delays	Quantify the delays in obtaining the data: 1 = request for measurement waits in a queue or inbox and is addressed sporadically 4 = request for measurement is processed at regular intervals but less frequently than daily 7 = request for measurement is processed at regular intervals more frequently than daily but not immediately 10 = request is processed immediately
Collector Availability	Quantify the degree to which the collector is involved in other activities and unable to take measurements: 1 = higher-priority activities require >75 percent of time 4 = higher-priority activities require >50 but <75 percent of time 7 = higher-priority activities require >25 but <50 percent of time 10 = this is the collector's highest priority or the data comes from an automated source
Total Metric Reliability	This is a calculated field, the result of summing the four previous fields.
Comments	Enter any information about the individual measurements that might explain low reliability scores.
Averages	This is a calculated field, the result of averaging each of the numeric columns. It is useful in pointing out areas for improvement.

Appendix F

The Quality Function Deployment (QFD) Matrix

It can be argued that the QFD matrix is the single most important tool used for DFSS projects, because it provides a clear linkage between requirements (the "what") and the features or characteristics that will satisfy them (the "how"). Because of its numerous sections, one of which resembles a roof, QFD is often referred to as the House of Quality (HOQ). Its strengths include the fact that it provides:

1. A single repository for key requirements and the methods in which they will be satisfied
2. The ability to cascade data from one phase of the project to the next, ensuring an unbroken linkage between phases

Exhibit F.1 shows the format of a QFD matrix. The remainder of this appendix outlines the use of the matrix and explains how to complete each section of the House of Quality.

- *Who creates it?* Although any member of the project team can create the QFD, the content is normally determined through brainstorming and other group meetings. It is advisable to assign one member of the team responsibility for transcribing the results of those sessions into the QFD format.

Exhibit F.1   QFD Matrix

Product Requirement/ Feature Correlation

PR1
PR2
PR3
PR4
PR5
PR6
PR7
PR8
PR9

Product Requirements/ Features

	PR1	PR2	PR3	PR4	PR5	PR6	PR7	PR8	PR9

Customer Requirements

Requirement | *Importance to Customer*

1 CR1
2 CR2
3 CR3
4 CR4
5 CR5
6 CR6
7 CR7
8 CR8
9 CR9
10 CR10

Exhibit F.1   QFD Matrix (continued)

Impacts on customer satisfaction

	M1	M2	M3	M4	M5	M6	M7	M8	M9
Impact on Customer Sat	0	0	0	0	0	0	0	0	0
Ranked Impact	0	0	0	0	0	0	0	0	0
How Measured / Targets									
Direction of Goodness									
Upper Spec Limit (USL)									
Lower Spec Limit (LSL)									

Exhibit F.1   QFD Matrix (continued)

Impact of All Features on Customer Req		**Competitive Assessment/Development Priorities**								
		Current Performance/Cust Sat	**Competitive Product 1**	**Competitive Product 2**	**Competitive Product 3**	**Performance/Satisfaction Goal**	**Improvement Required**	**Impact Multiplier**	**Development Priority**	**Normalized Development Priority**

Totals

- *When is it created?* The first version of the QFD is normally created during the Identification of Opportunities phase of DFSS. Although incomplete at that point, creating it early in the process helps the team quantify and prioritize customer requirements.
- *Who is responsible for updating the form?* Anyone on the project team can update the QFD; however, to avoid version control problems, it is advisable to assign one team member this responsibility.
- *How often is it updated?* Whenever information shown on the QFD changes, it should be updated.
- *Who can view the data?* Once the initial sections are complete, the QFD becomes part of the project team's information repository and should be available to anyone within the company.

Field	*How to Complete It*
Customer Requirements section:	This section lists each of the customer's requirements ("what") as well as the importance that the customer has assigned to each.
Requirement	Enter the requirements obtained from customer interviews or other sources. Each requirement is entered in a separate row. *Note:* On QFDs 2 through 4, the requirements are the CTQs identified from the Product Requirements/ Features ("how") section of the preceding QFD.
Importance to Customer	Enter the importance rating that the customer provided. To provide clear distinctions among requirements, a scale of 1-4-7-10 is recommended. *Note:* The importance rating for QFDs 2 through 4 is determined by translating the Impact on Customer Satisfaction from each column into a 1-4-7-10 scale.
Competitive Assessment/ Development Priorities section:	This section, which can be viewed as a continuation of the Customer Requirements section, records the customer's satisfaction with the current product and one or more competitive products. It also includes the company's performance targets and calculations to determine the priority in which individual requirements should be addressed.
Current Performance/ Customer Satisfaction	How well does the company's current solution satisfy this particular customer requirement? Enter the customer's level of satisfaction using a 1-4-7-10 scale.
Competitive Products	How well do competitive products satisfy this particular customer requirement? Enter the customer's level of satisfaction using a 1-4-7-10 scale.
Performance/ Satisfaction Goal	All requirements are not created equal in either the customer's or the company's mind. What would the company like the customer's satisfaction with this requirement to be? Enter the target using a 1-4-7-10 scale.
Improvement Required	As the name suggests, this field shows the difference between the company's goal and the current situation. It is a calculated field, the result of subtracting Current Performance/Customer Satisfaction from Performance/Satisfaction Goal. Negative results should be changed to zeros.

Field	*How to Complete It*
Impact Multiplier	Satisfaction of some requirements might, in the company's opinion, do more than simply satisfy one requirement. It may have an impact on the company's overall goals. This field allows the entry of a multiplier factor to indicate that increased importance. The default should be 1.0, with higher priorities indicated by larger numbers. Typically, only a few requirements will have an Impact Multiplier greater than 1.0.
Development Priority	This is a calculated field, the result of multiplying three fields: Importance to Customer, Improvement Required, and Impact Multiplier. As such, it assigns the highest priority to requirements that meet the following criteria: The customer has indicated it is important. There are large gaps between current satisfaction and the company's target. The company believes that satisfying this requirement will have a greater than normal impact on its operations.
Normalized Development Priority	This is a calculated field, showing each requirement's development priority as a percentage of the total. The calculation is Development Priority divided by the total for the Development Priority column.
Product Requirements/ Features section:	Each column in this section lists a product requirement or feature that is expected to satisfy one or more of the Customer Requirements. This is the "how" section of the QFD.
Product Requirement/ Feature	Enter one feature per column. Note that for ease of printing, the text is typically rotated 90 degrees.
Customer Requirement/Product Feature Intersection	Each cell represents the degree to which a particular feature will satisfy a specific customer requirement. A 0-1-4-7-10 scale should be used. Note the addition of 0 to the scale; some features will have no impact on a requirement. Also note that it is desirable to work with one feature (column) at a time and to disregard the Importance to Customer column as well as other Feature columns when rating each feature's impact.

Field	How to Complete It
Impact of All Features of Customer Requirement	As the name suggests, this field reflects the degree to which a requirement would be satisfied if all features were implemented. It is a calculated field determined by multiplying the Normalized Development Priority by the sum of all Customer Requirement/Product Feature intersections on each row. Note that an alternative calculation replaces Normalized Development Priority with Importance to Customer.
Impacts of Customer Satisfaction section:	As noted above, the most critical "hows" from each QFD become the "whats" for the next one. This section identifies those critical features.
Impact on Customer Satisfaction	This is a calculated field that shows how well a specified feature meets all customer requirements. To calculate this field, multiply each Customer Requirement/Product Feature Intersection in the column by the Normalized Development Priority for that requirement, then sum all the products. Note that an alternative calculation replaces Normalized Development Priority with Importance to Customer.
Ranked Impact	This field displays the rank of each Impact on Customer Satisfaction field and provides an easy way of determining which features are the most critical for satisfying customer requirements.
Targets section:	This section is used to identify the target values for each of the critical features.
How Measured	Enter the characteristic that will be measured (e.g., number of transactions processed, customer satisfaction level, number of screens available, hours of system uptime).
Direction of Goodness	This field indicates whether the upper or lower specification levels are the optimal values.
Upper Specification Limit (USL)	This field, combined with the next, indicates the acceptable range for the field being measured. The USL is the maximum value that the customer has indicated will meet requirements.
Lower Specification Limit	Enter the lowest value that will meet the customer's requirements.
Product Requirement/ Feature Correlation section:	This section, the "roof" of the House of Quality, indicates the impact that each proposed feature will have on the other. It reflects the fact that implementing some features may make it more difficult to implement others.

Field	*How to Complete It*
Feature/Feature Intersection	For each cell, enter the impact that those two features would have on each other on a five-point scale as follows: –– Implementing this feature will have a strong negative effect on the other. – Implementing this feature will have a mild negative effect on the other. 0 Neither feature will have an impact on the other. + Implementing this feature will have a mild positive effect on the other. ++ Implementing this feature will have a strong positive effect on the other.

Appendix G

List of Acronyms

Acronym	Meaning
AST	Accelerated Stress Test, a form of testing designed to determine under what conditions the product will fail.
C&E	Cause and Effect, a spreadsheet designed to show the relationships between two categories of data. Typically, customer requirements are one of those categories.
CASE	Computer-Assisted Software Engineering, commonly used in the phrase "CASE tools," referring to software products that automate one or more portions of the system development process.
CBT	Computer Based Training.
CFO	Chief Financial Officer.
CIO	Chief Information Officer.
CMM	Capability Maturity Model, the five-level definition of software process maturity.
COPQ	Cost of Poor Quality, the cost of defects, including inspection, rework, and lost sales.
COTS	Commercial Off-the-Shelf software, another term for packaged software.
CRUD	A matrix that indicates which processes can Create, Read, Update, and Delete a record on a database.
CSF	Critical Success Factor, the things that must go right if an organization is to meet its objectives.
CTQ	Critical to Quality, a requirement that must be satisfied.
DBA	Database Administrator.

Acronym	Meaning
DFSS	Design For Six Sigma.
DMAIC	The five phases of Six Sigma: Define, Measure, Analyze, Improve, and Control.
DOE	Design of Experiments, a method of testing that varies inputs to determine the corresponding effects on outputs.
DPMO	Defects per Million Opportunities, a measure of the overall quality of a process; calculated as number of defects observed divided by the number of opportunities to create a defect, with the result multiplied by one million.
DPU	Defects per Unit, a measure of quality; calculated as the number of defects observed divided by the number of units produced.
EIS	Executive Information System, typically a system that presents high-level information and allows successive drill-down to the underlying details.
ERD	Entity Relationship Diagram, a tool used to design databases.
ERP	Enterprise Resource Planning, a large integrated software package designed for manufacturing companies.
FAQ	Frequently Asked Questions, normally a document that provides answers to questions.
Five Ps	Prior Planning Prevents Poor Performance.
Five Ws	Who, What, Where, When, Why.
FMEA	Failure Modes and Effects Analysis, one of the most commonly used Six Sigma tools.
GIGO	Garbage In, Garbage Out.
GRACE	Items to be reviewed at the start of team meetings: Goal, Roles, Agenda, Code of Conduct, Expectations.
HOQ	House of Quality, a term that is sometimes used synonymously with QFD.
IDDOV	One definition of DFSS phases: Identify, Define, Develop, Optimize, Verify.
JAD	Joint Application Development, commonly used in the phrase "JAD sessions," where customers and IT work together to develop the specifications for a system.
JIT	Just in Time, frequently used to describe delivery of raw materials to a production line.
JRP	Joint Requirements Planning, the process whereby customers and IT develop the high-level requirements for a system.
KISS	Keep It Simple, Stupid, the premise that simplicity is the most valuable characteristic in communication and design.
KPA	Key Process Area, a component of a CMM level.
KPIV	Key Process Input Variable, an input that is critical to the output of the process.

Acronym	Meaning
KPOV	Key Process Output Variable, an output that is critical to the customer.
LCL	Lower Control Limit, the bottom of the normal processing range as statistically generated.
LSL	Lower Specification Limit, the bottom of the acceptable range specified by the customer.
MTBF	Mean Time Between Failures, a measure of a product's reliability.
NINO	Nothing In, Nothing Out.
PMAP	Process Map, a block diagram used to outline the steps in a process.
QA	Quality Assurance, the process of preventing defects.
QC	Quality Control, the process of monitoring and correcting defects.
QFD	Quality Function Deployment, a complex matrix relating requirements (whats) and the functions or features that will be used to satisfy them (hows).
QLF	Quality Loss Function, a measure of quality that includes the cost of customer dissatisfaction.
RAD	Rapid Application Development, a system development technique characterized by the use of CASE tools, JRP, and JAD.
RAIL	Rolling Action Item Log, a list of open items, normally with responsibilities and target completion dates.
RAVE	Characteristics of measurements: Relevant, Adequate to detect process changes, Valid and consistent from time to time, Easy.
RCS	Rumor Control Session, an informal communication method designed to help employees cope with impending change.
RFI	Request for Information, a request to potential suppliers for general information about the services or software they provide.
RFP	Request for Proposal, a formal request that a potential supplier present a proposal for services or software tailored to the requesting company.
RFS	Request for Services, a form typically used to request services from IT.
ROI	Return on Investment.
RPN	Risk Priority Number, a column on the FMEA, representing the degree of risk that a potential failure mode poses.
SARAH	The stages of coping with major change: Shock, Anger, Resistance, Acceptance, Hope.
SDLC	System Development Life Cycle.
SEI	Software Engineering Institute, the division of Carnegie Mellon University that developed the Capability Maturity Model.
SIPOC	A chart that provides a high-level understanding of a process. The components are Supplier, Input, Process, Output, Customer.

Acronym	Meaning
SLA	Service Level Agreement, a contract quantifying the work to be provided by IT or an outsourcer.
SMART	Characteristics of a problem statement or requirements: Specific, Measurable, Attainable, Relevant, Timebound.
S/N	Signal-to-noise ratio, a metric used when reducing variation in a process design.
SOP	Standard Operating Procedure.
SOW	Statement of Work, normally the formal contract that defines the work to be provided by an outsource supplier
Ts and Cs	Terms and Conditions of a contract.
Three Cs	Complete, Clear, and Customer-focused; applies to statements of work and service level agreements.
TMAP	Thought process map, a Six Sigma tool used to document the team's decisions, the reasons for those decisions, and the tools that were used in making them.
Two Ms	Meaningful and manageable, the characteristics Pande and Holpp recommend using when choosing projects.
UCL	Upper Control Limit, the top of the normal processing range as statistically generated.
USL	Upper Specification Limit, the top of the acceptable range specified by the customer.
VOC	Voice of the Customer, typically refers to customer requirements.
VOP	Voice of the Process, typically refers to the capability of a process.
WIT	Whatever It Takes.

Appendix H

Suggested Reading

Berry, Thomas H., *Managing the Total Quality Transformation*. New York: McGraw-Hill, Inc., 1991.

Breyfogle, Forrest W., III, Cupello, James M., and Meadows, Becki, *Managing Six Sigma*. New York: John Wiley and Sons, Inc., 2001.

Butler, Janet (Ed.), *Winning the Outsourcing Game*. Boca Raton, FL: Auerbach Publications, 2000.

Carnegie Mellon University Software Engineering Institute, *The Capability Maturity Model*. New York: Addison-Wesley, 1995.

Chowdhury, Subir, *Design For Six Sigma*. Chicago: Dearborn Trade, 2005.

Chowdhury, Subir, *The Ice Cream Maker*. New York: Doubleday Currency, 2005.

Chowdhury, Subir, *The Power of Six Sigma*. Chicago: Dearborn Trade, 2001.

Conner, Daryl R., *Managing at the Speed of Change*. New York: Villard, 1992.

Dertouzos, Michael L., Lester, Richard L., and Solow, Robert M., *Made in America: Regaining the Productive Edge*. Cambridge, MA: MIT Press, 1989.

Donaldson, Scott E. and Siegel, Stanley G., *Successful Software Development, second edition*. Upper Saddle River, NJ: Prentice Hall, 2001.

Eason, Ken, *Information Technology and Organisational Change*. Philadelphia: Taylor & Francis, 1988.

George, Michael, *Lean Six Sigma for Service*. New York: McGraw-Hill, 2003.

Harry, Mikel, Ph.D. and Schroeder, Richard, *Six Sigma: The Breakthrough Management Strategy Revolutionizing the World's Top Corporations*. New York: Doubleday, 2000.

Johnson, Spencer, M.D., *Who Moved My Cheese?* New York: G. Putnam's Sons, 1998.

Kanter, Rosabeth Moss, *The Change Masters*. New York: Simon and Schuster, 1983.

Lewis, William E., *Software Testing and Continuous Quality Improvement*. Boca Raton, FL: Auerbach Publications, 2000.

Martin, James and McClure, Carma, *Software Maintenance*. Englewood Cliffs, NJ: Prentice Hall, 1983.

McConnell, Steve, *Rapid Development*. Redmond, WA: Microsoft Press, 1996.

Moen, Ronald D., Nolan, Thomas W., and Provost, Lloyd P., *Improving Quality through Planned Experimentation*. New York: McGraw-Hill, 1991.

Pande, Peter S., Neuman, Robert P., Cavanagh, and Roland R., *The Six Sigma Way*. New York: McGraw Hill, 2000.

Pande, Peter and Holpp, Larry, *What is Six Sigma?* New York: McGraw-Hill, 2002.

Parikh, Girish, *Techniques of Program and System Maintenance*. Cambridge: Winthrop Publishers, 1982.

Pfluger, Shari Lawrence, *Software Engineering: Theory and Practice, second edition*. Upper Saddle River, NJ: Prentice Hall, 2001.

Somerville, Ian, *Software Engineering, Sixth Edition*. Harlow: Addison-Wesley, 2001.

Stamatis, D.H., *Six Sigma and Beyond: Design For Six Sigma*. Boca Raton, FL: St. Lucie Press, 2003.

Tayntor, Christine B., A Practical Guide to Staff Augmentation and Outsourcing, in *Information Management: Strategy, Systems, and Technologies*. Boca Raton, FL: Auerbach Publications, 2000.

Tayntor, Christine B., Software Testing Basics and Guidelines, in *Information Management: Strategy, Systems, and Technologies*. Boca Raton, FL: Auerbach Publications, 1998.

Tayntor, Christine B., *Successful Packaged Software Implementation*. Boca Raton, FL: Auerbach Publications, 2006.

Womack, James P. and Jones, Daniel T., *Lean Thinking*. New York: Free Press, 2003.

Index

A

P

Q

S